Advance Praise for

THE NEW LOCALISM

by Bruce Katz and Jeremy Nowak

"Katz and Nowak focus on solutions at a time when so much of public life is consumed by grievance. They remind us of the best traditions of American problem solving. If you care about cities and what you can do to make them more prosperous and inclusive, then read this book."

JOHN FRY, President of Drexel University

"With many national and state capitals struggling to adapt to a rapidly changing world, cities are increasingly responsible for shaping a future around innovation, inclusion, infrastructure, and the deployment of new technologies. Bruce Katz and Jeremy Nowak bring their unparalleled global and local expertise to create a New Localism—and provide cities, and anyone who cares about our future, a roadmap for cities to become the world's premier problem solvers with a mission to fulfill *all* of their citizens' human potential.

GREG FISCHER, Mayor of Louisville, Kentucky

"Federal and state governments are unable to innovate fast enough to keep pace with our changing needs. As mayors, we don't have the luxury of waiting for someone else to lead; we are expected to solve problems and we willingly lean in to that responsibility. Bruce and Jeremy understand this better than anyone and share their optimism for the way local leadership can be the antidote to the growing polarization and political dysfunction at the national level."

JORGE ELORZA, Mayor of Providence, Rhode Island

"*The New Localism* offers a new way of thinking about cities—one that seeks to harness their full potential in order to advance greater opportunity, inclusion, and growth that truly serves the public good."

CORY BOOKER, United States Senator for New Jersey
and former Mayor of Newark

"If *The Metropolitan Revolution* explained what was happening in the world's metros and why, *The New Localism* does the invaluable work of breaking down the 'how': what are the governance mechanisms, the leadership qualities, and most important, the new financing tools that enable metros to drive innovation, expand opportunity, and power the future. Katz and Nowak's careful deconstruction of new ways of getting things done leaves metros—and the national governments that should support them—with a wealth of ideas, and no excuses for inaction."

JENNIFER BRADLEY, Director, The Center for
Urban Innovation at the Aspen Institute,
and coauthor, *The Metropolitan Revolution*

THE NEW LOCALISM

THE NEW LOCALISM

HOW CITIES CAN THRIVE IN THE AGE OF POPULISM

BRUCE KATZ

and

JEREMY NOWAK

BROOKINGS INSTITUTION PRESS

Washington, D.C.

The Brookings Institution is a private nonprofit organization devoted to research, education, and publication on important issues of domestic and foreign policy. Its principal purpose is to bring the highest quality independent research and analysis to bear on current and emerging policy problems. Interpretations or conclusions in Brookings publications should be understood to be solely those of the authors.

Library of Congress Cataloging-in-Publication data are available.
ISBN 978-0-8157-3164-1 (cloth : alk. paper)
ISBN 978-0-8157-3165-8 (ebook)

9 8 7 6 5 4 3 2

Typeset in Electra

Composition by Westchester Publishing Services

Contents

Preface

This book evolved over many years of observation, engagement, and analysis. But the political events of 2016–17, from Brexit to the election of Donald Trump, from the United States pulling out of the Paris climate agreement to new populist movements in Europe and elsewhere, brought clarity and urgency to our central focus on the importance of local activity and prompted us to write the book now.

The two of us have spent our professional lives working to enhance the prosperity of cities and metropolitan areas and expand the opportunities of people who live there. We bring complementary but distinct experiences in urban practice and policy. One of us (Jeremy) has worked at the local level, primarily in Philadelphia, creating one of the largest community investment institutions in the nation, and then went on to chair the board of the Federal Reserve Bank of Philadelphia, as well as advise philanthropies, universities, and investment companies on urban development strategy. The other (Bruce) has focused on urban innovation, infrastructure, and inclusion at the national level, holding senior staff positions in the U.S. Senate and the U.S. Department of Housing and Urban Development and then starting a think tank on urban and metropolitan communities at the Brookings Institution.

Our different vantage points have given us a healthy respect for the power of national and state governments. We have also come to understand that the most forward-thinking initiatives in the nation, including those that deal with pressing social, economic, and environmental concerns, are emerging from local communities far more than from national policies or platforms. Why? The reasons are myriad and are based in deep structural changes in the economy and society more than in ephemeral political cycles.

Despite many positive expressions of change across the nation, American political discourse is largely (and understandably) focused on the dysfunctions of Washington, D.C., and many statehouses. Much less airtime goes to hard-working problem solvers in American cities and local communities. Discord plays better than collaboration; defining problems will always get more coverage than delivering solutions. Populism has cachet even when it supports a largely incoherent political agenda or loses most elections. Solutions, particularly those that involve deep institutional change, can be downright boring.

Yet a quiet but profound movement is under way in hundreds of cities, towns, and rural communities to meet the future head on. The time has come for those initiatives to take center stage. That is the purpose of this book. The movement that we call New Localism is analyzed in these pages, situated in its historical context, and framed in a future based on its successes and challenges. These stories are not reducible to political sound bites, nor are they the product of overnight success. But local activity is changing America in positive ways. And these actions draw from global innovations and have enormous implications for cities around the world.

Many see the times in which we live as concerning, even chaotic. We view this book as an act of optimism. Positive energy and affirmative possibility flow from the places and people we profile: vibrant, innovative, pragmatic, and relentlessly future leaning and progress seeking.

Acknowledgments

This book, like the work of cities, has been a collaborative effort.

We owe an enormous debt to the stellar research team of (or affiliated with) the Brookings Centennial Scholar Initiative. Julie Wagner urged us to write the book in the first place, believing that our views on New Localism as a counterforce to the rise of angry populism deserved a large audience. Her research with Jennifer Vey, Scott Andes, and Jason Hachadorian on the growing nexus between place making and innovation has been highly influential.

Luise Noring's distinctive views on the shifting nature and critical importance of urban governance and finance, breakthrough research on Copenhagen's public asset corporation model, and emerging methodology of urban problem solving have fundamentally transformed our thinking.

Alex Jones not only managed the process, but also provided daily guidance and innovative insights on all things urban, large and small.

We also benefitted from the research and practice contributions of Ross Tilchin, Brianne Eby, Alaina Harkness, Caroline Conroy, Jessica Brandt, Angela Blanchard, and Andy Altman and the work of three terrific interns at Brookings—Zhiyin Pan, Henry Eisner, and Adam Vieira.

The staffs of the Centennial Scholar Initiative at Brookings and the Brookings Institution Press were invaluable in the planning of the book, its release, and the campaign to spread New Localism throughout the United

States and the world. Ellen Ochs and Marikka Green have alone and to-gether mastered the art of stewarding networks of people and places. Their efforts have been amplified by the work of Grace Palmer, Shervan Sebastian, Charlotte Baldwin, Bill Finan, Yelba Quinn, Carrie Engel, Janet Walker, Valentina Kalk, Kristen BelleIsle, and Zoe Covello.

The Centennial Scholar Initiative itself would not have been possible without the remarkable leadership of Strobe Talbott, Kim Churches, and Martin Indyk. These individuals recognized the need for city-led, inter-disciplinary problem solving in the world and gave us the space to invent outside the traditional structures of the institution. To that end, Kemal Derviş and Bruce Jones helped us explore new linkages among cities, for-eign policy, and global governance.

The fine work of the Metropolitan Policy Program and the Reinvestment Fund—our former institutional homes—continues to inform and motivate.

Special thanks to the team at TSD Communications—David Dreyer, Ricki Seidman, and Eric London—who read early versions of the manuscript and kept our writing focused on the readers rather than the authors.

After months of writing, our peer reviewers—Eugenie Birch, Ira Goldstein, and Bob Weissbourd—provided the perfect mix of encourage-ment and criticism to keep us going, in the process adding their diverse expertise to this book. We also want to thank those who read and responded to specific portions of the manuscript at various times, including Bob Keith, Sean Closkey, Scott Jenkins, Michelle Kreisler-Rubenstein, and Mark Pinsky.

Susan Kellam provided a final structural review of the manuscript that sharpened our writing and brought the key points of New Localism to the surface. Marjorie Pannell, Kimberly Giambattisto, and the team at West-chester Publishing Services made sure we dotted our i's and crossed our t's with their final copyedit.

The stories of New Localism are best told by the leaders themselves, and in each city we are grateful for the guidance, fact finding, and reality checks from a number of very busy people who were beyond generous with their time. In Pittsburgh, Tim McNulty, Rick Siger, and Don Carter of Carnegie Mellon University, Rebecca Bagley of the University of Pitts-burgh, and the indefatigable leadership of the Heinz Endowments and the

Hillman Foundation, including Grant Oliphant, Dave Roger, Tyler Gourley, Andrew McElwaine, and Rob Stephany, added depth and color to one of the world's great tales of urban turnaround. In Indianapolis, David Johnson of the Central Indiana Corporate Partnership brought the largely untold story of Indianapolis's special institutional magic to life through personal recollections, meticulous detail, and access to primary documents. Jens Kramer Mikkelsen, the CEO of Copenhagen City & Port Development and the former lord mayor of Copenhagen, revealed the inner workings of his city's secret model of regeneration. In Philadelphia, Paul Levy of Center City District, John Fry of Drexel University, and John Grady of the Philadelphia Industrial Development Corporation showed how the building of cities depends on the continuous growth and dedication of their city builders.

On education reform, our work was informed by the leadership of practitioners such as Simran Sidhu, Kaya Henderson, Scott Gordon, and Alejandro Gac-Artigas. The field of public finance and community investment is filled with people trying to stretch the canvas between market relevance and public purpose. Many of those institutions are mentioned throughout the book.

Various other leaders of New Localism have shaped our thinking over the past several years, and their work has been an ongoing inspiration for this book: Julia Stasch and Deborah Schwartz of the John D. and Catherine T. MacArthur Foundation, Rip Rapson and Carol Coletta of the Kresge Foundation, Darren Walker of the Ford Foundation, Fred Kent and the inspiring team at Project for Public Spaces, and Dag Detter and Stefan Fölster, the co-authors of *The Public Wealth of Cities*. Detter and Fölster have created something rare in public policy—a genuinely new idea—and we hope we are able to promote their work in a small way in *The New Localism* by placing it in a broader political and civic context.

We want to thank the supporters of the Centennial Scholar Initiative at The Brookings Institution, without whom we would not have been able to write this book. Steve Denning and the Sage Foundation, Robert and Anne Bass, the Rockefeller Foundation, and the John D. and Catherine T. MacArthur Foundation have all offered both financial and intellectual support for our work and have pushed our thinking in the process. Jeremy also thanks

Catherine Murphy and members of the Berwind family, who provided him with time to write while also doing work for Spring Point Partners, a new initiative of the Berwind Corporation.

Finally, Jeremy wants to give special thanks to his wife and children, who give him the optimism and love to keep moving forward. Bruce is indebted to his family for their unwavering support of his urban obsession and tolerance of a peripatetic work life. He dedicates this book to his mother, who continues to inspire a passion for the written word and a commitment to turn ideas into action.

ONE

Power Reimagined

My interest is in power. How power works.
—Robert Caro, *The Power Broker*

This is a book about reimagining power.

For generations, the locus and nature of power seemed settled, reflected in the vertical lines of political authority. National and state governments sat at the apex, writing laws, promulgating rules, distributing resources, and running the country. Cities and metropolitan regions—the places where the overwhelming majority of the population lives and where national wealth is disproportionately generated—resided at the bottom, often acting as administrative arms of higher levels of government more than as agents in charge of their own future.

This picture, hierarchically neat and textbook tidy, is radically changing. The location of power is shifting as a result of profound demographic, economic, and social forces. Power is drifting downward from the nation-state to cities and metropolitan communities, horizontally from government to networks of public, private, and civic actors, and globally along transnational circuits of capital, trade, and innovation.

These changes are shattering traditional notions of where power lies, the people and institutions that wield it, and how transformative change occurs. New sets of leaders are upending conventional wisdom about who solves problems in an age with too much partisan conflict and not enough common purpose.

Power is not what it used to be. It is less confined to the authority of government alone and more fueled by the market potential that comes from the concentration of economic, physical, and social assets in real places. It is less defined by scales of influence distributed across layers of government and more derived from sources of civic strength that come from collaborating across sectors.

The exercise of power is also not what it used to be. The ability to get things done has shifted from command-and-control systems to the collective efforts of civil society, government, and private institutions. It is vested in and affected by leaders and institutions that convert market and civic power into fiscal, financial, and political power.

In sum, power increasingly belongs to the problem solvers. And these problem solvers now congregate disproportionately at the local level, in cities and metropolitan areas across the globe.

New Localism embodies this new reality of power. It is the twenty-first century's means of solving the problems characteristic of modern life: global economic competition, poverty, the challenges of social diversity, and the imperatives of environmental sustainability. To be clear, local action is not a replacement for the vital roles the federal government plays as a distributional and regulatory platform; rather, it is the ideal complement to an effective federal government and, in times such as the present, an urgently needed remedy for national dysfunction. New Localism also reflects the reality that cities are many things at once: geographic units; regional economies, markets for goods and services, networks of leaders from government, business, and civic groups, and places of shared culture and values.

Today, progress is evident among vanguard cities and metropolitan regions that are inventing new models of growth, governance, and finance. These novel and distinctive models focus intentionally and purposefully on inclusive and sustainable outcomes as measures of market success.

Growth. These vanguard cities are igniting growth by leveraging their distinctive sectors to commercialize research, seed and grow businesses, and create quality jobs. Local leaders are aligning their educational systems to provide workers with the skills they need to obtain jobs in an advanced economy and are seeking solutions to deep-seated poverty through early childhood education and school-to-career strategies. They are creating the civic and physical spaces that enable the seamless exchange of ideas and the continuous invention and deployment of products and technologies. And they are responding to the urgent environmental imperative to reduce carbon emissions by embracing renewable energies, developing more walkable, bicycle-friendly and transit-accessible cities, cleaning up watersheds through the use of green infrastructure, and converting public buildings to energy-efficient uses.

Governance. These vanguard cities are catalyzing growth through forms of governance that align the distinctive perspectives of government, business, philanthropy, universities, and the broader community. Governance is being driven by collaboration rather than coercion, stewarded by diverse networks rather than by elected decisionmakers alone, and characterized by iterative problem solving rather than by rigid and prescriptive rulemaking. Governance is also being exercised by new institutions that are designed to leverage the public legitimacy of government with the entrepreneurialism of the private and civic sectors.

Finance. These vanguard cities are capitalizing growth by using a vast array of tools to fund investments in innovation, infrastructure, and inclusivity initiatives. Cities are bankrolling the future by converting their market power into tangible, investable resources. In the process, a new field of metro finance is emerging that aggregates and deploys capital from community, national, and global sources to align investments with local economies and priorities. The public sector is embracing both traditional mechanisms such as voter referenda and new mechanisms such as value capture to invest in physical and human capital, infrastructure, and children. At the same time, private and civic capital is spurring innovation by investing in firms and intermediaries that translate research into tangible products. To make progress on these fronts, local governments are beginning to tackle legacy liabilities, to focus tax revenue on what works, and to manage public assets in more productive ways.

New Localism is a nascent phenomenon, a work in progress. The harsh reality is that the dramatic devolution of responsibility has not been met with a concomitant delegation of capacity or resources. Twenty-first-century problem solving is essentially taking place amid twentieth-century financial and institutional arrangements that are antiquated and inadequate. If cities, in short, are to be the world's problem solvers, municipalities must grow new sets of leaders and invent new intermediaries and institutions that align with this disruptive era and its heightened importance. Cities and their partners must think anew about everything from the fine print of financial instruments to the vehicles for cross-sectoral collaboration to the management and disposition of public assets.

There is no doubt that a growing number of cities are stepping up to this challenge with newfound confidence. A restructuring economy has placed a premium on high-skill and high-productivity industries clustered in more dense, urban environments. Together with changing demographic preferences, these economic dynamics have increased the market value and market power of such communities. New technologies that enable driverless cars and personalized medicine are not just being invented in cities; they are being tested and deployed there. Cities are on the front line of the next economy.

This shift in where and how America solves problems represents the formative stage of New Localism. While deeply rooted in American civil society, today's New Localism emerged out of crises in local economies and in response to the vacuum left by higher levels of government. Action had to be taken to rescue communities and cities from decline. New Localism exists as much because of need as by design, reflecting both the limited capacity of the local public sector and the narrow reach and vision of conventional private sector investors. The convergence of economic crises, the absence of solutions at higher levels of government, and the American inclination for subsidiarity makes New Localism urgent and inevitable.

New Localism has the potential to outlive this moment of crisis and change, to capitalize on the profound economic and demographic shifts of the past four decades, which have favored an urban resurgence in the

United States. Markets are revaluing cities and New Localism is the vehicle through which leaders can translate market power into the resources that can finance the future. This is how communities will survive and thrive in our current age.

POPULISM AND NEW LOCALISM

While the rise of a very vocal populism has received significantly more attention than the quiet problem-solving efforts of New Localism, both are the products of structural dynamics that have resulted in widespread fiscal distress, job insecurity, and cultural anxiety.

It is tempting to view New Localism as a mere side product of the angry populism that has swept the United States and Europe. At its core, populism is a revolt against elites, whether economic or political. And as populists have altered the national discourse, they have—sometimes intentionally, sometimes not—attacked and weakened the nation-state as well as supra-national institutions, and empowered local forces. The stated aspiration of the Trump administration to "deconstruct the administrative state" is ironically elevating the city-state as the locus of problem-solving activity.[1]

The collaborative networks of New Localism, we believe, act as a countervailing force and cultural antidote to the rise of right-wing populism. Populism has reenergized a politics—most prominently represented by Donald Trump in America and the Brexit coalition in the United Kingdom—that is nostalgic in focus, nationalistic in tone, and nativist in orientation. The rhetoric of this populist politics seeks to create walls, literal and figurative, that inhibit the flow of people, goods, capital, and ideas across borders; the essence of the modern economy.

The populism on the left, while devoid of national and ethnic chauvinism, often is characterized by a similar nostalgia for a world that no longer exists. Many of their positions take a far too simple view of multinational trade agreements and global economic institutions. Neither Bernie Sanders's view of the federal government as the realm of most solutions nor Donald Trump's notion of economic nationalism fits the new global or local reality.

Still, the populism that defined the 2016 U.S. presidential election shares much of its origins with New Localism. It is rooted in the long economic restructuring and social transition that has exacerbated national income inequality and rattled the meaning of national identity. The core difference is that while populism has evolved into a national political strategy to exploit these grievances, New Localism is a problem-solving philosophy geared toward alleviating them.

In contrast to right-wing populism, New Localism embraces diversity rather than ethnocentrism and is curious rather than closed. In contrast to the political extremes of both the left and the right, New Localism is guided by pragmatism rather than by ideological fervor. New Localism governs with a long-term view toward the future; much of populism campaigns on a shortsighted return to the past.

The problems of the new global age are significant. But the real solutions to these challenges will disproportionately come from the ground up. The more progressive variants of populism that seek to strengthen the safety net, reinforce investments in infrastructure and education, and protect consumers and the democratic franchise at large from the undue influence of money in politics are important complements to New Localism.

But, as this book explores, the practical solutions to economic growth, economic inclusion, and environmental sustainability are more within the local domain than the national. Modern national and state governments seem unable to mount sufficient or sustained responses to modern challenges. Excessive partisanship has poisoned Congress and state legislatures and put representative democracy itself in a seemingly intractable state of gridlock and polarization.

The stalemate is compounded by structural fiscal challenges. In *Dead Men Ruling*, the Urban Institute's Gene Steuerle shows how growth in the nonchild portions of Social Security, Medicare, and Medicaid programs and payment on the national debt are fueled by decisions made by prior Congresses; hence the title of his book.[2] He bases his assumptions on Congressional Budget Office forecasts that by 2026, the federal government will be spending $4.1 trillion a year on entitlement programs such as Social Security, squeezing investments in housing, infrastructure, education, and research and development.[3] In short, Congress has little "fiscal freedom" to shift investments to new challenges.

Thus, even prior to the onset of a divided Congress and the accession of the Trump administration, the federal government had diminishing ability to invest at scale in the future through research that would spur innovation, new infrastructure better aligned with the twenty-first-century economy, and the educational and other investments needed to support higher levels of economic inclusion. That responsibility had already devolved to society itself, to American cities and localities.

As politics has become nationalized, problem solving has become localized.

THE LOCAL ADVANTAGE

Cities and counties are solving problems because they can. The knowledge-intensive industries that increasingly dominate the U.S. economy seek the convergence of assets that many U.S. cities and metropolitan areas naturally possess: anchor research institutions and collaborative ecosystems of firms, entrepreneurs, investors, and intermediaries. The emerging economy is revaluing proximity, density, authenticity, and the solid bones—historical buildings, traditional street grids, access to waterfronts, cultural institutions—that can be found in the traditional downtowns and midtowns of communities large, medium, and small.

Increased technological innovation has also enhanced the role of cities. As the basic science and applied research conducted in universities, hospitals, and companies reach commercial markets, cities have accelerated the invention of new technologies. Such progress in recent years is giving cities new ways to grow firms, value, and jobs. Some examples are Chattanooga's efforts to create the smartest energy grid, Pittsburgh's decision to be a living laboratory for testing driverless cars, and Chicago's decision to open up public data for use by entrepreneurs and technology firms. The role of cities as markets enables them to also be market makers, in granular and novel ways.

Technological advances, more broadly, have sped up a city's ability to change and evolve, sharpening the contrast with sluggish legislative processes. As national and state governments have grown more sclerotic, the ability of traditional governments to act with agility and discretion has been lost. Cities, however, can accumulate public, private, and civic wealth to create alternative paths for the design, financing, and delivery of solutions rapidly. Localities are the test bed for a dizzying array of innovations—charter schools, smart meters, mobility apps, social enterprises—based on the simple premise, hubristic in some cases, that "I can do that better."

The nature of problem solving is also changing, further reinforcing the growing preference for local responses. Tackling complex issues such as climate change or social mobility or the deployment and employment impact of disruptive technologies should work toward solutions that are integrated and innovative rather than dictatorial and prescriptive. As the political analyst Yuval Levin has written, "The absence of easy answers is precisely a reason to empower a multiplicity of problem-solvers through-out our society, rather than hoping that one problem-solver in Washington gets it right."[4]

Cities that are characterized by multidisciplinary and multisectoral networks rather than by the narrow, specialized silos of federal or state bureaucracies can think outside the box. A national transportation agency tends to address transportation challenges—say, traffic congestion—with transportation solutions, often widening a road. To a person with a hammer, everything looks like a nail. A city is more likely to bring other solutions to bear—based in, say, housing or land use or technology—to solve the same problem.

Cities and other localities can craft and deliver better solutions to hard challenges since they match problem solving to the way the world works—integrated, holistic, and entrepreneurial rather than compartmentalized and bureaucratic. They can also put more players on the problem-solving field in ways that are quintessentially modern and imbued with new technological potential. Such mayors as Greg Fischer of Louisville and Rahm Emanuel of Chicago, for example, have successfully tasked entrepreneurs to take on social challenges and apply the ethos of the startup world to the urban arena.

A cultural affinity for public purpose and volunteerism is deeply rooted in localities. Cities are home to tens of thousands of mediating institutions—churches, community organizations, business associations, philanthropies—that play a critical role in addressing the most difficult challenges faced by families and neighborhoods.

As former New York senator Daniel Patrick Moynihan made clear throughout his long career, the federal government should set a strong platform for family and community success but cannot substitute for or take the place of community institutions. As he noted in a speech to the National League of Cities in 1985, "Federalism is not a managerial arrangement that the framers hit upon because the country was big and there were no telephones. . . . Federalism was a fundamental expression of the American idea of covenant."[5]

To be sure, the issues that many cities face—from deep-seated poverty and aging infrastructure to legacy liabilities that crowd out needed items from public budgets—are difficult to overcome. But the most creative solutions will come from local initiatives in the places where schools are managed, jobs are created, budgets are designed, contracts are negotiated, and infrastructure choices are made.

Cities share another advantage over the nation-state in their ability to respond nimbly and flexibly to challenges and opportunities. The federal government has very little discretion to make investments that respond to non-natural crises such as the Detroit bankruptcy or the Ferguson and Baltimore disturbances, or to adjust to broader demographic transformations or technological disruptions. The uninterrupted growth of entitlement programs and the proliferation of highly rigid programs have created a government that, like a fossil, is inflexible and stiff. Incredibly, a small city or regional philanthropy has more discretion to make smart, aligned investments than distant federal agencies do.

Problem solving close to the ground rather than policymaking from a remote national or state capital has the tangible benefit of customization. A local solution can be a more efficient use of resources since it is more aligned with the distinctive needs of a particular place. A weak-market city such as Detroit needs to demolish blighted housing in order to boost value; a hot-market city such as Boston needs to build and preserve more housing to meet demand. National and state legislatures, by contrast, tend to enact one-size-fits-all solutions and, for political reasons, prefer spreading public resources evenly, like peanut butter across a slice of bread.

New Localism is thus a brake on national uniformity. It allows places to focus on the challenges they actually have rather than on the issues du jour favored by national governments or national constituency groups more broadly. It recognizes and celebrates the differences between regions. The country draws its strength not only from being "one nation" politically but also from having multiple nodes of energy, innovation, and experimentation.

Finally, cities reflect a new circuitry of civic innovation, the ability to adapt, tailor, or replicate an innovative practice invented in one city in other cities. All cities, whether developing or developed, new or old, large or small, face similar challenges. The fact that multiple cities in radically different circumstances are simultaneously trying to solve challenges makes them more likely to innovate than hyperspecialized national agencies. And when cities join together to commit to common quantifiable outcomes, as is now happening with the response to climate change, the drive toward new replicable solutions and routinized financial mechanisms is accelerated.[6] The commitment of hundreds of cities to the climate goals of the 2015 Paris Agreement illustrates the growing power of New Localism. Collective accords and campaigns will inevitably engage such societal (and urban) challenges as early childhood education, crime reduction, and transportation choice.

WHAT FOLLOWS: OUR FRAMEWORK

This book chronicles the rise of New Localism. But it is as much about what must happen as it is about what has happened, reflecting our strong conviction that much work remains to be done if New Localism is to successfully fill the vacuum left by higher levels of government.

Five key points about New Localism provide the frame for this book.

First, *New Localism is not the same as local government.* New Localism refers to multisectoral networks that work together to solve problems, as well as the institutional vehicles they invent to get things done. Local governmental leaders increasingly understand the horizontal nature of power and how to involve and catalyze civic and private sector partners.

Second, *the devolution of power and problem solving to local levels is not an argument against the vital importance of federal and state governments.* Emerging changes at the ground level do make a strong case for reengineering aspects of federalism, including clarifying the strengths of different levels of government and considering how New Localism might provide a more agile approach to social equity challenges.

The federal government must do things that only it can do, including safeguarding national security, providing a stronger social safety net than it presently does, providing guarantees of constitutional protections and civil rights, making smart national infrastructure investments, protecting natural resources, protecting the integrity of markets, and funding scientific research, innovation, and postsecondary education to keep the nation competitive.

States also play a fundamental role, imbuing cities and communities with the ability to maximize the strength of their economies and use it to raise and attract new resources for change. States must also invest in public institutions of higher education and address the inequities that come about when local governments do not have the taxing capacity to fulfill basic education obligations or other services.

Third, *New Localism is the locus of problem solving that must by necessity be open to new ideas and a diversity of constituencies.* That the term "localism" often conjures up insularity and narrowmindedness is misleading in this context. New Localism occurs at the intersection of local capacity and global change, where innovation is primary and the status quo is no longer sufficient.

Fourth, *New Localism is occurring at multiple geographic levels—district, city, county, and metropolitan.* In theory, certain interventions should be designed and delivered at different geographic scales. In practice, U.S. cities and metropolitan areas, like others across the world, are highly fragmented and do not respect market, social, or environmental realities. Problem solving, therefore, occurs at different scales when the mutual interests of disparate stakeholders are recognized and organized. We are, at heart, urban realists: interested in the practical application of problem solving that makes a difference rather than the perfect identification of structural reforms that make a point and rarely happen. We also believe in natural sequencing: local solutions today often become metropolitan solutions tomorrow as the infectious allure of problem solving moves across artificial borders.

While this book is primarily about cities and suburbs, the material has clear relevance for rural areas. The lessons and principles that are extracted from successful urban initiatives, particularly regarding quality placemaking and inventive education, can be directly applied to the rural sphere. And many rural areas, despite conventional wisdom, are not out of sight and out of mind. In fact, as a result of the extreme decentralization of the population, half of the people who live in rural communities actually live in metropolitan areas and potentially benefit from smart and strategic metro solutions and heightened intra-metro linkages.[7]

Fifth, *New Localism has emerged in its most dramatic form in the United States as a result of the exceptional level of partisanship and the consequent withdrawal of the federal and state governments as reliable partners.* While most of our discussion, therefore, centers on U.S. cities, the book draws from important global examples, particularly in the governance and finance arenas. And, as with rural areas, the book has clear global implications because of the replicability of urban solutions and the interconnectedness of urban financing tools in the world today.

With these markers in mind, the book proceeds on the following plan:

Chapter 2 provides a more in-depth analysis of New Localism, its emergence and the transition from the early emphasis on placemaking and urban restoration to the wholesale repositioning of communities for the growth sectors of the global economy. The evolution of New Localism reveals qualitative differences from the top-down interventions of earlier eras, when problem solving was concentrated in higher levels of government. It is fueled by networks of institutions and leaders rather than reliant on the public sector alone. It is horizontal rather than vertical in organization, focused on replication of solutions across places. And it is simultaneously local and global, since smart solutions can be invented both at home and abroad, in large and small cities alike.

Chapter 3 begins with a simple statement: *Everything has changed.* Globalization, dizzying technological advances, demographic transformation, and financial restructuring have created a world of enormous dynamism and possibility but also one of economic insecurity and cultural anxiety. The confluence of forces has simultaneously driven political instability at the national level and transformative change at the local level. It has, on the one hand, created the conditions for the reemergence of populism and neonationalism, as people and places left behind have lashed out at what they perceive as ineffectual national leaders and inadequate protections. On the other hand, these forces have simultaneously enabled the rise of an affirmative localism. A nimble and networked economy rewards communities that are similarly nimble and networked while dramatically expanding the range of available solutions.

The next three chapters provide detailed stories of New Localism in action in three cities: Pittsburgh, Indianapolis, and Copenhagen, Denmark. Each story captures a new norm of practice that can be codified and ultimately replicated in other cities that are grappling with the same kinds of issues.

The Pittsburgh story, presented in chapter 4, focuses on new models of growth in a city that was one of America's quintessential old manufacturing centers. Today it is a global leader in advanced robotics and autonomous vehicles and the place to be for some of the world's most important companies, such as Google and Amazon.

In chapter 5, the story of Indianapolis represents the dynamism of that city as it reinvented itself over the past several decades, and more specifically on what can be learned from the deep system of networked governance that has emerged. Those networks function at multiple scales and with different levels of formality and focus.

Pittsburgh and Indianapolis matter because they demonstrate that organized leadership can elevate the distinctive assets of a place in ways that transcend the confines of the past, building linkages throughout the national and global economy. They represent the triumph of the public, private, and civic sectors working consistently in tandem, of communities recognizing and leveraging their own special assets, and of places perfecting a culture of collaborative action. They also reflect stories of quiet leadership exercised by individuals in private and civic institutions working behind the scenes over decades who combined the ability to collaborate, a demand for strategic intelligence, and a clear sense of public purpose.

Pittsburgh and Indianapolis also matter because both are industrial and heartland cities, and their stories are not another retelling of Silicon Valley's or New York City's story. There is no flyover country in America. Other parts of the book draw examples from the coasts but also note some of the extraordinary things happening in Chattanooga, Cincinnati, Kansas City,

Oklahoma City, and St. Louis as well. These stories reinforce what Steve Case has labeled "the rise of the rest" and reflect the strength of a national economy that is varied and distributed.[8]

New Localism will need to step up the pace of innovation and structural reform if it is to meet the extraordinary challenges of our times and address the fiscal pressures that accompany the decline in federal discretionary spending and the rise in local pension and other liabilities. For that reason, the Copenhagen experience described in chapter 6 is of vital importance. It is the story of how that city utilizes a publicly owned corporation with a private, profit-making mandate to manage public assets in smarter ways and generate capital for public infrastructure. It was natural to use a European example in this instance because the United States is well behind many European and Asian nations in using market mechanisms to achieve public ends. American public finance leaves far too much capital on the table. It is one thing to catalyze markets, something the public sector ought to do, but it is another thing to miss the opportunity to extract public value from the value the public creates.

Chapter 7 addresses the importance of economic inclusion as an integral part of urban growth, governance, and finance. Communities must be intentional about connecting residents to growth and opportunity, and this chapter highlights a series of strategies based on anchor-driven growth, reform of the educational system, youth programs, and social capital. Governance must also include broad networks of stakeholders from diverse communities; in many instances diversity is more aspiration than reality. There is no single path for advancing inclusion, but a lack of intentionality limits long-term economic success and ultimately degrades democracy.

Chapter 8 discusses finance and the challenges of building financial products and intermediaries at the local and regional level that have market discipline and public purpose. Philanthropy, impact investors, civic intermediaries, universities, and the public sector are all working to catalyze and maximize private investment. Their financial innovations are taking place at the boundaries of civic, public, and private investment and, in the process, creating a new field of metro finance.

Chapter 9 specifically addresses several big ideas that follow from the chapters on inclusion and metro finance, but also reflects the lessons of the three case studies. To drive the future, cities must find new ways to invest in innovation, infrastructure, and inclusion, both by harnessing local capital and by connecting to global instruments and institutions. The ideas presented in this chapter not only are doable, they should be done. Innovation districts, generally located near universities and medical campuses, can be their own investment sector, attracting capital from pension funds and university endowments. Public asset corporations can regenerate industrial areas and finance large-scale infrastructure by increasing the commercial yield of publicly owned land and buildings without raising taxes. Cities can be part of a national, locally resourced campaign to invest in children, based on objective research and proven models, so that every child gets a shot to be middle class by middle age.

These ideas show that cities, far from being broke, have the means to raise enormous amounts of public, private, and civic capital and dedicate these resources to advanced problem solving. The ideas are bold and designed to provoke debate. But that is the purpose of this book, to describe what is already happening that accelerates growth and inclusion and to imagine what is possible and necessary moving forward.

The final chapter is a call to action. If cities are where the local and global converge, the right leadership and civic culture are the engines of a productive convergence. Whether it's in Erie, Pennsylvania, or Abilene, Texas, the ways to move forward engage leaders from all walks of life and several layers deep. To this end, theories of network intelligence that have been created to enhance the performance of corporations can also be applied to multiply the number of city leaders and improve their problem-solving capacity.

Leadership and civic culture have maximum impact when they are expressed through effective institutions. The institutions that urban leaders inherit, both within and across cities, were built to serve a different market and a different political economy. At a time when so much is changing, it is important that local leaders not only act but also take on the difficult task of renewing institutions or building new ones to meet hard challenges.

Organizing for success, of course, is not a job for city leaders alone. If national and state governments, global corporations, financial institutions, and multilateral institutions are to be city-savvy in a city-driven century, then they too need to reform their practices and engage cities as true partners. A burst in the establishment of city-oriented capacity-building and knowledge-sharing intermediaries, as well as investment funds, is clearly on the horizon. Just as earlier eras of political instability and economic insecurity led to the creation of such national institutions as the Federal Reserve Bank and the Social Security Administration, New Localism will find its hard expression in new institutions built by and for cities. History is repeating itself, but in urban form.

With so much uncertainty and vitriol at the federal level, New Localism offers a pathway to national renewal and a more competitive, sustainable, and inclusive society. It can unlock and leverage trillions in private and civic capital as markets are created and individuals and institutions find ways to invest in social outcomes. It is a path toward liberating and galvanizing energy and capital across the nation to invest in the future. It can make the United States more democratic since it places decisionmaking closer to the ground, with greater opportunities for participatory engagement on a regular basis rather than limited to periodic voting.

Finally, and most important, as citizens see solutions to pressing challenges actually implemented rather than simply debated by polarized parties and ideologies, New Localism can restore political comity and sanity to the American system and thus restore faith in government.

This is how to rebuild nations and repair the world: from the ground up.

TWO

New Localism and the American City

Not everything that is faced can be changed. But
nothing can be changed until it is faced.

—James Baldwin, *New York Times Book Review,*
January 14, 1962

New Localism is a problem-solving practice and governing philosophy for the twenty-first century. It emerged out of pragmatism—out of the need to rescue communities in decline—but is increasingly focused on linking local communities to the growth sectors of the global economy in ways both inclusive and environmentally sustainable. It embraces the devolution of responsibility downward and reflects the multidimensional nature of how problems are solved over the long term. Its success will require the development of new norms of growth, governance, and finance.

Localism as a political concept has signified a variety of things, including a preference for local solutions and the devolution of funding and political authority to local or regional decisionmakers. In other contexts, localism refers to being attentive to local ecologies, traditional cultures, and small businesses. Rural concerns over the impact of agribusiness on traditional farming lifeways emphasize the importance of family enterprise under the flag of localism.[1] Environmental protection is increasingly a local issue. Today, more than a thousand land trusts nationwide maintain stewardship over watersheds that provide livelihoods to many local people and serve as habitats for wildlife. These land trusts, with help from local volunteers, teach communities about the resources that are being protected.[2] The rise of the local food movement and increasing interest in sustainable agriculture are reenergizing alternative ways to think about local control and enterprise.[3]

There are other well-known variations on the localism theme, including those that focus on local economies and appropriate technology. The capacity of new communications technology, while global in consequence and reach, also empowers local activists by supporting their communities of interest. Neighborhood associations are increasingly electronic town halls, and citizens' groups dedicated to local government accountability use electronic media to evaluate budgets and policy ideas in real time. Technology has the ability to elevate local or individual causes in real time.[4]

The phrase *New Localism* was used a few years ago in the United Kingdom as a way to forge a new social contract with local authorities and civil society. In the British system, New Localism was seen as a breakout set of ideas that departed from the traditional overreliance on a strong central government. Organized within the framework of the Localism Act of 2010, New Localism recognized that while national governments ought to set minimum standards for social well-being, the implementation and management of a host of functions could be better undertaken at a local level, and not necessarily even by local government in the narrow sense.

Academics have sometimes focused on localism and what it means in the context of global changes in the economy. The collection of essays, for example, edited by Edward Goetz and Susan Clarke and titled *The New Localism: Comparative Urban Politics in a Global Era* offers a wide perspective on the changing nature of local politics as it adjusts to or reacts to economic restructuring. While many of the essays identify the importance of nongovernmental interest groups, from civic associations to pro–business growth associations, the contributors to the volume largely focus on politics and political movements in the traditional sense, though with a sophisticated understanding of global impacts and conditioning.[5]

The rich political science literature on cities analyzes the ways in which governments and politicians mobilize or demobilize different constituencies or social movements to achieve legitimacy. Urban development literature and urban sociology have been slightly more attuned to informal civic and political organizations and their consequences for growth and development. That literature has largely focused on the struggles within cities by various groups to control their destiny, though it often does so within the context of national or global economic analysis.[6]

The use of the term New Localism in this book owes much to others within the public sector, academia, and civil society that have sought to rescue the distinctive qualities of local communities from perspectives that view everything through formal structures or assume that in the age of globalization, there is limited political or civic space for locally initiated social change.

The ability of local communities in the United States to become effective problem solvers should not come as a surprise. Cities and towns developed in the absence of any intentional federal urban policy during most of the nation's history. Historically, city building was more of a bottom-up and relatively chaotic enterprise, involving builders and investors, merchants and workers, civic associations, immigration and immigrant entrepreneurs, and local government. It was never the result of a top-down policy so much as it was a self-organizing market and civic practice.[7] Moreover, America's political culture favors bottom-up approaches, a result both of the constitutional suspicion of too much government and of Americans' embrace of civil society as both a counter and a complement to markets and government.

THE ORIGINS OF NEW LOCALISM

New Localism has its roots in the second half of the twentieth century, a time when cities and other localities lost economic vitality and were struggling to revitalize. During that period, suburban America housed the upwardly mobile, and most central cities became the poorer parts of metropolitan economies. Suburban counties were growing and expanding in population and economic power. The older historical cores had higher levels of poverty and were often overwhelmingly minority, with increasing shares of African Americans and then Hispanics. The economic decline of urban centers was especially notable in northeastern and midwestern cities, which lost population (and continue to do so) to many southern and southwestern cities.[8]

The causes of central city decline have been studied for years and include such issues as racial discrimination, zoning laws, political fragmentation, shifts in transportation and communications technologies, a decline in manufacturing employment, public policies that encouraged decentralization, tax policy, consumer preference for larger homes, high crime rates, and the decline of urban public institutions. With respect to national dynamics, there are many other issues to consider, including the relocation of northern industries to Sunbelt states where labor was cheaper and less unionized. Whatever the reasons or drivers, the result was unmistakable:

most cities declined over a period of thirty to forty years as residents moved out of central cores and from older regions to newer ones.

Federal urban policy in the 1960s and 1970s focused increasingly on poverty alleviation and ensuring civil rights, resulting in laws against housing and lending discrimination. While these were important policy efforts, far less federal attention was paid to urban economic growth. Moreover, federal and state infrastructure investments continued to overwhelmingly support suburbanization. In this context, urban policy and poverty policy seemed to converge in the mind of the public.

In the 1980s, with the advent of the Reagan revolution, it became clear that federal policy was not going to have much of a city focus with respect to either poverty or growth. Since Reagan, every administration has proposed boutique place-based revitalization programs, from enterprise zones to Promise Neighborhoods zones, but most have not added up to much. Moreover, poverty reduction, both inside and outside cities, has been more affected by general economic conditions and universal programs such as the earned income tax credit, food support, and the low-income housing tax credit.[9] Targeted, place-based poverty reduction programs have shown less impact.[10]

City renewal came about in the absence of intentional federal support. Demographic changes starting in the mid-1980s and picking up steam by the early 1990s showed central city population loss beginning to level off, partly reversing the large-scale declines of the 1960s and 1970s. By 2000, and especially by 2010, census and other data showed that many central cities were gaining population.[11]

What caused this change? The central city renaissance was shaped in large part by a changing global economy, niche demographic demand, and new cultural preferences.

The Economic Shift

Cities have always had the advantages of agglomeration. What changed in the past few decades is that many urban institutions have become more relevant to the global knowledge economy: cities now offer a high concentration of research, medical, and academic institutions that attract students and knowledge workers and anchor the commercialization of new technologies. This economic grounding has attracted startup firms, business support networks, and venture capital sources. The new civic and entrepreneurial energy that emerged has added to city building efforts.

There are few examples of urban revitalization that do not have university and medical centers playing some role: the University City district of West Philadelphia, the midtown institutions in Detroit, University Circle in Cleveland, Johns Hopkins in Baltimore, and Washington University in St. Louis are just a few examples. These prestigious community pillars create residential, business, and real estate multiplier effects for their local environment. But most important, these institutions act globally even as they retain their place-based emphasis.[12] This convergence of the local and global in singular institutions identified with place is one of the hallmarks of the global economy. Such institutions, working with allied institutions and companies, including major commercial real estate firms, have increasingly formed the basis for larger innovation districts throughout the world.

Demography

After the significant losses of population to suburban communities, new demographic trends have brought people back into cities. Some cities sustained losses of nearly half their population. St. Louis and Buffalo entered the twenty-first century with nineteenth-century population levels. Detroit continues to lose population, although there are signs that the exodus may be leveling off.

Now, many central cities are being resuscitated for reasons linked to baby-boomer and millennial lifestyle choices, economic opportunity, and immigration.[13] Aging baby boomers are attracted to the cultural amenities of cities, and their impact on urban housing markets has been compounded by the entry of large numbers of millennial workers who are not starting families and prefer the amenities of cities. New urban industries linked to technology and research are also attracting highly educated young adults.

Both retiring baby boomers and the rising generation of unattached young people contribute to a deep trend in American demography: an increase in the number of people who live alone or in households of two persons. This contrasts with the traditional suburban housing demand of larger families in single-family households, although developers are adapting to these demographic changes in suburban communities. But the changing nature of household composition has worked especially well in urban areas and has led to an increase in rental units in some downtowns.[14]

The most decisive demographic influence on urban redevelopment, however, has been immigration. While immigration has long contributed to population growth in U.S. cities, rates of foreign-born persons in the United States began to accelerate in the 1990s and have continued to escalate since. Immigration has fueled urban population replacement and growth. Cities are prime destinations for immigrants, and city gateways on the East and West Coasts, and increasingly throughout the Southwest, have benefited the most. American cities could not have revived as they have in the absence of large-scale immigration. Moreover, dramatic levels of immigrant entrepreneurship in cities as diverse as Houston, Miami, Philadelphia, and Minneapolis are powerful reminders of how cities were built and rebuilt over generations.[15]

The Culture of Cities

The cultural shifts that made city living desirable are complicated to track but are both a consequence and a cause of central city revival. Television and popular culture are good barometers of when those shifts began to happen. While cities have always been the setting for gritty crime shows and legal and hospital dramas, the formula for most soap operas and situation comedies was either suburban or placeless. Starting in the 1990s, television suddenly showcased cities as hip places for young singles to explore relationships and develop careers. The city became a playground for the characters of *Seinfeld*, *Sex and the City*, and *Friends*. Television had decided that the city was young again.

Why did the culture embrace dense urban living and the social value of urban places? Some of it has to do with the affiliation with universities and other institutions linked to the startup innovation economy. And some of it has to do with the connection between cultural creativity in the arts and media and the economy, for arts and the media remained urban even during periods of decline. By the 1990s creativity and knowledge were increasingly identified with urban communities and urban-based companies.[16]

But the linkage between culture and cities also has to do with environmental sustainability and how its associated values translate into imperatives to repurpose legacy places. Cities are ideal places for environmental stewardship, which is important to the culture: urban dwellers are not as car dependent as people in the suburbs, and urban life can be more energy-efficient. Urban dwellers can use public transportation, walk, or ride a bicycle to work. Thus urban civic activism based on retrofitting the older built environment emerged in concert with an environmental ethos.[17]

GOVERNANCE AND PLACEMAKING

While demographic and economic changes and cultural preferences contributed to reshaping American cities, new governance practices were also decisive in this regard. New models of governance were generally built on better uses of data for decisionmaking, a focus on outcomes, and the use of outsourced civic and private capacity. They also provided early examples of the solution sharing and replication among cities that is happening at an expanded pace today.

The transformation of cities and many other localities over the past several decades, in other words, was not a passive process resulting from a shift in economic opportunities or demography. Rather, the places best able to take advantage of opportunities either had existing advantages (major research universities and intact business districts) or else organized to take advantage of new economic realities by becoming the civic innovators and problem solvers of New Localism.

A reduction in crime rates through computer mapping, community policing, and targeted social interventions reflected one of the most important shifts in urban governance. Prior to the 1990s, police assumed they could respond to crimes but not prevent them. That perspective changed, first in New York City and then throughout the nation. The drop in the murder rate in New York City from 30 per 100,000 (2,262 in 1990) to 4 per 100,000 (335 in 2016) is staggering.[18] This decline was accompanied by a decrease in the number of people incarcerated and, recently, a decrease in the use of the controversial stop-and-frisk techniques.[19]

There are many aspects to changes in policing, ranging from the use of better technology to improved civic interactions. Crime mapping through geographic information systems is an important way to strategize the use of police resources. Community policing that involves civic participation can have a significant effect. The work of David Kennedy's National Network for Safe Communities demonstrates the impact of combining social services and criminal justice resources.[20]

Community renewal became the focus of new business and resident associations. Emphasizing clean and safe environments, many associations formed special service districts that collected fees from businesses and residents to perform additional public services. Hundreds of downtown, park, and neighborhood districts improved both the optics and the market viability of communities through partnering with public agencies. These efforts also became the cornerstone of physical revitalization by raising private and civic capital to restore public spaces.[21]

Similar community efforts to turn around schools emerged in traditionally distressed central cities through the advent of public charter schools, publicly funded but privately managed. Charter schools represent promising if controversial aspects of school reform, but they have transformed the landscape of education in many of America's largest cities. Today, large school districts are responding to consumer demand and creating an increasingly diverse portfolio of learning opportunities.[22]

American cities have also incubated local development organizations and community development financial institutions that play critical roles in revitalizing lower-income communities and helping to restore their market and civic viability. These institutions draw on both civic models of participation and market models of development and finance to invest and develop where others were unwilling. As early-stage risk takers, they cleared the way for other market and civic participants. Finally, these development entities became critical to the transformation of public housing in America, which, while driven by regulatory and budget changes in Washington, D.C., during the Clinton administration (particularly the HOPE VI program) was generally undertaken by local public-private partnerships.[23]

Many of these community-based efforts, reinforced by downtown associations, formed the early architecture of New Localism. They organized both at a grassroots level—among civic groups, church congregations, and tenant or homeowner associations—and at the grasstops level—among corporate, bank, and foundation leaders. They invested in communities that could not wait for an external force to save them. And they developed new institutions or intermediaries to attract capital or organize development.

The new governance institutions that formed the backbone of early New Localism efforts were involved in many facets of placemaking, creating livable places with distinct value by transforming communities in decline into places of greater vibrancy and public use.

Placemaking is largely an organic process that occurs in a context of renewed investment and market demand. The right design and planning efforts are also important. Many older city neighborhoods were first transformed by artists, designers, and artisans who could reimagine uses for older manufacturing buildings, or by civic activists who converted abandoned urban land into parks and gardens. The reuse of inherited industrial spaces to create distinctive user-friendly environments is urban redevelopment's calling card in the twenty-first century.

Placemaking uncovers the inherent value of a community and redefines its potential by integrating its historical identity with contemporary uses. As American cities lost population and dynamism, many of the grand institutions and buildings of the nineteenth and early twentieth centuries fell into decline or disrepair. Late twentieth-century placemaking rediscovered what still existed and repurposed it for a new era.

Some of the most interesting examples of placemaking have involved the reclamation of industrial buildings no longer viable as sites for routine manufacturing. Many had stood abandoned or underutilized for decades; others had been torn down without regard for their architectural or historical value. But today a few thousand of these older industrial buildings have been transformed into residential and commercial sites, artists' studios, and performance centers. In many areas they also represent types of gentrification that typically see tenant replacement as the value of the land and units changes—yesterday's artists' lofts become tomorrow's investment bankers' condos. But while issues of affordability have to be addressed in the fast-growing cities, many of those buildings were underused or abandoned, and their transformation into active use is a contribution to public and private wealth.

Waterfronts too have been reinvented in myriad ways as both private development sites and public amenities. As Joseph Riley, the former mayor of Charleston, South Carolina, declared, "Give the citizens their river once again!" In cities throughout the nation, waterfronts are becoming both publicly accessible and commercially viable.

In some places the battle over the use of waterfronts and industrial zones or buildings resulted in profound disagreements between different constituencies, from labor leaders to residential developers; from new residents to more established ones. But in the best of situations accommodations are made, and hence future spatial form becomes—as is often the case—a negotiation of social interests.

Rediscovering and reanimating place also means creating public spaces to enable people from different walks of life to mingle and connect so as to experience common urban ownership and belonging. Food markets and plazas, cafés and bike trails, festivals and parades, street performances and outdoor concerts all create shared identity. The regeneration of public spaces means that more people learn the informal negotiation of city life regarding the norms of place and community. The proliferation of farmers' markets and outdoor art exhibits or the marketing of special restaurant or late-night gallery openings may be a good deal more planned than what Jane Jacobs, author of the 1961 *The Death and Life of Great American Cities*, aspired to in her urban vision of the organic collision of residents, makers, and merchants, but it does the job nonetheless.

The more profound aspects of placemaking involve the reconfiguration of public institutions—schools, public transit, community colleges, social service centers, museums, playgrounds. This is a task that is a good deal more difficult than adding bike lanes, programming a public space, or declaring a First Friday art gallery evening. It involves the reinvention of institutions with deep cultures and legacy relationships.

Cities are built as a negotiation between private ownership and the collective use of public institutions and spaces. At their best, cities have a democratic character. A low-income resident and student should have access to great schools and great art, to recreation and music, to the possibilities of many cultures. At their worst, cities are segregated by race and class, and the unequal distribution of services creates fissures that fester in the collective memory and erode a sense of shared destiny. Placemaking in the twenty-first century must have as its intentional focus the reassertion of shared community and prosperity. This affects every institution, from how museums and orchestras open their doors to public school students to how new immigrants find a public voice for cultural expression to how schooling and lifelong learning become second nature to civil society and the public sector.

GLOBAL LEADERSHIP FROM THE GROUND UP

While many of the earliest examples of New Localism had to do with rescuing places in decline by investing in residential and commercial real estate and in community institutions, other forms of New Localism entailed reconnecting place to the economy in broader ways. Rebuilding place and catalyzing economic relevance are related, particularly in terms of attracting and retaining talent. But they involve different emphases and strategic intent and hence are generally driven by different constituencies.

What a place makes or how it contributes to global production and innovation becomes the relevant frame of reference as the conversation shifts from placemaking to creating economic value. Placemaking entails investing in physical and institutional assets, whereas renewed economic relevance requires investment in those sectors of the economy for which a place has shown advantages and global capacity.

Economically thriving urban centers and their larger metro economies are critical to national competitiveness. The United States is among the most urbanized nations in the world, if by urbanization we include the metropolitan regions within which central cities reside. Close to 85 percent of Americans live in urbanized or metropolitan areas. The concentration of population in a few major metropolitan regions in the United States is striking: one out of seven Americans lives in either the New York, Los Angeles, or Chicago metropolitan region, and one out of three Americans lives in the top ten metropolitan regions. All population growth in America is metropolitan.[24]

But just as important as the handful of mega-global cities is the fact that strong U.S. urban economies are far more numerous than in other nations, including Europe. The United States has a huge metropolitan advantage, although it is does not develop public policy around this fact. The only part of national government with an explicit urban mandate is the Department of Housing and Urban Development (HUD), which largely focuses on housing those living in poverty. Few other parts of the federal government take a spatial perspective, although many have subunits with spatial emphases. Programmatically, the basic architecture of the American federal government is in contrast to the fact that American demography and wealth are metropolitan.

When the McKinsey Global Institute studied the 259 largest American metropolitan areas (population of 150,000 or more), among the several observations that emerged was this striking fact: the per capita GDP premium among American cities is greater than that of their European counterparts, and the dynamism of the U.S. economy comes from the wide swath of middleweight cities across the nation. This broader base of metropolitan economies creates more flexibility and diversification for the U.S. economy as a whole. It can be one of America's greatest advantages, but only if we invest accordingly. Enhancing the value of those middleweights will be decisive for the American economy in the near future.[25]

How many of these middleweight cities become thriving communities is less about top-down prescription and more about local reinvention. What this means from city to city will vary, but the general thrust of investing in place, identifying points of global economic relevance, and creating higher levels of social cohesion must become an explicit part of any local action agenda.

Strong signs of economic restructuring in those middleweight cities often go unmentioned in the national press. Cincinnati, Pittsburgh, and St. Louis are becoming global centers of technology with industrial expertise in medical devices, robotics, and genomics. Other stories involve inclusive growth strategies. Communities such as Anchorage, Kalamazoo, and Louisville have launched cradle-to-career initiatives, integrated efforts that promote kindergarten readiness, elementary and secondary education, college completion, and workforce-oriented skills training. And Boise, Houston, and St. Paul are ensuring that new immigrants to the United States can "earn, learn and belong," maximizing their contributions to the broader community.[26]

Many local communities are becoming strong environmental stewards, making certain that growth does not come at the expense of the environment. They are committed to climate action plans that seek to lower carbon emissions and reduce waste. Dallas, Philadelphia, and Washington, D.C., are developing cutting-edge solutions to manage stormwater runoff and help restore watersheds. In Philadelphia, the William Penn Foundation, working in collaboration with civic groups and government agencies, has embarked on a long-term strategy to improve the quality of the Delaware River watershed, which provides drinking water to 5 percent of the nation's population.[27] The strategy leverages the scientific capacity of Philadelphia's Academy of Natural Sciences and the knowledge of civic partners, who are building a constituency for improving the river. The Delaware River Watershed Initiative knits together a wide range of social interests—suburban and urban, rural and recreational—over a four-state area.

These new economic growth initiatives on the part of middleweight cities are being designed by and delivered through networks of institutions and leaders that collaborate to solve problems. In Chattanooga, Indianapolis, and San Diego the public, private, and civic spheres are joining forces at the scale of the city and metropolis to catalyze new economy-shaping efforts, measure progress, and champion success. As with place-based initiatives, this is community organizing at the highest level. It underscores that in cities and other major population centers, it is difficult to know where the public sector ends and the private and civic sectors begin—far different from the visible hand and top-down control of federal government agencies.

Becoming global leaders also means that middleweight cities must identify new ways to finance the future, particularly under the constraints of conventional finance and the public sector. Despite local fiscal stress, the response in recent years to raising new public dollars for infrastructure and inclusion has been remarkable. Over the past three election cycles, for example, voters in cities and metropolitan counties have approved billions of dollars for infrastructure investments ranging from transit extensions to rail station redevelopment to road modernization. In the 2016 election cycle alone, voters from Los Angeles and Seattle to Wake County, North Carolina, and Indianapolis approved nearly $200 billion in additional taxes to spur ambitious transit and more sustainable patterns of development.[28]

Ballot initiatives passed in Broward County, Dayton, King County, and San Antonio are generating hundreds of millions of dollars in local revenues to provide children with high-quality early education and other proven investments in young adults.[29] The use of public referenda to raise public resources cuts across red and blue party lines, conservative and liberal communities. Oklahoma City is in many respects a leader in such financing, having successfully pursued a series of Metropolitan Area Projects (MAPs) referenda to invest in downtown sports, cultural, and civic facilities and the upgrading of public schools. These projects enabled the city to respond aggressively and project an image of unified determination in the aftermath of the bombing of the Alfred P. Murrah Federal Building in April 1995.[30]

New Localism extends far beyond traditional forms of public finance. Networks of public, private, and civic actors are trying to fill the void left by national governments with a wide array of innovative approaches to problem solving. Such cities as Denver and Washington, D.C., are using the appreciation in real estate values to help pay for transformative infrastructure projects, the remaking of Union Station, and the deck-over of a portion of a 1960s freeway. Business leaders such as Dan Gilbert in Detroit and Paul Allen in Seattle are playing the role of catalytic developers and restoring downtowns to prior glory, while other tech entrepreneurs such as Audible founder Don Katz in Newark are using their capital to seed start-ups and entice employees to live in the city.

These positive expressions of pragmatism show that the geography of New Localism is malleable, scalable, and fit to purpose. In some examples, initiatives are designed, financed, and delivered at the city or even urban district or neighborhood level. In other cases, usually those involving infrastructure or environmental concerns that cross jurisdictional borders, the county, metropolitan, or even regional scale is being invoked.

NEW LOCALISM: A GOVERNING PHILOSOPHY AND PRACTICE

The power of cities and counties is not like the power of nations or states. It is grounded in markets and civics more than in constitutions or charters. It is multisectoral rather than monosectoral. It is defined by pragmatism rather than by straitjacketed partisanship. And it is enmeshed in global flows of capital, labor, products, ideas, and practices.

As a governing philosophy and practice, New Localism in the United States can be defined by seven characteristics.

First, *New Localism holds as a basic tenet that cities and their metropolitan communities are the level of society that will address many of the economic, social, and environmental challenges facing the world today.* They can often do so in a way that is more efficient, more effective, and more democratic than can be achieved by national governments alone. Solutions are often more likely to succeed because they are customized to place, designed and delivered by cross-sectoral and interdisciplinary networks, and nurtured through local institutions that can transcend election cycles.

The mythology of an omniscient central power has grown since the middle of the twentieth century, even in federal republics where governance is multilevel and multichannel. This myth reaches fever pitch during presidential elections, when to all appearances it seems that the nation will rise or fall depending on the decisions of one individual.

National myths are hard to break, yet the data make clear that central governments are the dominant investors in only certain public activities while being junior partners in many others. In the United States, for example, the federal government is the prime investor in defense, in key components of the safety net, and in basic science through the National Institutes of Health, the National Science Foundation, and the Defense Advanced Research Projects Agency and other research arms. In many areas critical to our future prosperity and shared growth, however, Washington is a small player. It provides only 12 cents and 25 cents of every public dollar spent on K–12 education and transportation infrastructure, respectively.[31]

This mythology of national power has oriented problem solving toward national-level fixes when the answers lie instead at the local level. For years, researchers in the United States studied the salutary benefits of quality early childhood education, and presidential candidates and national representatives dutifully proposed legislation to make such education a universal reality. For years, nothing happened, as proposals fell victim to partisan gridlock and fiscal limitations. That's why corporate, political, and civic leaders in recent years have taken the matter into their own hands in city after city.

Correcting the confusion over who does what in societies is an essential act of civic education and a necessary first step toward national progress. The myth of a centralized national power as the main solution provider in earlier decades tended to infantilize cities. Solving problems has been associated for years with going to Washington and securing resources, reforms, or some combination. The proliferation of constituency groups for every interest and issue imaginable is testament to the power and persistence of the myth, even after years of federal drift and local activism. As in a relationship gone sour, cities have held out endless hope that the federal government would somehow miraculously heal itself when all the evidence said otherwise. No more. Cities' main message to the federal government today is "First, do no harm."

Second, *New Localism is a mechanism for converting the self-organizing power of markets and civil society into structured fiscal and financial resources and, ultimately, political power.*

Market power is enhanced by focusing with precision and discipline on the special competitive advantages of a particular place rather than on the assets of cities in general.

Fiscal power is gained by both cleaning up urban balance sheets, which are often encumbered by pension and other liabilities, and by making hard decisions on local taxes. This latter point often means dusting off the public referenda process and garnering voter support for large, transformative investments in the future, most notably in children and infrastructure. Taxes are often increased at the federal and state level when media scrutiny and public engagement are at a minimum. Cities are an "open book," requiring an interwoven mix of transparency and trust.

Financial power is gained by engaging sophisticated market actors, domestic and global, in economy shaping and placemaking. City leaders now routinely deal with a broad array of financial institutions (such as rating agencies, commercial banks, investment banks, pension funds, even sovereign funds) and corporations (in arenas as diverse as technology, manufacturing, real estate, and sports and entertainment).

Political power is gained both through the ballot box and through the building of strong coalitions within and across cities, within and across sectors. The collective commitment of cities to carrying out the climate goals of the Paris Agreement represents the new form of political power that cities are wielding in the world today.

The conversion process is multilayered. It is a game of chess played by leaders who must combine substantive knowledge of issues with a keen understanding of the interplay among markets, civics, and politics. This is a far cry from the days when cities were seen as the backwater for pothole politicians and second-tier business leaders.

Third, *New Localism reflects a commitment to a new kind of problem solving that is distinct from the uniformity of policymaking.* It adapts the risk-taking attitude of individual entrepreneurs and investors to the collective sphere. It is experimental and tolerant of failure. It is the twenty-first-century embodiment of Franklin Roosevelt's words in his famous 1932 speech: "It is common sense to take a method and try it. If it fails, admit it frankly, and try another. But, by all means, try something."[32]

New Localism is multidisciplinary in focus and collaborative in practice, enabling cities to leverage the expertise and experience of disparate sectors and diverse sets of people. The world's challenges today simply do not follow the twentieth-century model of compartmentalized thinking and stove-piped action.

New Localism is practice- and task-led, focusing on tangible action and visible, measurable results.

Cities are thus able to learn from both successes and mistakes and make course corrections in real time. This also engenders trust building as the combination of quick wins and structural reforms convinces multiple stakeholders that change is actually possible and progress is actually measurable. Trust is earned from tangible success, from the results of action rather than talk. The accumulation of trust is like a savings account in which interest compounds. Its growth is not linear, and careful stewardship enables larger payoffs over time.

Fourth, *New Localism has elements of both representative and participatory democracy.* Municipalities and counties elect mayors, county executives, and members of city and county councils. These elected officials have formal roles and responsibilities and commensurate powers. They also have the imprimatur of democratic legitimacy. Elections confer on these officials the authority to represent the body politic. No other institution or constituency group, no matter how influential or well resourced, can claim this mantle.

Yet problem solving in communities does not end with the passage of a local ordinance or regulation. Solutions are often designed by and financed and delivered in close cooperation with the private, civic, and community sectors. Participatory democracy means that relationships across sectors are often natural and reinforcing: institutions are partners rather than antagonists in getting things done. There is a qualitative difference between the role of a mayor or city councilperson and the role of a governor or state legislator, or the U.S. president or member of Congress.

Cogoverning also helps explains why New Localism is nonpartisan. The regular engagement of business, civic, and academic leaders elevates pragmatic thinking and commonsense discourse and crowds out the inflammatory rhetoric associated with partisanship and ideology. This creates a healthy group psychology that rewards creative tinkering (the essence of problem solving) rather than obstructive action (the essence of partisanship). Localities, in other words, engender group innovation; legislatures reward groupthink.

Fifth, *New Localism is intensely focused on maximizing value for long-term prosperity rather than short-term private profit or political gain.* Cities are not exclusively governments but represent broader networks of institutions and individuals—homeowners, universities, hospitals, philanthropies, private businesses, utilities—which are committed to and depend on the betterment of their place.

In the early stages of the 2016 elections, politicians on the left and right were raising alarm bells about the dangers of short-termism. Hillary Clinton often recited the risks for the private sector, but former House majority leader Eric Cantor captured the breadth of the issue, saying, "If you think about short-termism and what is infecting so much of the public discourse today, there is this trend toward short-termism in both the corporate and business arena as well as in government and politics. Where they have something in common, it is this lack of trust or faith in institutions."[33] Much of the problem can be traced to the nationalization of politics and finance, which has divorced ideology and decisionmaking from the realities on the ground.

But unlike national institutions, corporate or political urban stakeholders are fundamentally grounded and patient investors, committed to long-term value appreciation and broad prosperity rather than to the quick buck or political win. They are both stewards of the past and foundation builders for the future. They see cities as a unified asset portfolio and recognize the holistic effect of disparate investments to strengthen and reinforce each other's value.

Sixth, *New Localism simultaneously embraces the local and the global, the latter being a source of immense and still unrealized benefits and power.* While institutions are deeply rooted in the distinctive economies, priorities, and culture of local communities, they are also remarkably connected to global investments, interests, and intelligence. The web of connections is intricate and complex. Universities draw talented students and faculty from all over the world and engage in transnational research projects. Companies depend on global supply chains and sell their products and services into global markets. Global capital doesn't respect borders and invests sometimes through arm's-length instruments, sometimes through direct, hands-on engagement. Cities simultaneously exist within nations and transcend nations.

Finally, *New Localism reflects a new horizontal rather than vertical mechanism for societies to solve hard problems.* Cities are constantly crafting new ways to address challenges that are urgent, immediate, and often highly visible. Solutions that are concrete, imaginative, and tested on the ground do not stay local for long. Instead, they are adapted to other cities' situations, tailored to the different economic and social starting points and the fiscal conditions of different cities. Cities may be on their own, given the abdication of responsibility by national governments and states, but they are not alone. Other cities are continuously inventing solutions that are ripe for replication or adaptation.

This is a far cry from twentieth-century notions of problem solving, which depended on experts in specialized bureaucratic agencies designing new programs or promulgating regulations and then imposing them from above. Problem solving today, by contrast, occurs within a broader framework of collective urban action. It is an exercise carried out by cities across multiple institutions and across a vast cohort of collegial innovators. Cities borrow heavily from other cities as they develop solutions. Peer learning is the primary way city builders perfect their craft.

The growing interaction of global cities, because of trade patterns and other affinities, further enhances the creativity of solutions. Here the response to climate change is a good example. A city like Copenhagen leads in public sector and process innovation (such as structural shifts in renewable and distributed energy), whereas a city like Tel Aviv excels at product innovation (such as green tech). When these two cities work together, not only are there obvious opportunities for mutual exchange and benefit but also a new platform is created for breakthroughs. This is the new urban calculus: "$2+2=5$," in the memorable phrasing of Henry Cisneros, the former HUD secretary.

The replication of solutions is also being accelerated by new city intermediaries and networks. The C40 Cities Climate Leadership Group, for example, "supports cities to collaborate effectively, share knowledge and drive meaningful, measurable and sustainable action on climate change."[34] In 2015, C40 Cities reported that 30 percent of their climate actions were delivered as a result of collaboration with other cities.[35] The Rockefeller Foundation's 100 Resilient Cities, for its part, enables cities to share lessons on how to tackle natural shocks and socioeconomic stresses.

New Localism is a reminder that power in countries as powerful as the United States—or Germany or France or China—has never been as simple as the conventional picture painted by hierarchical command-and-control systems. Millions of decisions are made by subnational leaders and ordinary citizens, and these decisions build communities, drive economies, educate children, catalyze innovation, and change lives. New Localism is both representative of and restorative of the democratic ideals and principles on which the republic was founded and which sustain Americans in good and bad times.

Yet New Localism is still nascent and emerging; it is neither fully formed nor fully operational. And, to take a cue from Shakespeare, it is more honored in the breach than in the observance.

While competing in this global economy requires new thinking, many cities continue to pursue zero-sum economic development strategies that subsidize stadia and steal businesses rather than incent innovation. These strategies are rarely aligned with smart education and workforce strategies that give workers the technical skills they need to succeed in growing occupations. And reinvestment in neighborhoods, downtowns, and waterfronts still has a long way to go to make up for decades of disinvestment, depopulation, and decentralization.

Acting effectively also requires structural reforms. Many cities must come to terms with legacy liabilities, most prominently unfunded pension fund and health care costs, that continue to eat away at present-day budgets and make it increasingly hard to deliver high-quality public goods. They must also address the proliferation of legacy public authorities—airport authorities, port authorities, water and sewer authorities, convention center authorities, stadium authorities, redevelopment authorities, public housing authorities, land banks, and independent school boards—that populate cities in their singular fiefdoms and undermine the design of and execution of integrated strategies.

Finally, the financing of New Localism must overcome the chasm that still exists between cities and financial capital. U.S. cities are mature economically but immature governmentally and financially. In most U.S. cities there is little information on what the public owns and no mechanism for disposing of public assets in ways that maximize long-term growth and public return. There are few trusted intermediaries that can bridge the gap between local communities and large sources of capital. The result is that private and civic capital sits on the sidelines and fails to invest.

Addressing these challenges cannot, for the most part, be legislated, regulated, or mandated from above. Rather, it rests with cities to use and organize the powers they have rather than wait for powers they will never receive.

THE STRUCTURAL ROOTS OF NEW LOCALISM

New Localism emerged as a necessary response to the dramatic decline of core cities in the latter part of the twentieth century. The related dynamics of depopulation, deindustrialization, and racial segregation compelled many cities to respond in novel and networked ways when it became clear that the challenges were too large and structural for ill-funded national programs—model cities, urban development action grants, empowerment zones—to address.

But the roots of New Localism run much deeper. Large forces have placed cities at the center of a new global economic order. They are both the generators and the recipients of an unprecedented flow of goods, people, capital, and ideas across national and continental borders, all facilitated by new, ubiquitous technologies. The economic, environmental, and social externalities of these flows help explain some of the economic insecurities of the twenty-first century and the rise of populism. But they also give cities unique and central roles to play as hubs of innovation and problem solving.

The next chapter explores the forces that have birthed both New Localism and populism and demonstrates the ways in which cities are at the epicenter of the new global narrative.

THREE

Everything Has Changed

History does not crawl, it jumps.
—Nassim Nicholas Taleb, *The Black Swan*

The rise of populism and the emergence of New Localism share common drivers: dramatic shifts in the economy, an increasingly global society, widening gaps in income and social status, and the new economic advantages of urban institutions and business development ecosystems. Yet among the least understood consequences of globalization is how it foregrounds the importance of locale. The global and the local have converged in new ways. This chapter explores that convergence and its consequences for political discontent and local problem solving.

The integration of local and national economies into a worldwide system of investment, consumption, and production has produced more than a globally connected economy. We are a global society, with common communications platforms, multinational companies, shared news sources, global universities, and an increasingly diverse population. Globalization has also remade the significance of locality while converting cities into the dominant settlement pattern.

The depth of global change today rivals the transition from a majority rural society to the large-scale industrialization and urbanization that occurred during the latter part of the nineteenth century and the first decades of the twentieth century in the United States. As was true then, today everything is in play: the meaning of national identity, the nature of familiar institutions, how we make a living, and the conviction of our politics and values.

The new hyperglobal economy emerged from the triumphs of America and its allies following World War II. Advanced digital technology, the ascendance of market economies, and free trade flowed largely from American innovations and strategic values, which prevailed during the Cold War and eventually brought nations into a unified economic sphere.

With the collapse of East European communism, China's transition to a market economy, and a reawakened Indian economy, global capitalism rapidly absorbed millions of new workers, owners, and consumers. Advanced communications made the world shrink even as more economic participants enlarged its reach, resulting in a shakeup in wealth creation, income distribution, and global politics.

Global economic change upended numerous local economic arrangements, from small-acreage rural farmers who could not compete with agribusiness, to incumbent industries overwhelmed by large-scale enterprises and unable to afford investments in new technologies, to companies protected by public subsidy and trade barriers, to small manufacturing towns transformed by technology and trade.

The diminished status of routine manufacturing and the generally lowered earning capacity of non-college-educated workers was a profound change for many American communities and households. Manufacturing still contributes significantly to the U.S. economy, but the share of manufacturing jobs in the overall labor force and the contribution of manufacturing employment to entry-level middle-class jobs will never return to their former state.[1]

A restructured global economy produces winners and losers. Several Asian nations emerged with a stronger middle class and more competitive export economies. In economically advanced nations such as the United States and some European countries, inequality has increased over the past four decades. In his study of globalization, the economist Branko Milanovic details how economic elites and many highly educated professionals across the world are profiting, as are many poor and moderate-income workers in nations formerly excluded from market economic growth.[2]

Inequality within the United States has widened more rapidly than in other advanced economies. After a period of increasing income convergence extending from the 1950s through the early 1970s, American incomes have diverged significantly over the past forty years. Today the top 10 percent of U.S. earners average about nine times the income of the bottom 90 percent of earners. In terms of wealth, the top 10 percent of Americans have about $51 trillion in net worth, while the bottom half has about $1 trillion.[3]

Why did this happen? Multiple reasons have been put forward: the decline of industrial labor unions, an inadequate social safety net, the changing role of higher education in securing middle-class employment, declining levels of entrepreneurship, employment disruptions from auto-mation and global trade, and the capacity of economic elites to influence tax policy and other regulations. All of these answers contain some kernel of truth and have clearly contributed to the renewed populist atmosphere.

America still has a large middle class, but, as a Pew Research analysis of household income since 1971 shows, the middle is shrinking because of changes at both ends of the income scale.[4] The precarious nature of middle-class life is one of the major causes of political discontent. And as a large middle class is important to democracy, the lack of income security for large numbers of people in the middle class is a civic as well as an eco-nomic problem.

Many of the jobs that disappeared from the United States, Europe, and other large industrialized economies around the world were lost through automation and changing work processes rather than through offshoring or labor substitution with low-cost foreign labor.[5] Technology both de-stroys and creates new jobs, but the dislocations are hard to manage, par-ticularly for middle-aged or older workers with limited skills applicable to new, higher-wage job opportunities. Although we benefit from techno-logical innovation in fields ranging from communications to health care, downside risks also exist. They are just experienced differently depending on skills, economic sector, and even geography.

New technologies have also shaken the foundations of familiar institu-tions, from banks to bookstores. This in turn has contributed to the sense that everything has changed and that the rate of change will continue to accelerate. The capacity to eliminate core functions of private firms, civic institutions, and even government by removing middle-tier roles and directly connecting customers and providers has revamped commerce.

Disintermediation emerged first in finance but spread rapidly along the electronic lines of the internet. The apps on a simple handheld device allow one to enroll in a course, invest capital, find a date, buy a book, download a film, view a live broadcast, read an X-ray, communicate on social media, or make a travel reservation—all without speaking to anyone or going anywhere.

As Tom Friedman once noted, nobody would have predicted that the largest cab companies in the world (Uber, Lyft) would no longer own cars, the largest hotelier (Airbnb) would own no buildings, and the largest book and music seller (Amazon) would build its business without retail outlets.

With rapid advances in 3-D printing technology, robotics, and artificial intelligence, the transformations of the past few decades will be dwarfed by what is coming. Current debates over the implications of self-driving automobiles, for example, reflect both aspirations for and fears of new technologies. It is coming; we just don't yet know what it means.

Transformations in the economy and technology have been accompanied by changes in local demographics. The past fifty years were a time of unprecedented immigration from Asia, Latin America, Africa, and the Caribbean. In 2016, the highest levels of immigration into the United States were from Mexico, India, China, the Philippines, and El Salvador. The percentage of persons in the United States with European immigrant heritage declined significantly from 1970 through today.[6]

By 2014, non-Hispanic whites were a minority of public school students, and by 2020 it is estimated there will be more minority children overall than non-Hispanic white children.[7] The transformative role of immigration can be observed throughout America: from small towns in the Midwest to the South to Anchorage, Alaska, where 100 languages are spoken in the public school district.[8]

Most studies on acculturation rates find today's rates to be similar to those of past eras of high immigration.[9] Moreover, as intergroup marriage rates grow, the nation is changing in even more profound ways. Seventeen states had miscegenation laws before 1967.[10] Now interracial marriages in the United States represent over 8 percent of all marriages. In 2015, 17 percent of new marriages were interracial.[11]

The combined effect of new demography and a changing economy has created, for some, a crisis in national identity. As the nation becomes more diverse, incumbent identities are sometimes challenged in uncomfortable ways. Cultural transformation through immigration and economic change is a constant theme of American history. But rapid change during a period of wage stagnation and widening income inequality generally has political consequences. The public policy stop signs go up.

CONVERGENCE OF GLOBAL AND LOCAL

The relationship between globalization and populism has been heavily discussed with regard to electoral discontent. The connection between globalization and localism as an arena of enhanced civic action has not been as well explored as the general theme of global economic change and populism. However, there is an explicit link between globalization and New Localism.

An important logic within globalization leads back to the local. Globalization not only creates a hyperconnected world, it also opens up new means for expressing local identity and new possibilities for local development strategies. The importance of local capacities and action is augmented by global and technological change. The local and the global, we claim, converge in several ways.

One aspect of the convergence has to do with the structural power of economic integration and what it means for nation-states and political decentralization. A second aspect of the convergence has to do with the increased importance of cities within the global economy—the spatial effect—and what that means for the relationship between urban communities and the nation-state. And a third aspect of the convergence has to do with the leveling effect of technology and how that generates common challenges for economic growth, which are ultimately shaped and actualized locally.

Taken together, these three inflection points may reshape the nature of economic growth and political affiliation throughout the twenty-first century not only in the United States but also globally. They are the undercurrents of a major wave of change. The wave is evident, but not the undercurrents, which may ultimately be more consequential.

Structural Effect
The confluence of global commercial rules and advanced technological capacities results in a centrifugal force and a centripetal force. National economies are being pulled onto a transnational platform even as there is increased potential for new types of political autonomy within existing nation-states.

As multinational systems assume many of the nonsecurity functions of nation-states, prenational social solidarities are more easily expressed. If the functions of the nation-state are diminished economically, then local cultural sovereignty will more readily renegotiate a new structural position. Global commercial integration could thus make it easier for Quebec to leave Canada or Catalonia to leave Spain. That may never happen. But the point is that a globally organized market comprised of legacy political systems enables subunits of those political systems to seek autonomy. And even if those subunits do not want independence, they may negotiate new power-sharing arrangements.

An ethnic or regional group may decide it no longer needs the existing national system for economic and social protection if there is a global substitute or alternative. In fact, it may find that the existing national framework works against its economic self-interest, in addition to the barrier of differences in cultural or historical identity. Hence the group may either try to exit or, at the very least, try to negotiate substantive autonomy from the center. That is why some federalist systems may be more resilient: they have the potential to hold the nation-state together by providing greater levels of governmental authority to the subnational parts.

The tension between the parts and the whole within the nation-state were on display during the Brexit referendum. It was no accident that London and other large British cities voted so heavily in favor of staying within the EU while much of the rest of England voted to leave.[12] A diverse and cosmopolitan city that recently elected its first Muslim mayor, London is a global hub for finance and related professional services. Its growth is based on global commerce, drawing, in part, on Britain's historical role as a world colonial power and its related cultural influence. To make matters more complex, the Scots voted to stay in the EU in part because it functions as a counter to U.K. power. The question now is to what extent a renewed Scottish movement toward full independence will carry forward as the United Kingdom exits the EU.

Spatial Effect
The autonomy of subgeographies within national systems is further complicated by the global economy's increasingly becoming an urban economy. There are two aspects to global urban ascendance.

First, there is only a limited number of urban hubs dominating the global economic system. That number will increase and its composition will change over time as Western and northern dominance is challenged by the rise of global cities in Asia, Latin America, and Africa. But no matter where global cities are located or how many global urban centers there are, economic divisions within nations between the most globally connected metropolitan centers and the less economically significant cities, let alone rural or small-town communities, are one consequence of globalization.

Second, today's dramatic levels of urban population growth, whether that population resides in the most globally significant cities or not, is a remarkable and accelerating phenomenon. Globalization is driving more people into cities and urbanized areas than ever before. As this happens, urbanism becomes the dominant spatial form and hence a shared cultural artifact of the global system. Cities are the workshop of a proto-global culture.

There has been a great deal of scholarship on the development of global cities in the context of globalization. Perhaps best known is Saskia Sassen's classic study of New York, London, and Tokyo.[13] One of the arguments expounded in Sassen's work, as well as that of other economic geographers, is that as supply chains extend across the globe, there is an accompanying concentration of administrative and financial hubs, the control centers of the supply chains. This results in a spatial architecture in which some cities are economically dominant globally. We can track this dominance through the siting of multinational headquarters, the geographic clustering of certain firms, rates of innovation, and other indicators.

Dominant urban regions form the most dynamic part of the economy of their nation, enabling a de facto autonomy that does not require a renegotiation of status but emerges organically through cultural and economic distinctions. That is true of such diverse cities as Paris, Toronto, and Los Angeles.

The world today is a global economy defined increasingly through the mediation of places where cultural and economic qualities are hardwired for connectivity. Those cities or metros are generally more diverse than their respective nation-states and larger than most other cities; they attract a greater share of young people, immigrants, and workers in industries with global linkages. The same cities tend to engage politically and through civic and business networks across national boundaries. Their universities, cultural institutions, and medical centers are also increasingly global in how they distribute knowledge and market products, in the makeup of the student body and the employee corps, and in their access to donor and investment capital.

But the trend toward urbanization in general is far more pronounced than the rise of the twenty-five or fifty most globally important urban centers might suggest. Buoyed by the economics of agglomeration, the expansion of market economies, and the industrialization of agriculture, cities and their surrounding urbanized areas, particularly in the developing world, are growing exponentially. Demography follows jobs and other social opportunities whether those opportunities are linked to livelihoods, kinship, refugee displacement, or the availability of public goods. In advanced economies such as the United States, most people lived in cities by around 1920. For the world as a whole, that point was reached in 2008, according to UN data.[14]

The share of people living in cities is expected to grow to about two-thirds of the global population by the middle of the twenty-first century.[15] This represents a complete reorientation of human settlement patterns in a relatively brief period of time. In 1800, only 3 percent of the world's population lived in cities; by 1900 the percentage had climbed to 14 percent, and 100 years later, half the world was urban. Much of twenty-first-century urban growth will be in the developing world, as much as 90 percent in Asia and Africa.[16] Rapidly growing cities create enormous challenges for infrastructure, governance, and social stability. They also pose challenges in terms of national identity.

The rise of urbanization as the dominant economic and demographic force in the world changes the role of the nation-state as the exclusive political body for international relations. The city-state is reemerging. In the United States, examples of city versus federal debates on hot-button issues such as immigration and environmental protection have recently made the news. But just as important, the uptick in global city-to-city exchanges in everything from economic growth and trade to the diffusion of new governance strategies reflects the changing value of global urbanism.

Leveling Effect

The third aspect of convergence has to do with the leveling of economic advantages as a result of technology and the global diffusion of production. In an era when something can be produced anywhere and workplaces are increasingly virtual, the qualities of locale are a major component of economic competition. Local amenities are major driving forces of change. Localities compete for investment, talent, and business growth, and the quality of place, particularly for people and firms with choices, has become more and more critical.

There are, of course, already vast advantages for some communities, advantages rooted in history, political economy, and institutional capacity. It is easier to build out a dynamic local economy if MIT and Harvard are in your backyard and if the transportation, cultural, and recreational infrastructure is ample. And of course, resource location still counts, whether in energy-rich regions or locales proximate to major ports.

But even historical advantages can be replicated or replaced by new technologies or the right investments. That is what makes globalization so powerful and in many ways so manic: incumbent nations and regions, like incumbent companies, can be overtaken by places that are better at innovating and smarter at investing. Legacy advantages have increasingly short shelf lives unless they are elevated by the right actions and investments.

China, for example, is massively investing in its own universities (particularly its elite nine), which are now moving up in the global rankings.[17] These investments will slowly curtail the demand by Chinese students for a Western education. The same is happening among the most elite universities and medical centers in India, Singapore, and elsewhere. And many American universities are opening campuses throughout the world as part of their growth strategies, in essence selling their brand and expanding their demographic and tuition reach. This is also happening with legacy institutions such as orchestras. If they cannot sustain themselves in their original communities, they partner with other cities across the globe that can support them.

Even a lack of natural resources can be overcome by the right innovations and investment. Israel's technological prowess, for example, has converted what was once viewed as a resource-poor nation into a global energy (Mediterranean natural gas) hub and a water resource power through drip irrigation, desalination, and other forms of water generation.[18]

So while the world may not yet be flat as Tom Friedman provocatively noted some years back, it is moving in that direction, and this has important consequences for local communities, particularly those without preexisting historical advantages.[19]

A globally dynamic economy requires that any locality that wants to thrive must invest in the qualities of place that attract and retain residents and firms, in human capital, and in an enterprise environment that enables innovation and business growth. As we noted earlier, federal investments in infrastructure, education, and research are critical. But the local capacity to drive effective change through both public and private actions and sources is the most important factor. As the economy becomes more globally connected, the interventions and activities of locality become increasingly decisive.

NEW LOCALISM AND POPULISM

The three kinds of forces that favor a convergence of the local and global—structural, spatial, and leveling—have both a New Localism effect and a populist effect. They each represent opportunities for political disruption and local change.

As the role of the nation-state changes, the potential for higher levels of local political autonomy grows. As urban centers become the universal human settlement, the local becomes anchored to a more universal culture. And as technology and trade disrupt existing economies, the potential emerges for new types of competitive advantage that require the reorganization of local public and private capacity. Each of these dynamics drives the need for New Localism as a problem-solving practice, while also placing cities in the crosshairs of populism, from both the right and the left.

From the perspective of the populist right, cities are the sites of cosmopolitan identity that do not necessarily share the traditional values of the rest of the nation. From the perspective of the populist left, cities embody globalization's flawed economic outcomes: a wealthy upper class connected to finance, technology, and higher-paying professions such as law and medicine, socially isolated from an economically insecure working class of service, public sector, and manufacturing workers. Cities are both incubators for economic opportunity and repositories of people less connected to the benefits of economic growth.

Today's populism is a national political response to a local social and economic dislocation that is both metropolitan and rural. This was reflected in the results of the national referendum in the United Kingdom concerning EU membership, in recent political contests in Europe, and, in the United States, in the popularity of Bernie Sanders and the election of Donald Trump. Though the populist candidates on the European continent lost, the campaigns were a wake-up call alerting to some unanticipated results of uneven growth.

No matter who wins a national election, coming to terms with the nature of discontent and the necessity of locally focused change becomes paramount. While the centrist, pro-EU candidate Emmanuel Macron won an important election in France, he will have to figure out what to do with sections of the nation that are deindustrialized and with the restive suburbs of Paris and other cities, where high unemployment rates fuel immigrant discontent.[20] The sources of populist grievance on the left or right do not disappear after an election. But change can no longer be mandated through national rules. Macron must come to terms with the connections between national discontent and local solutions within the new global reality, or little will change.

In a book about local problem solving during a period of populist discontent, it is useful to reflect more deeply on today's populism. In general, populism refers to a loosely associated group of political movements that have flourished both on the political right and on the left, emerging especially during periods of rural displacement and rapid urbanization.[21] In general, populism emerges outside the established political order and seeks to transform the economic status quo, or at least establish new types of popular participation and economic inclusion. Because populism emerges during periods of significant change, it is often characterized by an uneasy mix of tradition-seeking momentum and future-facing reform. Most important, populism is fueled by grassroots organization even as it coalesces or may be stoked by singular political leaders.

Diverse political views are encompassed by populism in the context of globalization. Two things are important to note. First is the tendency by some to view populism on the right and left as similar, insofar as they share some common antiglobalist rhetoric and points of view. But they differ significantly on a variety of things, from the role of the nation-state to the importance of ethnic diversity. Second is the tendency to relegate populism—of the left or the right—to the realm of nonrespectability or even irrationality, as the French political scientist Pierre Manent notes, and thus to delegitimize all of its content, while assuming that the political center— either center right or center left—occupies the realm of reason.[22]

The delegitimizing of populism as outside the mainstream ignores the historical power of populism to transform societies by bringing issues to the fore or eventually evolving into more significant governing platforms. Examples of these transformations can be found throughout the world, from Latin America to Asia to the United States.[23] If we consider the social movements and politics of the antiglobalists, the distinctions between right-wing and left-wing populism in Europe and the United States are clear.

The antiglobalist populism of the right is focused on national sovereignty and cultural identity in the context of a changing economy and national demography; it is nationalistic and often ethnocentric. It views the declining role of the nation-state as reducing the rights of native citizens. The antiglobalist populism of the left focuses on the oversized power of capital, the declining power of labor, and the economic marginality of some ethnic minorities. The two sides meet in their dislike of multinational trade agreements and their interest in renewing the traditional manufacturing base. And each in its own way questions the fact that citizens do not have enough institutional or political protection from the vagaries of the economy. Populists seek stronger protection or mediation, whether through the nation-state, city-state, ethnic associations, class solidarity, or trade unions.

Populists on the right and left are also united in their disdain for elites, viewed as benefiting from and leading globalization without having to suffer its negative consequences. What is meant by "elites" is not always the same thing for the left and right. For the left of the Democratic Party, for example, elites are generally the super-rich, especially Wall Street executives. For many Republicans and conservative independents, elites are about culture as well as capital and are represented by a variety of social types from media, universities, and business.

But most important, elites are those whose fortunes and identities are no longer bound to the nation or to their conationals, as might have been the case in an earlier era. This resentment was presaged by Christopher Lasch in his 1994 book, *The Revolt of the Elites*. Playing off Ortega y Gasset's 1929 publication *The Revolt of the Masses*, which described the ascent of the mass movements that were overtaking Europe, Lasch looked at the other face of the dynamic. He identified our time as a period when well-educated and wealthy elites with common backgrounds and affiliations were withdrawing from local and national life, adopting more cosmopolitan and global relationships, and living in geographically and culturally protected enclaves. Their revolt was an exit from ordinary public life, an exit that most of us do not have as an option.[24]

Right-wing populism in the United States and Europe unite around anger toward global elites, a defense of national sovereignty, and anti-immigration sentiment. Culture, race, and immigration play a significant role in those populist reactions. During a period of economic insecurity and high levels of immigration, the coexistence of declining wages and shifting demographics can lead to a dangerous political brew.

In Europe, the large numbers of Muslim immigrants and refugees translated into fears of terrorism, which were justified for many when attacks occurred on the streets of Paris, Brussels, London, Manchester, and Nice. Those attacks helped resurrect national sovereignty politics across the continent, and not only among right-wing groups. Nationalist parties and many in the political center scorn the Schengen border agreement that eliminated internal border controls among EU member nations. In the United States, fears of terrorism were linked to border security, refugee policies, and sanctuary city policies throughout Trump's campaign. Warnings about the next Orlando or San Bernardino were part of his campaign.[25]

Populism does not have to succumb to ethnic antagonisms. It can instead highlight systemic issues that constrain equity and social mobility, including bringing a stronger labor and environmental focus into global trade agreements, creating a stronger national safety net, and insisting on upgrading incumbent skills to take advantage of new jobs. But it cannot assume that many of the contemporary changes in economic, technological, or demographic reality will be reset. They will not.

New Localism emerges from the same global economic changes but concerns itself more with local practices and repositioning than with national policies. New Localism is a less overtly political movement and as such is more accepting of the terms of global economics than populism is. But a populist perspective and a New Localism practice may merge in the future when it comes to creating new institutions to manage change and growth. Ultimately political discontent might find expression in more tangible social and institutional arrangements.

History provides numerous examples of large-scale transitions in the economy and politics that led to the creation of new institutions to manage change. In the late nineteenth and early twentieth centuries, for example, the United States was rocked by economic and social upheaval. In rural America, predatory financial institutions had weakened the tradition of family-owned farms. Rural populism led to the creation of cooperatives, a new system of national farm credit, and even America's only state-owned bank. Grassroots groups elected mayors and governors throughout the South and Midwest, almost elected a president, and created a national economic platform, some aspects of which were adopted decades later in a different form.[26]

In cities and small towns, rapid, unfettered industrialization transformed the built and natural environments and spawned industrial models of wage exploitation, which culminated in labor struggles that often ended in tragedy—New York's Triangle Shirtwaist Factory fire in 1911, for example, or the bloody coal mine battles of West Virginia, whose most violent moment emerged at the battle of Blair Mountain in 1920. In both cases, labor unions emerged as the mediating institutions that stood between workers and corporations during most of industrial capitalism.

Rural and urban populism in the United States also helped usher in one of the greatest periods of legislative reform. The disruption in rural America led to the search for new institutions and policies that could provide small farmers with access to low-cost capital. The disruption in cities and industrial towns led to the rise of progressivism, which sought changes in work safety rules, eight-hour workdays, child labor protections, and ultimately a system of retirement, health care, and welfare benefits. Many of those reforms originated in cities and states and only later were embraced by the national government.

Many of the instruments and institutions created 100 years ago and again during the New Deal had local policy origins but soon became federal in scope, from the national system of government-sponsored enterprises to the social security system and Medicare. We believe that many of the new instruments and institutions being generated in cities today to match capital to new opportunities and challenges or to create higher levels of economic inclusion may one day become new national institutions that reflect the best we are learning from the local level. It is too early to know.

This is a moment of accelerated institutional innovation, and for good reason. The most radical restructuring of federalism—the division of responsibilities across multiple levels of government—since the New Deal is under way. The national changes that emerge may eventually be forced to come to terms with gaps in the safety net that were not corrected earlier. Those gaps are currently being filled by some cities and states but may eventually become the subject of a national debate driven by many of the populist voices that are clamoring for raises in the minimum wage, investment in children's learning, and better health care. Those national reforms may prepare citizens for global economic participation and ultimately contribute to the energy and possibilities of New Localism.

If there is to be a shared history of populism and New Localism, we have to start by asking, what is going to change in a new period of economic and social upheaval? As before, new political and civic ideologies are emerging that cater to economic insecurity and social disaffection. But can new instruments and institutions be created that will allow capital to flow unimpeded to new sectors of the economy and forgotten sectors of the nation? Should institutions be repurposed if they served their original purpose in an earlier stage of growth but have much less potential as change agents today? Are new models of governance needed to accelerate the potential for change?

The three case studies that follow in chapters 4, 5, and 6 and the subsequent chapters on finance and economic inclusion look at new institution building and social intermediation in a variety of ways. It is from observing what is happening on the ground that we can begin to answer some of these questions and project the trajectory of change for the near future.

FOUR

Revaluing Urban Growth

PITTSBURGH CASE STUDY

A city must think like a system and act like an entrepreneur.
—Matthew Taylor, Chief Executive of the Royal Society
for the Encouragement of Arts, Manufactures
and Commerce

Economic growth is a precondition for urban prosperity, but
old models of growth are insufficient in today's global economy. Pittsburgh's renaissance—from a rust belt victim of
deindustrialization to a high-tech global hub—is a prime
example of what is needed, a model that differentiates a regional economy globally and prioritizes long-term investments
in innovation assets, talent, and quality places. Pittsburgh's
position in the global economy stems from an understanding
of the drivers of modern competitiveness and leaders' and
citizens' willingness to adapt to new economic realities.

Pittsburgh's storied revival emerged from the rubble of a nuclear disaster.

On March 28, 1979, reactor 2 of the Three Mile Island Nuclear Generating Station experienced a cooling malfunction and a partial meltdown of the reactor core. A complicated combination of stuck valves, misread gauges, and poor decisions led to the discharge of a small amount of radiation into the atmosphere.[1] It also precipitated a mini-tsunami: thousands of gallons of water rushed into the basement of the reactor, carrying fuel pellets, radioactive materials, debris from the damaged core, and water from the Susquehanna River. In an eerie coincidence, the situation mirrored the plot of *The China Syndrome*, a movie that had been released just twelve days prior to the Three Mile Island disaster.

The plant remained shuttered for four years as a group of companies, including Bechtel Group and Westinghouse Electric Corporation, started the dangerous process of entering the reactor's basement to assess the full extent of the damage. The hurdles to cleaning up the disaster site were immense. No person could safely set foot in the flooded basement. And there were no sensors or cameras to record an accurate picture of the hazards.

Enter Red Whittaker, a newly minted robotics professor at Carnegie Mellon University. With Bechtel support, Whittaker and his team of twenty-something graduate students (what Whittaker recalls as an "army of youth") built mobile robots that could travel the corridors of the crippled reactor under remote control. These new robots boldly went where no human could venture.[2]

The Carnegie Mellon roboticists transformed the stationary robot used for repetitive tasks into a new class of technology and application: robots on wheels outfitted with cameras, lights, radiation detectors, vacuums, scoops, scrapers, drills, and a high-pressure spray nozzle.[3] Sealed and submersible (the basement was flooded) and powered by hundreds of feet of electrical cord that snaked through the containment building, these remotely operated robots surveyed the site, sending back information and drilling core samples to measure the radiation level of the basement walls. The most expensive machines cost $1.5 million to build, which was considered "low cost and low risk" by the global companies in charge of the project. The robots worked for four years inside the reactor building, playing a major role in the cleanup.[4]

The robotic heroes at Three Mile Island galvanized the fledgling robotics industry in the United States and the world. The foundation of technological expertise, however, was local and regional.

Carnegie Mellon had just established the Robotics Institute as part of the university's School of Computer Science, funded in part by a $3 million grant from Westinghouse. The institute's driving force was Raj Reddy. Born in Madras, India, and the holder of engineering and technology degrees from universities in India and Australia, Reddy received his doctorate in computer science from Stanford and arrived at Carnegie Mellon in 1969, attracted by Nobel laureate Herbert Simon, who, along with Alan Newell, was a pioneer in the field of artificial intelligence.[5]

Reddy encouraged researchers at the Robotics Institute to tackle both the development of increasingly complex technology and its commercialization. As Red Whittaker recalls, "There was nothing else like it that had the undiluted, unbridled commitment to the future of automation. Robotics was envisioned as a bold future. At the time, it was the stuff of fantasy and science fiction." By 1986, Whittaker had a Field Robotics Center that was deploying mobile robots into active volcanos in Alaska, searching for meteorites in Antarctica, and surveying an 1,800-acre area of Nevada for buried hazards.[6]

Ten years of invention led to the establishment of the National Robotics Engineering Center (NREC) as an operating unit within Carnegie Mellon's

Robotics Institute in 1996. Initially funded by NASA, NREC pioneered the brave new world of autonomous vehicles. From the flooded basements of Three Mile Island to the city streets of Pittsburgh, the farms of California, and the surface of the Moon and Mars, the roboticists at Carnegie Mellon married theory and practice, basic science and applied research, wild dreams and practical realities. A convergence economy emerged: a fusion of academia and industry with electrical and mechanical engineering, computer science, and multiple other fields. When disciplines collide, magic happens.

In September 2015, Clive Thompson captured the accomplishments of Reddy, Whittaker, and their colleagues in a *New York Times Magazine* article:

> There's a useful high-tech concept called the Technology Readiness Level. NASA came up with this scale to gauge the maturity of a given field of applied science. At Level 1, an area of scientific inquiry is so new that nobody understands its basic principles. At Level 9, the related technology is so mature that it's ready to be used in commercial products. "Basically 1 is like Newton figuring out the laws of gravity, and 9 is you've been launching rockets into space, constantly and reliably," says Jeff Legault, the director of strategic business development at the National Robotics Engineering Center. . . .
>
> In effect, Carnegie Mellon used the NASA scale to carve up its robotics research. The Robotics Institute would handle research from Levels 1 to 3 or 4, while the [National Robotics Engineering] center would take technology from there and move it to 7. If John Deere approached the center for help with a self-driving tractor, the center would produce a prototype that could be mass-produced while publishing its research publicly.[7]

Pittsburgh's robotics ecosystem increased its capacity to commercialize and productize new research rapidly in 2010 when the NREC's John Bares assumed the role of CEO of Carnegie Robotics, a new spin-off dedicated to scaling up the commercial design and manufacturing of robotics systems and components. Bares's professional move showed the evolution of robotics from the laboratory to the market. Pittsburgh was ready to compete.

By 2015 Pittsburgh had become known as Roboburgh.[8] Dozens of companies with thousands of jobs formed a cluster, drawn by the gravitational pull of Carnegie Mellon's campus in the Oakland neighborhood and the NREC in the Lawrenceville neighborhood, along the Allegheny River. Fittingly, the center is housed in a renovated, 100-year-old foundry building on a reclaimed industrial brownfield site.

The rise of co-working spaces, incubators, and accelerators encouraged more entrepreneurship. Innovation Works, for example, has emerged as the most active seed-stage investor in the Pittsburgh region. Since its launch in 1999, Innovation Works has invested $72 million in more than 300 local companies. Those startups have gone on to raise another $1.8 billion in follow-on funding. Innovation Works also operates two accelerator programs, AlphaLab and AlphaLab Gear (for hardware companies). AlphaLab was ranked the sixth best accelerator in 2014 by researchers at Rice University, the University of Richmond, and MIT.[9]

RE2 (Robotics Engineering Excellence) offers a good example of how robotics clustering in Pittsburgh helps build an ecosystem for entrepreneurs. RE2 Robotics develops robotic arms to help the military dismantle explosive devices in far-off wars or local bomb squads to do the same closer to home. "These arms are put on robots to do the dull, dirty and dangerous," said president, CEO, and founder Jorgen Pedersen, a graduate of Carnegie Mellon.[10]

RE2 Robotics, a spin-off from Carnegie Mellon, has garnered multiple grants from the U.S. military, seed funding from Innovation Works, and venture funding from Draper Triangle. Located less than a mile from the NREC, RE2 Robotics recently expanded its purview to work with the University of Pittsburgh and the Veterans Administration to develop what it calls a Patient Assist Robotic Arm to "help people with disabilities better navigate the logistics of a world not designed to accommodate them."[11]

A broad network of institutions and intermediaries dedicated to turning ideas into products provides support for fledgling firms in Pittsburgh. This network is powered by "connectors," professionals who link individuals with smart ideas to other individuals with talent in firm management and entrepreneurial finance. Vaish Krishnamurthy, the founder of Clean Robotics, captured these opportunities in a blog post, "Could my dream of starting a robotics company have come true had it not been for Pittsburgh?"[12] No, she wrote. A transplant from India by way of California, Krishnamurty describes the ease and speed with which she was able to build a management team and obtain modest seed funding to bring her idea for Trashbot, a robot that separates recyclables from waste, to market.

The key issue here is talent. Companies have been well served by Pittsburgh's intentional effort to serve as a talent greenhouse (growing skilled workers from within) and a talent magnet (attracting skilled workers from outside). Talent sprouting is being done as part of a partnership among Carnegie Mellon University, the University of Pittsburgh, and a broad group of community colleges. A two-year associate degree in robotics engineering technology is being offered by regional institutions such as California University of Pennsylvania, Butler County Community College, and Westmoreland County Community College. The Community College of Allegheny County in Pittsburgh is also building a program on mechatronics, which combines electronics and mechanical engineering since every piece of machinery now has a digital component. In advanced degree programs in mechatronics, students learn how to design robots or computer-based systems; in associate degree programs they learn how the system functions and how to maintain and operate these machines. The demand for mechatronics credentials is growing: computer-operated physical devices will soon be in every car, house, stoplight, office building, and delivery vehicle (car or drone).[13]

The magnetic effect of Pittsburgh is seen in its ability to attract and retain the millennial population. From 2000 to 2014, according to a study conducted by the Pew Charitable Trusts, the number of young college graduates grew by 53 percent while the city's overall population dropped by 9 percent. The growth in millennials was the third best in the country, behind that of Jersey City and Washington, D.C.[14]

Pittsburgh's distinctive quality of life and historical character are major draws for millennials. As Rebecca Bagley, the University of Pittsburgh's vice chancellor for economic partnerships, observed, "I think we've made the transition from the Rust Belt to the new economy city."[15]

But Pittsburgh's revival is also a remarkable testament to the power of immigration and open borders. Raj Reddy's prominence at Carnegie

Mellon reflects the critical role that talented global migrants have played in the Pittsburgh revival.

Indians began their migration to Pittsburgh in the 1970s, lured by Westinghouse Electric Company's recruitment of engineers. A small trickle of migrants became a wave, attracted by the research and entrepreneurial possibilities at Carnegie Mellon, the University of Pittsburgh, and the University of Pittsburgh Medical Center.

Pittsburgh was seen as a welcoming place where talented immigrants could commercialize ideas and grow companies. Vaish Krishnamurthy, the young entrepreneur mentioned earlier, was born in Chennai, India, and earned her graduate degree in electrical engineering at the University of California, Riverside, before making her way to Pittsburgh. And she is just the latest in a long list of dynamic business leaders.

Priya Narasimhan, for example, is the founder of YinzCam Inc., a Carnegie Mellon spin-off focused on mobile live event streaming (a perfect match of business and passion, given that Narasimhan is a die-hard Pittsburgh Penguins fan). As of December 2016, YinzCam's software had been downloaded more than 30 million times. Narasimhan and her team were also responsible for the iBurgh app, which complements the city's 311 service by letting users file complaints about graffiti around town. It was the first iPhone application to enable such complaints to be communicated to municipal government.[16]

Sunil Wadhwani earned a master's degree at Carnegie Mellon and cofounded iGateCorp, an IT business solutions firm. After iGateCorp was acquired by the Paris-based CapGemini for $4 billion in July 2015, Wadhwani and Ashok Trivedi created a $40 million special venture fund called SWAT Capital LLC to invest in startups in Pittsburgh and elsewhere. Wadhwani also serves as a Carnegie Mellon trustee, an example of how Pittsburgh's immigrant entrepreneurs remain loyal to their new hometown.[17]

What's interesting about the Indian presence in Pittsburgh is that the Steel City has a far lower percentage of diversity than the national average. That's not the case with the Indian community, however. The share of Indians in the city is slightly above the national average, reflecting the strength of the universities and next-generation industries.

The rise of robotics in Pittsburgh is a classic tale of smart economy shaping by means of a strong research platform, a tight-knit ecosystem of academic researchers, entrepreneurs, investors, and incubators, and a large talent pool. But the success of robotics ultimately brought competition and disruption. In February 2015, Uber and Carnegie Mellon announced a strategic partnership to develop self-driving vehicles. The idea of the partnership was to provide a forum for Uber technologists to work closely with Carnegie Mellon faculty, staff, and students on various technological challenges in the arenas of mapping, vehicle safety, and more. Uber built its Advanced Technologies Center literally blocks away from the NREC along the Allegheny River.[18]

Three months later, the *Wall Street Journal* reported that Uber had poached four professors and thirty-six researchers and technical staff to work at the company. (At the time, the NREC had about twenty-five faculty and 100 researchers and technical staff).[19] News reports described the NREC as being "decimated," "gutted," and "in a crisis." Indeed, the impact of this move in the small, close-knit world of Pittsburgh roboticists cannot be overemphasized. The director of the new Uber center was John Bares, who had been part of Red Whittaker's initial "army of youth" on Three Mile Island and who had run the NREC from 1997 to 2010 before leaving to found Carnegie Robotics.

But while the Uber raid was disruptive on many levels—research was interrupted, capacity diminished, and relationships strained—it was also a sign that Pittsburgh had arrived. As the urban studies theorist Richard Florida observed:

Uber's move to Pittsburgh and its hiring of CMU talent is good for the city. Universities are the talent magnets and anchors of the innovation-driven knowledge economy. But for decades, CMU has been generating talent and technology and subsequently losing them to more mature tech hubs like Silicon Valley. Uber's location in Pittsburgh—and indeed its hiring of top CMU researchers—signals that Pittsburgh has finally become a player in commercial technology. This will likely strengthen Pittsburgh's talent magnet effect, attracting more top researchers and graduate students to the city and spurring the creation of more technology, more startups, and perhaps even a leading-edge industry cluster with Uber and CMU as its twin anchors.[20]

Florida's predictions are coming to fruition. Carnegie Mellon has methodically rebuilt its research base, aided in part by Uber donating $5.5 million to the university to fund new faculty positions and graduate research. Tier 1 automotive supplier Delphi entered Pittsburgh in 2015 through an acquisition of Ottomatika, a 2013 spin-off from Carnegie Mellon.[21] In February 2017, Ford Motor Company announced it was investing $1 billion in Argo AI, a firm founded by two engineers formerly with Uber, Google, and Carnegie Mellon. The goal: to develop a virtual driver system for the automaker's autonomous vehicle, scheduled for 2021.[22] And in May 2017 it was reported that Aurora Innovation, a new autonomous vehicle startup founded by former Tesla, Google, and Uber engineers, had quietly set up shop in the city.[23]

While Carnegie Mellon was rebuilding and Ford was buying, the city government was greenlighting Uber's effort to introduce a fleet of self-driving cars on city streets. As Mayor Bill Peduto said, "It's not our role to throw up regulations or limit companies like Uber. You can either put up red tape or roll out the red carpet. If you want to be a 21st century laboratory for technology, you put out the carpet."

The mayor's actions, however, were calculating rather than submissive. As Peduto observed, "The three areas that the world is moving [toward] is shared, electric and autonomous. [Pittsburgh] will be at the forefront of the building of this new economy."[24]

Robotics did not fall under Uber's wheels. Early in 2017 the Department of Defense awarded $80 million to the Advanced Robotics Manufacturing (ARM) Innovation Hub, an independent, public-private partnership institute founded by Carnegie Mellon. Overall funding for ARM is set for just over $250 million, with an additional $173 million in matching funds committed from a variety of partner organizations, including industry, state and local government, universities, and nonprofit organizations.

ARM is positioned to leverage the strengths of Carnegie Mellon and the broader Pittsburgh region in artificial intelligence, autonomous vehicles, 3-D printing, and other emerging technologies to make industrial robots more affordable and adaptable for businesses. As part of the Manufacturing USA network, the institute will transform U.S. manufacturing through innovations and education in robotics and automation technologies, with the aim to help create 510,000 new manufacturing jobs in ten years. The institute's headquarters is slated to locate in a massive brownfield along the Monongahela River, the site of the old LTV Steel's Hazelwood Works.

The rise of robotics exemplifies the repositioning of Pittsburgh as a hub of advanced technologies. Carnegie Mellon's prowess in computer science, artificial intelligence, machine learning, and digital media has made the city a magnet for an interesting wave of domestic direct investment. Amazon, Apple, Autodesk, Oculus, Rand, and Intel all have outposts in town, and Disney has partnered with Carnegie Mellon University for years on cinematic graphics. In 2011, Google opened a 40,000-square-foot office in an old Nabisco factory in the city's East Liberty neighborhood. Now quadrupled in size and numbering over 500 employees, the firm started with just two employees in a rented office on Carnegie Mellon's campus. Andrew Moore, a professor of computer science and robotics, took a ten-year leave from the university to lead Google's new Pittsburgh campus before returning in 2014 as the new dean of the School of Computer Science.[25]

The allure of these leading companies for western Pennsylvania is not hard to discern. As Vaish Krishnamurthy boasted, "Pittsburgh has the talent of Silicon Valley at the mid-west cost of living."[26]

PITTSBURGH AND MEDICAL ADVANCES

While Carnegie Mellon was establishing itself as the robotics center of the universe, its Oakland neighbor, the University of Pittsburgh, was fast becoming one of the world's leading centers in biomedical research, innovation, and clinical excellence. The university has a long history of medical advances, most prominently the crafting of the Salk vaccine for polio in 1955 (Jonas Salk was a virologist at the university), the perfection of liver transplantation techniques under Thomas Starzl, and the development of a radioactive compound in 2008 that enables the early diagnosis of Alzheimer's disease. In 2016 the university was the fifth highest recipient of NIH funding nationally, the gold standard of biomedical research, and the top recipient of funding from the National Institute of Mental Health.[27] Overall, academic research investment in medical sciences is 350 percent of the national average.

As with Carnegie Mellon, expertise at the university cuts across multiple domains—drug discovery and design, organ transplantation and immunology, cell therapy, tissue engineering and regenerative medicine—and is enhanced by deep competencies in related fields such as genomics, bioinformatics, and computational systems. The depth and breadth of the university's academic reach—as well as the growing reputation of Pittsburgh as a tolerant community for foreign-born researchers—are a major reason why leading global researchers such as José-Alain Sahel, the head of the Vision Institute in Paris, has chosen Pittsburgh as the U.S. base for their pathbreaking work.[28]

The university's close affiliation with the University of Pittsburgh Medical Center (UPMC) not only provides a clinical base for drug trials but also supplies an enormous customer base for the study of using big data to change the way diseases are prevented and how patients are diagnosed, treated, and engaged in their own care. To that end, in March 2015 UPMC announced the Pittsburgh Health Data Alliance with the University of Pittsburgh and Carnegie Mellon. This partnership deploys technology and research from the University of Pittsburgh and Carnegie Mellon University—in big data, personalized medicine, or data security—to accelerate changes in the health care system. UPMC's vast provider base offers the perfect test bed to bridge the gap between academic computer science and commercial application.[29]

Pittsburgh, in short, capably blends its multiple sources of expertise to create new technologies, products, services, companies, and jobs. But the success of the city is not guaranteed: a Brookings report released in September 2017 confirmed the strength of the innovation ecosystem but also identified several challenges. The rate of employment growth in key technological areas lags the region's research competencies. The nascent startup scene has yet to produce the types of high-growth companies that can feed capital and expertise back into the ecosystem. While Carnegie Mellon University and the University of Pittsburgh effectively attract and supply high-skill entrants to the workforce, the region faces an undersupply of mid-career professionals.[30] Even the relationship between Uber and the city government turned sour in 2017 owing to the combative nature of the company, its controversial former CEO, and the broader issue of worker protections and benefits in a rapidly changing economy. As Mayor Peduto said in a statement, "In Pittsburgh, we have a saying—if it's not for all, it's not for us."[31]

City and metropolitan competitiveness, in short, is a game that never ends. The pace of economic restructuring, the intensity of global competition, and the challenges associated with growing and attracting talented workers require cities to be simultaneously strategic and agile, moving fast to capitalize on assets and advantages that have been honed and stewarded for decades.

WHAT PITTSBURGH TEACHES OTHER CITIES

The Pittsburgh story is exemplary of a new growth model that is increasingly being practiced by U.S. and global cities. It reflects a change in how many places think about economic growth—from a disproportionate concern with subsidizing consumption and tourism to a new emphasis on accumulating and leveraging distinctive productive and innovative assets.

To make that change, as Matthew Taylor of the U.K.'s Royal Society for the encouragement of Arts, Manufactures and Commerce often says, it's necessary for a city to "think like a system and act like an entrepreneur."[32] Thinking like a system requires taking a long and broad view of the regional economy, including identifying and cultivating assets and core regional competencies; investing in education, workforce development, and talent attraction; and creating quality places by maximizing historical downtowns, distinctive neighborhoods, and, in Pittsburgh's case, a confluence of rivers and a unique topography.

What makes a city act entrepreneurial?

Economists such as Edward Glaeser and AnnaLee Saxenian have looked at a variety of economic metrics.[33] But entrepreneurialism also has cultural dimensions. The sociological and psychological literature shows that entrepreneurs generally share similar personality characteristics, from tenacity to passion to flexibility to the ability to tolerate risk, that are crucial to a successful venture. Cities, of course, are not individuals but collections of people. And just as there is groupthink, there are cultural norms and modes of behavior in leadership groups that make them more or less likely to undertake bold and transformative efforts. Successful entrepreneurial cities are characterized by a culture of "positive reinforcement" whereby networks of institutions and leaders celebrate individual and collective wins and are small and agile enough to move quickly to leverage market and demographic dynamics.[34] But arriving at this point can be difficult.

Both sides of Taylor's advice are crucial: without a system view, cities pursue a reckless course to be the next Silicon Valley; without the spirit of an entrepreneur, even cities with a solid economic foundation could be left behind in the modern economy.

Through a decades-long iterative process, leaders from government, philanthropy, academia, and business have brought a systemic and entrepreneurial approach to Pittsburgh's economic evolution, providing fertile ground for the growth of important twenty-first-century sectors such as robotics and automation.

Pittsburgh's story offers multiple lessons for other cities.

First, *many cities have the potential to become "brainbelts" by strengthening collaboration across universities, workers, companies, entrepreneurs, and investors.*

As championed by Antoine van Agtmael and Fred Bakker in their 2016 book, *The Smartest Places on Earth: Why Rustbelts Are the Emerging Hotspots of Global Innovation*:

> Each brainbelt is a tightly woven collaborative ecosystem of contributors, typically composed of research universities, community colleges, local government authorities, established companies with a thriving research function and start-ups, usually supported by a variety of supporters and suppliers, including venture capitalists, lawyers, design firms and others. These different types of entities establish their own unique identity as they share knowledge, interact, form a community, grow and improve.[35]

According to van Agtmael and Bakker, economic restructuring has rewarded the "sharing of brain power." Rather than breakthroughs being engineered by the lone genius or "the brilliant pair of geeks in a garage," they argue, the process of innovation involves "collegial collaboration, open exchange of information, partnerships between the worlds of business and academia, multidisciplinary initiatives and ecosystems composed of an array of important players, all working closely together."[36]

At the same time, technological innovation has enabled the making of things. The integration of hardware and software, of mechanics and electronics, has resulted in "smart, complex products that delivered value far greater than products that could be created using the outdated, low-cost model [of outsourcing]."[37] In sum, the era of cheap is over and the era of smart has begun.[38]

Van Agtmael and Bakker's work reflects growing evidence of the critical role played by advanced industries in modern economies. Recent research led by Mark Muro shows, for example, that research- and STEM-intensive manufacturing, energy, and service sectors have an outsized impact on the U.S. economy. They employ 12.3 million people or 9 percent of total U.S. employment but generate 17 percent of GDP, account for two-thirds of exports, and represent 80 percent of private sector R&D investment. They create not only more jobs but better jobs. The average compensation in 2013 across advanced industries sectors was $90,000, nearly double that of workers in other industries.[39] And as Jonathan Rothwell has found, advanced industries have enormous potential for inclusive growth: half of all STEM jobs are available to workers without a four-year college degree.[40]

Van Agtmael and Bakker were unusual messengers for this new gospel. Van Agtmael was the person who coined the term "emerging markets" during a storied career in global finance. Bakker had been the editor in chief and CEO of the *Financial Times* of Holland. Their conclusions, however, portray a very different metropolitan geography of innovation than the usual trio of Austin, Boston, and Silicon Valley. Besides Pittsburgh, former industrial powerhouses such as Akron, Buffalo, Dayton, Rochester, and St. Louis in the United States and Dresden, Eindhoven, and Lund in Europe have emerged as new brainbelts.

A new epoch has arrived, which makes this economic period a moment for places like Pittsburgh. Technology and globalization have accelerated product cycles, extended market reach, and amplified impact. And they have fundamentally revalued places that invest at scale in the right stuff rather than trying to recreate a high-tech model that has already been played out in Silicon Valley.

Second, *success requires a radical ambition that is forward-looking: to be on the ground floor of new technologies that are reshaping nations, markets, and lives.*

In May 2013 the McKinsey Global Institute put out an influential study titled *Disruptive Technologies: Advances That Will Transform Life, Business and the Global Economy.* This prescient report identified roughly a dozen technologies—such as robotics, autonomous vehicles, genomics, energy storage, and cloud technology—that were moving from the laboratory to testing to prototyping to ubiquitous adoption.[41] The authors of the report predicted that the economic ramifications of this transformation have the potential to reach half of global GDP by 2025.

The McKinsey report captured an essential truth: technology shapes economies in long waves of innovation. It often takes decades for scientific discovery to translate into new products and services, but the transition from niche markets to global extent can occur rapidly. For example, it took more than fifty years to move from basic semiconductor research to the modern smart phone but less than a decade to go from the first iPhone to 2.16 billion smart-phone users. As with all disruptive technologies, there will be winners and losers. The economist Joseph Schumpeter long ago observed that innovation is usually accompanied by "creative destruction," which shifts the competitive balance sheet of firms, cities, and nations.[42]

The McKinsey report has enormous implications for cities. As recounted by Carnegie Mellon's Tim McNulty, the economic history of the twentieth century shows how a small group of cities—industrial centers such as Detroit, finance centers such as New York City and London, information technology hubs such as Silicon Valley and Boston—can occupy the ground floor of new technology platforms and reap the benefits for decades to come.

The cities at the forefront of the twelve economy-shaping technologies identified by McKinsey will benefit dramatically, attracting the global capital and talent that will allow firms to grow and scale up within the region. This growth and investment will in turn lead to more and better-paying jobs, with varying skill-level needs and across multiple sectors of the economy. These jobs will assuredly be in the tech sector, but they will also be found in other parts of the economy—in finance, insurance, real estate, and retail—that intersect with technology. The cumulative effect of being a first mover would be higher gross metropolitan product, and increased city and county tax revenues that can be reinvested in education, workforce development, infrastructure, and neighborhood revitalization.

The price of entry for being a future city are obvious: stellar research institutions, an ecosystem of firms, entrepreneurs and intermediaries, a concentration of talented and diverse workers, accessible risk capital, a global orientation, vibrant places to live and work, and the ability to act with intentionality and purpose.

Pittsburgh clearly has these assets. And, as robotics and autonomous vehicles have shown, a disruptive moment scrambles and reorders the playing field to the benefit of those communities that not only have the chops to invent technologies but also the knowhow to deploy them in the market and on the street. The supply of communities that have the ability to be future players is more substantial than has been recognized or realized.

Third, *a successful revival reflects the fortitude of investors focused on the long term.*

The largest investor by far has been the U.S. federal government. In 2014, roughly one-half of Carnegie Mellon's Robotics Institute's funding came from the Defense Department, including DARPA, the Army, the Air Force, and the Navy. The National Science Foundation was responsible for almost 15 percent of this funding, and other federal agencies, among them the Department of Agriculture, the Department of Energy, the Department of Homeland Security, and the National Institutes of Health, also made important investments. In comparison, the private sector contributed about 15 percent in sectors that included manufacturing, mining, and agriculture.[43]

Robotics represents only a small portion of the federal research largesse that is invested every year. Together, Carnegie Mellon and the University of Pittsburgh receive more than $1 billion in federal research dollars. Pittsburgh, in essence, represents the central thesis of Mariana Mazzucato's

2013 book, *The Entrepreneurial State*. Mazzucato makes a powerful argument that the U.S. federal government has been the innovative economy's most underappreciated and indispensable entrepreneur.[44] She documents the leading role that the government played in funding all the technologies that make the smart phone smart, including the internet, wireless systems, global positioning systems, voice activation, and touch-screen displays. The federal government has played a similar role in spurring technological breakthroughs in aviation and space exploration, pharmaceuticals and biotechnology, nanotechnology, and robotics.

Even so, Pittsburgh would not have soared as it did without the willingness of local philanthropies to take risks. The city has a long history of deep engagement among a robust philanthropic sector, advanced universities, and the broader innovation ecosystem.

These partnerships have supported a host of research and other related activities that have become pivotal to the Pittsburgh economy. One reason for this is the sheer size of the philanthropic community. As of October 2014, the Richard King Mellon Foundation was the thirty-fifth largest foundation in the United States, with assets of $2.3 billion.[45] The Heinz Endowments was the ninety-sixth largest foundation in the United States, with assets of $1.6 billion.[46] The impact of philanthropy on the city is even clearer on a per capita basis: the Pittsburgh metropolitan area benefits from $9,126 in foundation assets per person. The U.S. average is only $2,857.[47]

Pittsburgh foundations view technology-based economic development as a critical component of their social missions and invest accordingly. According to officials at Carnegie Mellon University, foundation grants were instrumental in starting such fields of study as machine learning, computational finance, and robotics. More recently, local philanthropy investments were critical to attracting the ARM Institute through more than $200 million in public, private, and civic capital. And support for all kinds of institutions—incubators, co-working spaces, technology councils, accelerators—is routine.

Even smart real estate investments can be a sign of long-termism. In 2002 the Heinz Endowments, the Richard King Mellon Foundation, the Benedum Foundation, and the McCune Foundation purchased the 178-acre Almono brownfield site, the remnants of LTV Steel's Hazelwood

Works. This site has now become a testing ground for driverless cars and will become the headquarters of the ARM Innovation Hub.[48]

To some extent, Pittsburgh's deep bench of focused philanthropies has enabled the city to assume responsibilities that were once the purview of the Commonwealth of Pennsylvania. For many decades the commonwealth, across Republican and Democratic administrations, was the center of economic development, investing in public university centers of excellence, technology transfer, initiatives such as the Ben Franklin Technology Partners, and trade-oriented efforts to boost exports and foreign direct investment. With budgetary scalebacks, the responsibility for these efforts has now largely devolved to public, private, civic, and university leaders at the city and metropolitan scale.

Fourth, *public and philanthropic investments must be part of a broader political, business, civic, and university alliance.*

The slow rise of robotics followed the fast collapse of the steel industry and the radical depopulation of the city. Between 1970 and 1990, one-third of Pittsburgh's population disappeared, along with more than 100,000 well-paying manufacturing jobs. These dynamics drove the formation in 1985 of Strategy 21, a collective effort of the City of Pittsburgh, Allegheny County, Carnegie Mellon, and the University of Pittsburgh, in close collaboration with city philanthropies and business leadership through the Allegheny Conference on Community Development. Strategy 21 placed strong emphasis on diversifying the economy and prioritized a series of high-profile projects so that the leadership in Pittsburgh could speak with one voice and advocate together for federal- and state-level investments. Four high-profile projects were eventually targeted: winning the federal competition for the Software Engineering Institute at Carnegie Mellon (1986), receiving one of five federally funded supercomputers (1996), building a new international airport terminal (1992), and (later) creating the NREC.[49]

In 1993, Carnegie Mellon president Robert Mehrabian launched another regional vision with the publication of a white paper. This paper, commissioned by the Allegheny Conference, sparked a major public engagement effort that resulted in the 1994 report, *The Greater Pittsburgh Region: Working Together to Compete Globally.* The Working Together Consortium was then formed to implement the plan and push through a sales tax increase of 1 percent.[50] With public support, a Regional Asset District was able to provide $1.5 billion over a twenty-year period for a wide range of quality-of-life investments, including investments in parks, libraries, sports stadia, and museums.[51]

Visionary public leadership was critical to the process, particularly that of Mayors Richard Caliguiri and Tom Murphy in the 1980s, 1990s, and early 2000s. Mayor Bill Peduto and County Executive Rich Fitzgerald have continued this legacy into this decade.

Fifth, *an entrepreneurial culture is crucial to success.*

Especially at Carnegie Mellon and the University of Pittsburgh, this culture has led to a highly productive "revolving door" between the academy, government, and industry whereby knowledge gained in one sector is used to facilitate the invention and deployment of products, catalyze the growth of entrepreneurs and companies, and extend the boundaries of scientific application. Andrew Moore's move from Carnegie Mellon to Google and back again to Carnegie Mellon has been noted, as well as John Bares's move from Carnegie Mellon to Uber (with an interim stop at Carnegie Robotics).

The city's revolving door has influence far beyond its boundaries. Subra Suresh, the president of Carnegie Mellon until June 2017, was the director of the National Science Foundation from 2010 to 2013. Patrick Gallagher, chancellor of the University of Pittsburgh, was the director of the National Institute of Standards and Technology from 2009 to 2014. Significantly, several of their top aides have served in senior government positions at the national and state level.

The phrase "revolving door" is, of course, generally seen as pejorative. But Pittsburgh's intermixing of people from disparate backgrounds and with diverse experiences—corporate, government, and university—is clearly having a synergistic effect in spurring initiatives and technologies and is a major reason why Pittsburgh is punching above its weight.

Sixth, *a city must build on rather than discard its historical legacy.*

As Don Carter, director of Carnegie Mellon's Remaking Cities Institute has noted, "There is a DNA of the region from 100 years ago. Being ahead of the curve is the key. Carnegie was all about reinvesting profits and automation. The key was to keep investing in technologies."[52] Andrew Carnegie himself said a successful businessman in any industry must "lead in it; adopt every improvement, have the best machinery, and know the most about it."[53]

Durable, long-term investments in innovation capacity are core to the Pittsburgh experience and its current competitiveness. Carnegie Mellon was founded in 1900 as the Carnegie Technical Schools to make engineers out of the children of low-skill workers in steel factories. The predecessor of the robots that cleaned up Three Mile Island basements could be found in 1939, when Westinghouse Electric took the World's Fair by storm with its robot called Elecktro. As Andy Masich, CEO of the Heinz History Center, recounted, "He can walk, talk and recognize colors. He can smoke cigarettes like it's going out of style. He's the hit of the World's Fair." As Masich summarized, "We were innovative in 1939 and imagined futures that have come to pass. Now Pittsburgh is seen as a robotics capital of the world."[54]

"The big point is that we are not going against our core brand," says Ilana Diamond, founder of AlphaLab Gear, the nonprofit that provides workspace, funding, and network opportunities so students can turn high-tech hardware inventions into start-up companies. "We have always made stuff here. . . . That's what the mills were, right? It's in our genes—we don't have to argue with anyone that Pittsburgh is a place where stuff gets made." Or as Whittaker says, "I like this city because it has blood in its veins."[55]

Finally, *cities must make their innovations visible to the world.*

In many respects, Pittsburgh has become a veritable playground of innovation. The community retains the wonder, awe, and excitement that were once associated with technological improvement and powered iconic moments such as the 1939 World's Fair. Peter Thiel, the cofounder of PayPal, has achieved notoriety for remarking, "We wanted flying cars, instead we got 140 characters."[56] In many respects, Pittsburgh has become the land of flying cars (or at least driverless cars).

Even a cursory visit to Pittsburgh exposes this cultural embrace of continuous innovation. Many cities describe their research prowess and commercial applications in nondescript meeting rooms through traditional PowerPoint presentations. In Pittsburgh, visitors are taken right to the source—university labs and startup companies—where the innovators

describe what they are researching or inventing with a passion and enthusiasm that is truly infectious.

If you ever want to feel positive about America (and the world), go lis-
ten to a group of student inventors at Carnegie Mellon or the University of
Pittsburgh, whose sense of technological possibility and real-world impact
knows no bounds. On a recent visit, we met Hahna Alexander, the CEO
and cofounder of SolePower. The company invented shoes and boots that
capture wasted energy from human motion (walking) and use the power
to charge portable electronics such as cell phones. There is enormous
potential to apply this simple but powerful invention in areas where the
energy grid is absent or unreliable, such as in developing nations, remote
areas, or war zones.

The last word belongs to Red Whittaker: "I chose Pittsburgh to build this
class of machines that I call field robots. What was needed was a place that
had a good future in computing, an excellent industrial base where good
people were available and where you could start with nothing much and
could grow to the best in the world."[57]

HOW PLACEMAKING REVALUES GROWTH

There is another critical piece to Pittsburgh's growth story, and that is how
smart, vibrant places, usually located in city cores and near major anchor
institutions, have become the sites of innovative economies.

Nationally, the spatial geography of innovation is shifting. Pittsburgh exemplifies how research- and innovation-intensive activity, once conducted on
isolated corporate campuses and in science parks located far from urban centers, is now moving toward denser, more dynamic areas. These innovation
districts are colocating leading research institutions, medical campuses, and
R&D-intensive companies with startups and business incubators; transit,
broadband, and quality public space; and a culture that promotes collaboration through formal and informal programming, meet-ups, and networking
events. Strong in sectors such as bioscience, technology, and creative industries, these districts are physically compact and historically significant,
and offer mixed-use housing, office, and retail space.[58]

The district's core is home to two world-class research institutions, the University of Pittsburgh and Carnegie Mellon University, along with UPMC, dozens of startup companies, and co-working spaces such as NoWait, Peptilogics, and Revv Oakland/StartupTown.

In South Oakland along the Monongahela River are clustered the Pittsburgh Technology Council, Carnegie Mellon and University of Pittsburgh research facilities, and large scientific and technology firms such as Thermo Fisher Scientific. Companies and research centers have gravitated toward Carnegie Mellon and the University of Pittsburgh, and spaces suitable for corporate partners (Carnegie Mellon's Collaborative Innovation Center) and workspaces (Revv Oakland) act as magnets to entice startups and other partners.

Pittsburgh's Greater Oakland district occupies roughly 5 percent of the city's land area but represents 12.8 percent of residents and 23.6 percent of jobs, which are concentrated in the city's growing education and health care sectors. The 1.7-square-mile district accounts for more than one-third of the entire state of Pennsylvania's university R&D output.[59]

Almost as important as the institutions within the district are the innovation assets adjacent to its porous borders. To the northeast is Chatham University and Bakery Square, home to Google and the University of Pittsburgh's Human Engineering Research Laboratories. To the northwest is Lawrenceville, anchored by Carnegie Mellon's NREC and home to perhaps the fastest-growing cluster of robotics startups in the country (such as Argo, recently acquired by Ford for $1 billion). To the south is the 178-acre Almono site. Just southeast of the district is downtown Pittsburgh, with over 45,000 jobs and the national headquarters of such companies as PNC, UPMC, Highmark, and U.S. Steel.

The district is also undergoing a virtual explosion of new construction. Carnegie Mellon is undertaking its largest building boom since the mid-twentieth century, with more than a half billion dollars invested in new real estate construction. In 2016 the university opened three new buildings, including Scott Hall, a $108 million home for its Energy Innovation institute and the Department of Biomedical Engineering. It even includes a facility for researching nanofabrication. Planning or construction is under way for several other buildings, including a new home for the Tepper Business

School, a "maker-space" renovation of a historic building, and a new engineering building, the Tata Consultancy Services Hall, that will serve as a collaboration space for students and industry. Among the major talent contributions that the Indian population has brought to Pittsburgh, the Mumbai-based Tata Consultancy Services has also made a $35 million gift to the university, the largest industry-funded gift in Carnegie Mellon's history.[60]

For its part, the University of Pittsburgh has already spent tens of millions of dollars renovating key research and medical spaces. As of the time of writing (summer 2017), the university was completing an ambitious ten-year capital plan to underwrite new facilities to house computing and information systems, immune transplant and therapy research, and other multidisciplinary endeavors.

The emergence of innovation districts like the one located in Greater Oakland is occurring as a result of profound demographic, economic, and social forces that spotlight the importance of place for innovation, job creation, and economic growth.

Demographic trends in the United States are fueling a demand for more walkable and transit-accessible neighborhoods that integrate work, housing, and recreation. A significant portion of the millennial generation, for example, measures quality of life in terms of access to urban amenities such as restaurants, retail establishments, and various cultural and social institutions. For this reason, the number of young college graduates living within three miles of city centers has surged in the past decade, not only in talent magnet cities such as New York, San Francisco, and Denver but also in older industrial cities such as Buffalo, Cleveland, and Pittsburgh.[61]

Meanwhile, the open, innovative economy increasingly craves density so that companies, researchers, and entrepreneurs can share ideas rather than invent in isolation. No one company can master all the knowledge it needs, so it must rely on a network of industry collaborators. The United States has entered a convergence economy in which industries are both inventing technologies at the intersection of formerly siloed disciplines and applying technology to traditional industries such as retail, health care, media, advertising, fashion, and finance. These shifts reinforce the importance of proximity as companies strive to be physically close to their company and organizational partners.

Rick Siger, director of strategic initiatives and engagement at Carnegie Mellon, emphasized the importance of space in an interview with the *Pittsburgh Business Times:* "We envision the robotics Ph.D. standing in line at the café that bumps into the Tepper MBA. We want to foster that kind of serendipitous interaction that could lead to the next great breakthrough or company."[62]

Finally, innovation districts are nestled in cities that boost multiple hubs of creativity, entrepreneurialism, and vibrancy. The Project for Public Spaces, for example, has played a major role in championing public food markets and reimagining Main Streets, where local entrepreneurs and "makers" are stimulating local economic development by energizing public spaces with pop-up stores, food trucks, and community markets. They and other groups, such as Smart Growth America and the Congress for New Urbanism, have been strong advocates for mixed-use activity centers near transit stations, as well as entrepreneurial communities that specialize in arts, culture, and craft manufacture.

These trends highlight the importance of advancing innovation—at multiple scales and in multiple sectors—across the United States. They also emphasize the role of placemaking in creating authentic and inclusive places to attract young talented workers and fuel idea generation and social connectivity. Together, they demand an approach to urban economic development that does more to cultivate environments—within buildings, in public spaces, across streetscapes, near transit hubs—where the economic, physical, and networking assets of a place collide in ways that inspire idea generation, foster collaboration, and spur a sense of invention and entrepreneurship.

Many innovation districts are emerging organically near advanced research institutions located in the cores of cities. In these communities— Pittsburgh's Oakland district, Midtown Atlanta (the location of Georgia Tech), Kendall Square, Cambridge (the location of MIT), St. Louis's Cortex district (the location of Washington University), Birmingham's near downtown (the location of the University of Alabama–Birmingham), Cleveland's University Circle (the location of Case Western University and the Cleveland Clinic)—the growth of research-driven companies and the influx of talented workers are creating a demand for a dramatic improvement in placemaking. In some respects, innovation has come first, creating a demand for and spurring the development of quality places, which in turn have driven more innovation—a virtuous cycle.

Yet most cities in the United States and abroad do not host Tier 1 research institutions. In these communities, a reverse phenomenon is starting to happen.

CHATTANOOGA: REVERSE ENGINEERING

Chattanooga, Tennessee, is the most compelling example of this reverse engineering. In 1969 the city was declared the most polluted in the United States: "People had to drive with their headlights on all day," according to one recollection.[63]

Nearly two decades later a community planning process, Vision 2000, began to envision an urban core based on its distinctive natural asset, the Tennessee River. The Tennessee Riverpark Master Plan, published in 1985, called for $750 million of mixed-use development and conservation along twenty-two miles of the river.[64]

During the 1990s the city government and its partners turned the plan into action. The Tennessee Aquarium opened in 1992, the Walnut Street Bridge (renovated as a walking bridge) in 1993, and the Creative Discovery Museum in 1996. In 2005 the city unveiled another $120 million in riverfront improvements spanning 129 acres. (Half of the funds came from private donations; the other half came from the sale of publicly owned properties and an increase in the taxes on hotels and motels.)

Enter Gig-a-byte. In 2009 the Electric Power Board of Chattanooga (EPB), the city's public utility, simultaneously built one of the world's most extensive municipal high-speed internet networks and smartest energy grids. Smartly deploying $280 million in local revenue bonds and federal stimulus funds, EPB installed more than 9,000 miles of fiber throughout its metropolitan service area and 180,000 smart meters and 1,400 intelligent switches throughout its energy grid.[65]

Chattanooga mayor Andy Berke quipped that the Gig City now has "the fastest, cheapest, most pervasive internet in the Western Hemisphere."[66]

The effort had two transformative effects: it created an enticing lure for tech entrepreneurs and a host of other businesses and families, and it resulted in the development of a truly smart grid.[67] The utility built one of the world's first modern electrical grids, capable of being a laboratory for smart responses to climate change and severe weather conditions throughout the United States and the world. EPB has gone from 2 million meter reads per year to 17 million meter reads per day.[68]

With high quality of life and high-speed connectivity, the city took the next step, designating a 140-acre enclave in the heart of the downtown as an innovation district. The Innovation District is the product of genuine, enthusiastic collaboration—not often seen in bigger cities—among public, private, and civic institutions and leaders. These players included the city and county governments, EPB, the Lyndhurst and Benwood Foundations, the University of Tennessee–Chattanooga, the Enterprise Development Center, and an entrepreneurial mix of investors that included the Lamp Post Group, startups such as Bellhops, incubators such as Co-Lab, and real estate developers such as River City Company.

After decades of sprawl and decentralization, Chattanooga is rediscovering the benefits of density. The number of residents living downtown has doubled and locally grown coffee shops (probably the best new metric for urban vibrancy) are plentiful. The final sign that Chattanooga's innovation day had arrived came in October 2016, when Oak Ridge National Laboratory, the Department of Energy's largest national facility, opened an office at the EPB.[69]

This reverse engineering is being repeated in hundreds of other cities, large, medium, and small. Cities have historical physical assets— downtowns, Main Streets, buildings, waterfronts—that can be repurposed both to spur new innovative growth and to boost civic pride and community participation. Older industrial cities, in short, have "good bones." As Steven Johnson wrote in *Where Good Ideas Come From,*

> Just like the skeletal structure left behind by dead coral forms the basis of the rich and thriving ecosystem of the reef, abandoned buildings and rundown neighborhoods are often the first homes of innovative urban subcultures. Their unconventional thinking and

experimentation often has no place in glitzy mainstream malls and shopping centers initially. Old buildings allow subcultures to interact and generate ideas that then diffuse and spill over into the mainstream.[70]

Just as technologies, disciplines, and sectors are converging to create new products, so too disparate parts of cities are blending to generate new geographies that mix culture, creativity, and innovation at all levels of the economy. In Oklahoma City, an older medical district is now merging with Automobile Alley, one of the city's most vibrant commercial and entertainment corridors. In Philadelphia, the boundaries between Center City and University City are being erased as a result of the location decisions of companies such as Comcast (which is building new towers at the western edge of the traditional downtown) and the centrality of the 30th Street Station.

Providence, Rhode Island, is knitting together the Jewelry District (which concentrates the ample medical research and design competencies of Brown University, the Rhode Island School of Design, the University of Rhode Island, and local hospitals), College Hill (where the main campuses of Brown and RISD are located), the traditional downtown (where Johnson and Wales, a top culinary school, is located), and the newly emerging River District (where Waterfire and various food and other creative efforts are under way). The merged district blends classic research-driven biosciences commercialization with design and arts and food, all within cycling distance. And a new pedestrian bridge is being built across the Providence River on a former federal highway.

Despite these examples, much work remains to be done to rebuild communities in ways that are truly innovative, sustainable, and inclusive. The majority of university-led innovation districts, for example, lack authentic and inclusive places to attract young talented workers and to fuel idea generation and social connectivity. At the same time, other urban hubs that may function as amazing places often have untapped economic assets that are currently more oriented toward consumption than toward innovation and have very little connection to districts anchored by universities and research-intensive companies. Meanwhile, low-income residents—many of whom live in high-poverty neighborhoods near these emerging areas—continue to be left out of the equation.

Realizing the full potential of cities will also require a radical overhaul of transportation infrastructure. The cores of many cities are scarred by legacy highways built in the decades after World War II and rail infrastructure built in the decades prior. These highways and railways destroyed the traditional urban fabric, often dividing waterfront areas from downtowns and downtowns from universities and other employment centers of the city. Many highways and railways located in urban areas are either coming to the end of their useful life or have ceased to play a vital economic role, offering opportunities for transformative infrastructure investments (such as the replacement of elevated freeways with boulevards) that are more supportive of the new demand for vibrant places and creative economies.

These challenges are daunting but not insurmountable. What Pittsburgh, Chattanooga, Oklahoma City, Philadelphia, and Providence have in common is the ability to emerge from an urban decline following industrial-era prosperity into newfound global relevance by applying the tenets and principles of New Localism. Pittsburgh in particular illustrates a new growth model driven by distinctive sectors such as robotics and by the dynamic, sustained interaction of government, academia, entrepreneurs, and philanthropists. The depth and breadth of innovative anchor institutions have spurred a virtuous cycle of talent attraction, company growth, and restoration of the core of the city as a vibrant place.

In Chattanooga, a citizen base recognized that the only way to transform would be through a physical makeover of its river frontage and the broader historical downtown area. With so much invested in a major master plan, the city's public utility overhauled the power grid, building a high-speed internet that sent a signal that Chattanooga was ready for twenty-first-century businesses and twenty-first-century lifestyles.

In all these stories, the critical element is collaborative governance across networks of public, private, civic, and university institutions and leadership. No one sector can alone power a city and metropolis forward in today's complex and competitive economy. Inventing and sustaining a new model of networked governance is the topic of our next chapter and requires a sojourn to Indianapolis.

FIVE

Rethinking Governance
INDIANAPOLIS CASE STUDY

Be an ecosystem rather than an ego-system.
—Chris Cabaldon, Mayor of West Sacramento

New Localism entails a broad definition of urban governance that reaches beyond the mayor's office and into local universities, philanthropies, businesses, and civic organizations. The evolution of such networked local governance has been rapid and widespread. It has emerged at different geographic scales and with different limits of focus. A key challenge that remains is cultivating a governance structure that is more than just a loose affiliation or informal network but remains flexible and democratic. Indianapolis is one city that has gotten it right. Its structured, formal collaboration has been yielding rewards for more than thirty years.

Indianapolis's revival started with sports.

By the time Bill Hudnut was elected mayor in 1975 the situation was grim: Indianapolis was flat on its back, weakened by deindustrialization and excessive suburbanization. "Downtown Indianapolis had become so desolate that men with shotguns hunted pigeons on Sundays among empty buildings and along a trash strewn canal," read the former mayor's obituary in the *Washington Post*. "Novelist and native son Kurt Vonnegut described the city in 1970 as a place where 'it was no easy thing to be an optimist' and the passage of time was marked by the '500-mile speedway race and then 364 days of miniature golf.'"[1]

Mayor Hudnut had entered office with momentum. Just a few years earlier, in 1970, to mitigate issues stemming from municipal sprawl and fragmentation, the state legislature had consolidated the city and county governments of Indianapolis and surrounding Marion County. In one act, "Unigov" increased Indianapolis's population by about 250,000 and its land area by about 275 square miles, establishing it as one of the top U.S. cities (its population of 853,000 in 2015 made it the fourteenth most populous city in the United States).[2]

But just making a city bigger doesn't make it better. Hudnut and a high-level group of community leaders (including Ted Boehm, a future

Indiana Supreme Court justice) targeted sports as a potentially winning strategy to uplift the city and revitalize the urban core. The federal government had just enacted the Amateur Sports Act of 1978 to promote amateur athletics and require each Olympic sport to have its own governing body. One year later, the mayor and a small group of business leaders, in close collaboration with the locally based Lilly Endowment, created the nonprofit Indiana Sports Corporation. The sole mission of this first-of-its-kind regional sports corporation was to turn Indianapolis into the "Amateur Sports Capital of the World" by luring the newly mandated Olympic governing bodies and big spectator events.[3]

Its success proved astonishing. In 1982, Indianapolis played host to Olympic hopefuls during the National Sports Festival. The Indiana Sports Corporation organized and carried out the event with the help of 3,000 volunteers. More than $100 million invested in new facilities transformed the campus of Indiana University-Purdue University Indianapolis (IUPUI).[4]

In 1987, Indianapolis hosted the Pan American Games, stepping in when Santiago, Chile, backed out for economic and political reasons. Indianapolis was the first host city to break even financially: in fact, hosting costs tallied at $30 million but filtered $175 million into the local economy.[5]

The city's athletic venture did not stop with amateur sports. In the early 1980s the city began construction on the $80 million Hoosier Dome stadium, even though it had no professional football team. But a scheme was in place. After negotiations over Baltimore's Memorial Stadium improvements reached an impasse, Hudnut convinced the owner of the Baltimore Colts to move his team to Indianapolis. What followed is often considered the most notorious relocations in American sports, a secretive operation that involved the mayor's neighbor (the CEO and chairman of Mayflower) and the dispatch of fourteen tractor-trailer trucks in the middle of the night to the Baltimore Colts' facility in Owings Mills, Maryland; drivers weren't told their destination until the next day.[6] Baltimore fans knew nothing until they woke up the following morning to the news.

The sports acquisitions frenzy crested in 1997 when Indianapolis successfully persuaded the National Collegiate Athletic Association (NCAA) to move its headquarters from its suburban campus in Overland Park, Kansas. Indianapolis offered the NCAA a reported $50 million ($10 million from the Lilly Endowment, $15 million from private individuals, businesses, and organizations, and $25 million from state and city taxpayers). The city also built the NCAA a 142,000-square-foot headquarters and the Hall of Champions, a 35,000-square-foot exhibition hall and museum. The deal included 500 free parking spaces and first-class landscaping. The NCAA paid a rent of $1 per year. A Kansas City representative expressed his opinion that the Indianapolis organizers "may be a little beyond sane in what they have done."[7]

As David Johnson, president and CEO of the Central Indiana Corporate Partnership and BioCrossroads, later recalled, "The NCAA move came up suddenly and got done marvelously well by a loose, enterprising, effective but self-appointed confederation of community leaders; a cooperative and creative Governor (when it came to providing the land); and an extremely generous Lilly Endowment and corporate community (when it came to finding the money and encouraging others to do likewise)."[8]

FROM BASKETBALL TO BIOTECH

At this point in the story, Indianapolis reflects a high-end version of a sports and stadia strategy that is commonly implemented in the United States. The country is littered with dozens of stadia built with public subsidies, even though there is strong evidence that the return on these investments leaves much to be desired.[9] Still, Indianapolis played the sports hand as well as it can be played. The city's success in luring major sporting events, a major sports team, the Colts, and the foremost college sporting association, the NCAA, helped boost civic pride, altered the identity of the city, and provided a much-needed platform for urban revitalization. But the real impact of the events of the previous two decades was to illustrate how effective a collaborative governance network could be. Indianapolis's experience shows that when the entirety of the regional leadership, from public, private, and civic sectors, gets behind one vision and aspiration, concrete results follow.

But Indianapolis leaders recognized that a sports-based development strategy can take a city only so far. Sports attract tourism and visitors.

Game time enhances demand for lodging and restaurants. Name teams may have an intangible effect on the attraction and retention of innovative firms and talented workers. But in the end, the sports industry thrives on low-wage jobs and does not represent a model of economic growth for a city or metropolis. Beer and hot dogs are not the stuff of a sustainable middle class.

Indianapolis leaders—particularly the Lilly Endowment and the Corporate Community Council, the key business organization—also recognized that the informal method of bringing corporate, civic, and government leaders together to take advantage of discrete opportunities, while enormously successful, was not an optimal way to address more fundamental economic and social challenges facing the city and metropolis. As David Johnson recalled, "Even when deals like the NCAA move made great sense and brought terrific economic return, the dollars and stakes were just getting too high to be left to opportunistically organized volunteer leaders, without a broader plan or mandate, embarking on bold, spontaneous moves that carried a high price tag which someone else would need to pay and really begging the question of a comprehensive strategy for growth."[10]

In 1998, in the wake of the NCAA deal and in close collaboration with Lilly Endowment president Clay Robbins, two leaders of the Corporate Community Council—Larry O'Connor, the head of one of the largest banks, and Sallie Rowland, president of a regional architecture and design firm—established a task force and retained a consultant to help assess the problem and design potential solutions. A real consensus for change emerged among the regional corporate CEOs over the course of a year.

The task force members recognized that creating a prosperous region would be a big lift, requiring "a fundamental transformation of the region's human resource endowment to support a vigorously entrepreneurial, high value-adding, knowledge based economy that can create economic and social mobility for residents and world class competitiveness for businesses." And achieving this goal would necessitate an institutional shift: "As a loose knit and informal association (which is what most of the major corporate CEOs historically have wanted), the [Corporate Community] Council has been in previous years a low key but effective instrument to help coalesce CEO leadership around major civic projects and events. But the big challenges that now face the region are not projects and events. And the group's informal structure is not well suited to shaping and implementing complex long term strategies."[11]

Accordingly, the task force recommended in its report that the Corporate Community Council disband and establish in its place a new, CEO-only, invitation-only "coordinating organization to guide the corporate community in maximizing the use of corporate funding in the Central Indiana economic arena. It would provide funding, leadership and oversight of economic development activity in Central Indiana by establishing policy, priorities, strategic focus and synergy."[12]

After twenty years of success, and immediately after landing a big win with the NCAA headquarters, Indianapolis leaders were recommending shifting away from its sports-based strategy because they recognized it didn't offer the region long-term sustainability. They also recognized that the governance institution that had delivered that success was inadequate to the tasks that lay ahead. Although it was highly unusual for a successful task force to take these actions, their efforts proved prescient.

The Central Indiana Corporate Partnership (CICP) formed in 1999 as a 501(c)(6) organization with membership limited to fifty (later expanded to sixty) CEOs and presidents of the region's leading companies, philanthropic foundations, and universities. Currently the partnership has fifty-nine members, comprising fifty corporate CEOs, three heads of philanthropies, and six university presidents.[13]

From the beginning, the CICP was designed to be exclusive and impactful; the organization does not allow any substitutes or delegation to subordinates. The CEOs and presidents are the only members and participants. The idea is to "make the CICP Board synonymous with the most influential individual and corporate stakeholders in the State, empowered to make the kinds of strategic and investment decisions that are uniquely the province of those who actually lead organizations. The strength of the CICP's Board has always been the organization's single most compelling characteristic."[14]

Significantly, no elected officials serve on the CICP board, and none of the organization's core funding comes from public dollars. The organization is nonpartisan, avoiding political engagements or endorsements, political action committees, or other partisan behavior while collaborating closely with elected officials regardless of party.

An internal CICP document recounting the evolution of the organization from 1999 to 2017 summarized the CICP's mission as follows:

> CICP was intentionally structured to be the region's premier strategic economic arm for community leadership, providing oversight and guidance for our key business, university and philanthropic leaders, helping to prioritize resource allocation and leverage investment into those programs and institutions that could best advance regional development. Consequently, CICP was seen, from the beginning, as a strategic platform that could research, present for discussion and alignment and *then implement an effective long-term strategy*, impervious to political whim and elected official turnover, with the capacity to first define and then secure the next chapters of Central Indiana's future.[15]

Given this mission and its distinctive leadership model, CICP works closely with but is separate from other business and civic organizations. Like many metropolitan areas, Indianapolis has a large chamber of commerce, with a membership of 2,500 businesses.[16] That organization continues to do what it does well: represent the interests of businesses large, medium, and small before local and state governments, as well as coordinate business attraction efforts with city and regional economic development officials.

However, the CICP's work to spur economic growth is qualitatively different from the chamber of commerce's. Over the past eighteen years, the CICP has developed a playbook for maximizing collaborative leadership and engendering a new kind of collective serial entrepreneurialism. First commission an intensive, objective analysis of a leading cluster or important economic or social challenge. Then craft a detailed business plan for leveraging opportunities and addressing critical shortcomings. Only then stand up a special branded initiative, with sufficient resources, broad corporate buy-in, professional staff, and knowledgeable oversight. Repeat, again and again.

As David Johnson, CICP's current president and CEO, noted in the 2016 *Annual Report*, "CICP is truly providing both the workshop to develop and then runway to launch the best collaborative opportunities for our region's future success."[17] It has perfected a method of assessing the economy, devising practical solutions, and working the civics to translate analysis and ideas into action.

Since 2002 the CICP has designed and housed five sectoral initiatives to fill gaps and pursue strengths through a relentless focus on driving talent and investment to "verticals."[18] These initiatives are BioCrossroads, for life sciences (2002), TechPoint, for software development and information technology (2006), Conexus Indiana, for advanced manufacturing and logistics (2007), Energy Systems Network, for clean and alternative energy technologies (2009), and AgriNovus Indiana, for agriculture-related innovation (2014). The CICP created a sixth initiative, Ascend Indiana, in 2015 to address workforce development issues across regional sectors. Through these six initiatives, the CICP has allowed central Indiana to leverage its existing regional assets.

By design, each initiative has its own brand, marketing, and communications presence, often more prominent than that of the CICP itself. Each initiative also has its own advisory board of directors, which is not restricted to CICP members. Members provide financial support, community access, and, frequently, broad engagement across their respective organizations.

Beyond the branded initiatives, CICP has also led the formative stages of various regional initiatives that deal with such related issues as STEM education, innovation districts, defense-related research, and the economic development of adjoining metropolitan areas.

TURNING ANALYSIS INTO ACTION

A close look at the development and impact of the CICP's life sciences initiative, BioCrossroads, illustrates the distinctiveness of the Indianapolis model. One of the CICP's first actions was to commission Battelle Technology Partnership Practice to assess the region's position in major industry clusters such as advanced manufacturing, life sciences, and information technology. "At the time, public and private stakeholders had a general, though often anecdotal, knowledge of the sectors of strength in the regional economy," according to an internal CICP document.[19]

As home to several major companies, including Eli Lilly, the best known, but also Roche Diagnostics, the Cook Group (a major medical device concern), and Dow AgroSciences, the region's emphasis on life sciences was obvious. The Indiana University School of Medicine (today the largest MD-granting program in the country) and Anthem, the nation's largest health insurance company, also strengthened their positions.[20] And just a couple of hours north, Warsaw, Indiana—a small town of 20,000 people—hosted three of the five largest global orthopedic companies, representing one-third of the annual $45 billion in revenues from the orthopedic and related biologics industries.[21]

Upon its December 2000 release, the Battelle report, *Nurturing Central Indiana's Pillar Industries for 21st Century Midwestern Pre-Eminence*, had a galvanizing effect. It revealed a region bursting with assets—companies, research institutions, philanthropies, skilled scientists and workers—that were hidden in plain sight and significantly underleveraged.[22] As David Johnson recalled, "There were all these major players in the life sciences, but they weren't talking to each other. These were people who ought to be sitting at the table and putting new things in place."[23]

In February 2002, a coalition of organizations, including Indiana University, Purdue University, Lilly, the Indiana Health Industry Forum, and the mayor's office, again working in close collaboration with the Lilly Endowment, established the Central Indiana Life Sciences Initiative under the CICP umbrella. Later renamed BioCrossroads, this initiative has zeroed in on the four imperatives identified by the Battelle report as key to unlocking the state's life sciences future: providing better information about and brand identity for the sector; stimulating training and talent development by local government, vocational, and academic institutions; linking talent and business through effective collaborations; and finding sufficient venture capital to build a real local market.[24]

Generating a pool of local and regional venture capital became a top priority. In 2003, BioCrossroads launched the Indiana Future Fund with

$73 million in return-driven venture capital raised from a group of corporate investors, research universities, and state pension funds.[25] This was followed by the Indiana Seed Fund Program in 2006, which has gone through two rounds of funding, investing nearly $12 million in twenty-six companies, investments that have triggered follow-on funding of more than $100 million.[26] Without the seed fund, it is unlikely that leading innovations from both Purdue University (SpeechVive, SonarMed) and Indiana University (Assembly Biosciences, Anagin) would have found funding traction. Finally, in 2009, a third fund, the INext Fund, was capitalized with $58 million to provide nationally managed but locally accessible venture capital for promising startup companies.[27]

The Indiana Biosciences Research Institute (IBRI), founded in 2012 as the first industry-led research institute in the United States, best illustrates the links between talent and industry. Capitalized at over $150 million, the nonprofit corporation's goal is to attract global talent to Indianapolis to carry out basic and applied research in diabetes, metabolic disease and nutrition.[28] IBRI partners include life science companies such as Lilly, Roche, Dow, Cook Medical, and IU Health (the state's largest health care provider), plus academic institutions such as Indiana University, Purdue University, and the University of Notre Dame. Research is both basic and applied, and the industry partners have developed a framework to identify "rules of the road" with respect to shared intellectual property. IBRI also coordinates with its industry partners to identify faculty working on industry-sponsored contracts and leverages firm partners to bring those researchers to Indianapolis, both as IBRI fellows and as colleagues at member universities, increasing the collaboration between Indiana universities and firms.

This region, like Pittsburgh, needed to offer specialized educational opportunities to its residents to prepare them for the new jobs being created by developing industries. In 2006, BioCrossroads launched I-STEM/Indiana Science Initiative to ensure that Indiana elementary and secondary students receive exposure to science, technology, engineering, and math to gain the technical skills necessary to compete for jobs in the life sciences industry.[29]

Finally, the city needed to rebrand and expand from being primarily known as a sports capital to also being known as a center of health care collaboration and innovation. On the collaborative front, in 2004 Bio-Crossroads launched the Indiana Health Information Exchange as a sustainable enterprise with the collaboration of such health care organizations as IU Health, Community Health Network, St. Vincent Indianapolis, and Franciscan St. Francis Health, which until then had been serious competitors.[30] Today the network connects 100 hospitals, 30,000 clinicians and physicians, and more than 12 million patients to aggregate and deliver lab results, reports, medication histories, and treatment histories to all providers, regardless of hospital system or location.

And just as stadium building left its imprint on the earlier era, a major life sciences–based innovation hub is becoming the physical manifestation of the city's newest raison d'être. In 2015 BioCrossroads, in collaboration with the CICP, launched the 16 Tech innovation district to turn a sixty-acre site located near the downtown into a vibrant hub for tech-oriented enterprises in multiple sectors, starting with IBRI as the anchor tenant.[31] The city of Indianapolis approved $75 million in bonds to develop public infrastructure, to be serviced with revenue from tax increment financing. A portion of the funds would be used to create a community investment fund to benefit the neighborhoods surrounding the 16 Tech area.[32]

The cumulative effect of a disciplined focus on these efforts has been enormous. As of 2016, the state of Indiana's life sciences had grown to a $63.3 billion industry, second only to California for life science exports in the United States.[33] The industry is diverse, covering not only pharmaceutical and medical device companies but also agriculture/biotech research and testing services, and biologistics. It is home to nearly 1,700 companies and more than 56,200 workers (a 22 percent increase in employment since 2001). Perhaps most significant, the industry pays an average wage of approximately $99,000; by contrast, the average private sector wage in Indiana is $44,000.[34]

The Indianapolis case exemplifies how a globally competitive, advanced industry can emerge in the twenty-first century through a vision that recruits skilled workers, engages universities and companies in common goals, leverages strong philanthropic support, motivates novel public-private partnerships, invites smart placemaking, and affords ready access to risk capital. Indianapolis is a key model of New Localism for its collaborations within sectors, technological innovations, and investment in the workforce of the future—and for being launched into the global sphere through civic efforts and strong local leadership.

WHAT INDIANAPOLIS TEACHES OTHER CITIES

The Indianapolis story represents where local governance in the United States is headed. The current suite of supersized challenges and de facto devolution of responsibilities demands new models of networked governance and a fundamental reframing and refocusing of the leadership class in cities. The most effective local governance occurs in places that not only deploy the formal and informal powers of government but also create and steward new multisectoral networks to advance inclusive, sustainable, and innovative growth.

The logic is incontrovertible: if cities are networks of institutions and leaders, then institutions and leaders should cogovern cities.

The Indianapolis story stands apart in several respects, including the continuity of leadership, the impact of strategic philanthropy, the professional capacity that has been built and nurtured, the culture of collaboration, the level of capital deployed, and the progression of thinking and action. Its strong lessons serve as examples of how New Localism can work for other cities.

First, *a city must perfect the mechanics of collaboration, often through new formal structures.*

In most cities, stakeholders such as local government, chambers of commerce, large companies, universities, hospitals, and philanthropies engage and even collaborate informally on many projects. But they remain primarily siloed and separate. The heads of different organizations view collaborative projects as a form of corporate social responsibility: nice to do but not central to their organization's mission or bottom line. For that reason, collaboration often starts with CEO involvement but generally diminishes with time as lower-level corporate representatives who are not empowered to make decisions take the place of their principals.

Informal collaborative efforts that do not involve everyone's full support underscore the limitations of part-time volunteerism. The country is replete with task force recommendations, consultancy analyses, community needs assessments, and more beginnings that never develop further. Many cities, not surprisingly, suffer from report fatigue. As Richard Reeves, a senior fellow at the Brookings Institution, has pointedly observed: "Task forces typically do few tasks and have little force."[35] Many efforts are strong on diagnostics, weak on prescription, and nearly powerless on execution.

Indianapolis has brought structure to the practice of collaboration. It has moved business and social networks to a higher level of productive connectivity. *CEOs are not only pulled together to discuss, they convene to decide.* Collaboration is treated as a serious business that advances the broader prosperity of the city and metropolis and offers businesses real opportunities for expansion and differentiation. The professionalism of the organization helps ensure that busy leaders come together and stay together and that they concentrate on long-term impact rather than on the imperatives of four- or even two-year election cycles.

Because of the CEO-only requirement, members' time is requested sparingly and jealously guarded. CICP's board of directors meets three times a year in meetings that last two hours each. Meetings are generally scheduled two years in advance, and the schedule is not changed. Other than a seven-person executive committee, there are no other CICP committees that require members' time, though most members have substantial involvement with one or more of the initiatives and projects that originate from the organization. (About half of CICP board members sit on one or more of the branded initiative advisory boards.)

The CICP board delegates responsibilities for commissioning research, measuring progress, and crafting new initiatives to the professional staff. The organization also engages outside consultancies to do the due diligence and help design initiatives based on evidence rather than impulse. As the BioCrossroads example demonstrates, evidence gathering and data analytics form the foundation for development, financing, and delivery of disparate initiatives. Success is not left to chance or exclusively dependent on having exceptional individuals, although formal collaboration makes it more likely that an organization will attract or retain such people.

An examination of the mechanics of collaboration seems contrary to the usual emphasis on transformative urban policy ideas and practices. Yet if New Localism is to succeed and networked governance models at the city and metropolitan level are to replace command-and-control legislative models from federal and state governments, it becomes essential to study how organizations like the CICP rely on sharp and precise analysis to catalyze action. Government functioning is well known. Less is known about how networks of institutions and leaders transcend community activism to design, finance, and execute major initiatives and ensure continual progress. Understanding the details of successful governance networks deserves more attention.

Second, *city networks must compile the elements of a modern metropolitan strategy for global competitiveness.*

Like many U.S. cities, Indianapolis invested heavily in sports and stadia; unlike most other places the city used its initial sports strategy as a platform to take the next step and do grand things.

Shaping a metropolitan economy requires from the outset a dedication to distinctive clusters of companies, research institutions, entrepreneurs, technical institutes, and investors that give a community its special advantage. These clusters must be real rather than imagined; initiatives that aspire to make a community the next Silicon Valley may grab a few ephemeral headlines but are not a recipe for long-term success.

The evolution of the CICP has also shown that it is not sufficient for business and civic led efforts to attend merely to strengthening leading sectors through expanding local businesses and attracting companies from outside the region. Rather, networks must now ensure that their education and workforce development systems produce locally grown talent with the specialized skills that align with local advantages. And they must also create quality places that not only attract and retain workers and companies with a rich set of amenities but also provide a platform for the seamless and collaborative exchange of ideas.

In other words, there is an interesting line that runs from BioCrossroads in 2002 through 16 Tech in 2015, from a cluster-oriented initiative to a placemaking exercise. Economy shaping is not for the faint of heart. It requires an unwavering commitment to continuous improvement and a relentless curiosity to take on new topics and challenges that sit outside the original paradigm. CICP is, in essence, a learning organization comfortable with the iteration and refinement demanded of sophisticated economies.

Third, *city networks must act with intentionality and regional awareness.*

The United States is a large, differentiated economy with multiple competitive cities and metropolitan areas with strong, distinctive assets. Most communities inventory their assets but rarely leverage them. Indianapolis knows what it is based on objective evidence. It follows the Dolly Parton axiom: "Figure out who you are and do it on purpose."

The 2000 Battelle report showed, for example, that "Central Indiana's life sciences industry is more manufacturing-intensive than the nation as a whole including, besides pharmaceuticals, surgical and medical instruments and medical laboratories, all primarily export industries."[36]

As described above, steps were taken to leverage the distinct competitive assets of the corporate and research base. But the CICP went further, establishing regional networks that leverage complementary strengths. In 2007 it launched the BioCrossroads Linx initiative to help Indianapolis connect with other regions in the United States and beyond. One of the first metropolitan areas targeted for collaboration was San Diego, owing to the two regions' resources in biotechnology innovation. As Mary Walshok, the associate vice chancellor of public programs at the University of California, San Diego, observed:

> We've been really focused on helping grow clusters of entrepreneurial life science companies. Not just one or two or three, but hundreds in order to create high-paying jobs. At BioCrossroads they are doing a lot of that kind of start-up assistance as well, but they are also linking their manufacturing and entrepreneurial capabilities to places like San Diego and Research Triangle Park in North Carolina and saying, 'Let us be your partner.' They are branding themselves as a state that is good at partnering, and letting people know that you don't have to go to India or China to find help. *What I admire about Indiana is that they took stock of what they are good at and also identified their gaps, and then designed significant components of their plan around that.* We should all do more of that.[37]

Fourth, *successful governance networks must operate at or be cognizant of multiple geographic levels—regional, metropolitan, city, the greater downtown, and even the district.*

From the very start, the focus of the life sciences effort has included central Indiana, stretching seventy miles north to pick up West Lafayette and Purdue University and fifty miles south to pick up Bloomington and Indiana University (the university's original and largest campus). The engagement with Warsaw, Indiana, and its orthopedics cluster has pushed the region 135 miles further north.[38] Other CICP initiatives not discussed in detail in this chapter, among them Conexus Indiana and AgriNovus Indiana, have enabled the effort to engage with and benefit the entire state, owing to the broad reach of logistics and supply chain networks in advanced manufacturing and the scale and broad distribution of agribusiness throughout Indiana, respectively.[39]

The CICP's focus on the city and metropolitan area is equally smart and targeted. Advanced industry companies require a steady supply of mid- and high-skilled workers to perform increasingly technologically sophisticated jobs. These workers are primarily drawn from labor pools in cities and broader metropolitan areas. The CICP's effort to increase the postsecondary credentials of central Indiana's population through recent initiatives such as Ascend will benefit workers, companies, and anchor institutions throughout the city and beyond.[40]

The CICP's engagement with Indianapolis's greater downtown is particularly intense since this area boasts a remarkable concentration of the region's life science and tech companies, research universities, research institutes, hospitals, and support institutions. Multiple CICP efforts, therefore, interconnect in a relatively small geographic area, which further magnifies their impact in light of the benefit of density and the seamless exchange of ideas that occurs when innovative firms and talented workers are located in close proximity. These efforts build on the central aspiration of former Mayor Bill Hudnut, who asserted memorably: "We don't want our city to become a doughnut, with all the development on the periphery. We want to be like a cookie, solid all the way through."[41]

With 16 Tech, the CICP has narrowed its scope even further to the geography of a small district. The effort to create an innovation district in an area that is strategically located near the downtown but largely vacant and unutilized will compel the organization to engage issues of quality placemaking and neighborhood regeneration, issues generally outside the scope of traditional cluster-led economic development.

Fifth, *successful network governance models show the complex and varied interplay of the public, private, and civic.*

The models eviscerate the cartoon version of an efficient private sector taking the place of an inept and incompetent public sector. Rather, network governance combines the entrepreneurial capacity and capital of business and philanthropy with the legitimacy and broader concerns of local government.

In Indianapolis, the smart consolidation of city and county and the disciplined execution of a sports strategy in the 1980s and 1990s provided the strong platform on which the private and civic sectors could create the CICP.

Indianapolis consolidated the city and Marion County governments in 1970, setting up an intelligent governance structure. Unigov allowed Indianapolis to have only one governing city-county council (no separate county commissioners) and consequently a single and very powerful regional executive in the person of the mayor, who is in a position to make a real impact. Being mayor of Indianapolis has attracted strong candidates. Some of Indiana's (and the nation's) best political talent, from both parties—including Richard Lugar, Bill Hudnut, Steven Goldsmith, and Bart Peterson—have sought and served in this office.

Consolidating fragmented governments is a proven way to drive efficiencies in the delivery of government services.[42] In Indianapolis, this gave private and civic leaders the space to grow an advanced economy rather than fixing fragmented government, a topic that has consumed private and civic leaders in other metropolitan areas.

Yet Indiana's negligible funding for economic development has forced the CICP to assume responsibilities that in other states would be the remit of the state government. As David Johnson has written:

Indiana [has had a long] tradition of relatively minimal state-level economic development funding based on a deep culture of fiscal conservatism and an unusually broad constitutional prohibition against state-incurred debt. . . . [The Indiana Constitution] bars the State of Indiana from incurring or issuing virtually any form of public debt, including general obligation bonds for economic development. This provision was added to Indiana's constitution of

1851, after the state defaulted on bonds issued to finance a failed series of canals attempting to link the Great Lakes to the Ohio River through Indiana's growing cities.[43]

The CICP is essentially standing in the shoes of the state, funding activities that range from research and commercialization to seed and venture investment to trade-oriented relationships. To this end, Indianapolis and the CICP have had a head start on other cities and metropolitan areas in the country that only now are beginning to take on these roles.

Sixth, *successful governance networks are an interesting combination of silo busting and culture busting.*

Silo busting represents an effort to expand beyond the narrow interests of specialized agencies, which dominated the mid- to late twentieth century. Transportation agencies became notorious for treating all mobility (and congestion) challenges as engineering problems. Housing agencies reduced their effectiveness by addressing housing challenges through one lens (lack of supply) rather than multiple lenses (lack of income, location of supply, inadequate access to education and employment centers).

Cities function best when public, private, and civic leaders see problems and hence solutions in new, multidimensional ways. The trajectory of the CICP in Indianapolis—from an initial focus on sectors to a broader focus on skills and spaces—reflects the benefits of multiple perspectives and continued learning, a twenty-first-century approach to problem solving.

Indianapolis's and the other cities' stories mentioned in this chapter also represent a form of culture busting. In his book *Why the Garden Club Couldn't Save Youngstown*, Sean Safford highlights the ineffectiveness of an old-guard business and civic network in Youngstown, Ohio, that was too entrenched in the past to adapt to new economic realities. He contrasts the failed revival of Youngstown with the effective transformation of Allentown, Pennsylvania, a metropolitan area very similar in size and economic profile but where a broader mix of industry leaders, entrepreneurs, and civic leaders was more willing to embrace change and redirect the city's economy along different lines.[44]

Culture busting can operate in multiple ways. The CICP's success in Indianapolis, for example, required moving from voluntary associations to a structured organization and from the reliance on traditional government leadership and resources to the design of private and civic initiatives that blended public, corporate, and philanthropic capital. Culture busting is a form of risk taking and a fundamental shift in understanding that many responsibilities in a city and metropolis lie with the community broadly rather than with the government narrowly.

Finally, *networked governance requires continued support over a sustained period of time.*

Many leadership entities in the United States rely on member dues to cover the operating expenses of the organization. The CICP has gone further, creating an institutional vehicle, the CICP Foundation, to leverage philanthropic with corporate resources for each special initiative. The CICP Foundation has provided the platform for supporting projects over the long term to ensure that their success is not dependent on the shorter-term horizons of elected public officials.[45]

In this way, the CICP is one of the few governance organizations that has stepped up to the challenge identified by Indy Johar, cofounder of project00 in London: "While investment into tech start-ups has scaled at an increasing pace, our investment in developing governance for a networked age has been limited."[46]

Indianapolis, however, benefits from the presence of a globally significant philanthropy, the Lilly Endowment, which has assets of around $10.3 billion and is now the fifth largest philanthropy in the United States.[47] From 2000 to 2016, the Lilly Endowment made grants totaling over $550 million toward building the foundation for the region's advances in life sciences and contributed nearly $85 million to the CICP Foundation.

The grant-making focus of the Lilly Endowment has shifted during Indianapolis's growth period. After making large contributions in the 1980s to the building of such sports facilities as the Hoosier Dome, Market Square Arena, the William F. Kuntz Memorial Soccer Stadium, and the Indiana University Natatorium, the endowment began to invest in the growth of talent and opportunity based on the special sectoral strengths of the Indianapolis economy. Essentially, both the Lilly Endowment and the CICP made large bets on innovation, entrepreneurialism, and other essential ingredients of "regional prosperity."

Although the Lilly Endowment is by far the largest philanthropic foundation in the region, it is not the only one. Other philanthropies have provided nearly $15 million in grant funding to the CICP Foundation. They include the locally headquartered Richard M. Fairbanks Foundation, the Lumina Foundation, the Central Indiana Community Foundation, the Eli Lilly and Company Foundation, and Guidant Foundation, as well as the JP Morgan Chase Foundation and the Joyce Foundation, which have national reach.

BEYOND INDIANAPOLIS: NETWORKED GOVERNANCE LARGE AND SMALL

Indianapolis is the leading U.S. example of networked governance. Yet the transition from a primary role of city government to an emphasis on collaborative local governance has been under way for some time. As the Johns Hopkins University scholars Lester Salamon and Odus Elliott noted in their 2002 book, *The New Governance and Tools of Public Action*, "Public administration has leaped beyond the borders of the public agency and now embraces a wide assortment of third parties that are intimately involved in the implementation and often the management of the public's business."[48]

The cogovernance of a city or community does not simply refer to the outsourcing of service delivery to the private or nonprofit sectors, though that is a growing trend. Rather, citizens and corporate and civic leaders across the city conduct a vast majority of what could be broadly called policymaking efforts at the local level, outside city hall. The most successful cities are those that can coordinate and collaborate, aligning individual decisions in the service of a shared vision. Existing models of networked governance provide the framework for that alignment and serve as evidence that the New Localism is already under way in many places throughout the country.

The transition toward increased networked governance is partly a result of the expanding remit of cities.[49] They face such complex challenges as the mitigation of climate change effects, the execution of growth strategies that are innovative and inclusive, the financing of infrastructure, and the deployment of new technologies. Resolving these hard issues requires building coalitions of institutions and leaders that cross disciplines, sectors, constituencies, and, in some cases jurisdictional boundaries.

Globalization and the consolidation of industry have become enormous challenges to the creation and stewardship of governance networks. As regional firms are acquired and consolidated within larger institutions, particularly in the financial sector, many medium-sized metropolitan areas are left without robust and tenured business leadership. In their 2006 report on corporate citizenship and urban problem solving, Royce Hanson and Donald Norris found that "as Baltimore has become a 'middle-market' town, executives on their way up the corporate ladder to other cities have no incentive to become engaged in the city's affairs."[50] Sam Williams notes similar tensions in his 2014 book, *The CEO as Urban Statesman*, which he witnessed firsthand in Atlanta: "An increase in restructuring and consolidation within certain industries and the globalization of business also raise red flags for some observers about the future of CEO involvement in civic issues."[51]

Nonetheless, the practice of networked governance is well ahead of the scholarship, and the various examples throughout the country defy easy classification.

Some networks are very informal, their main organizational feature being monthly breakfast roundtables or loose coordination on regional priorities. Others have become highly formalized, in some cases being institutionalized through legislation, in other cases being granted powers of revenue and spending ability by local governments. Networks also exist at multiple geographic scales, from the district-level business improvement district (BID) to regional and supraregional business entities. Finally, networks may be general-purpose convening organizations or may have highly specialized missions based in a specific industry, research cluster, or service. There is no perfect organization. The best network is fit-to-purpose for its place and moment and is composed of the most active and committed leaders in a given community.

CLEVELAND TOMORROW

The Indianapolis model had strong antecedents in efforts undertaken in Cleveland several decades ago. In the early 1980s, Cleveland Tomorrow was organized to create a common action agenda for a corporate community in a city that had fallen through the economic trapdoor. What followed had important similarities to the CICP. An exclusive group of corporate CEOs formed a business leadership with three central objectives: to make manufacturing competitive, to foster the creation of new companies, and to assist in rebuilding the center city.[52]

With the close collaboration of leading philanthropies such as the Cleveland Foundation and the Gund Foundation, Cleveland Tomorrow's leaders were capable of mobilizing resources in support of key projects. They maintained a small staff but could take on large projects and spin off new organizations. An example is the Cleveland Advanced Manufacturing Program, a partnership among state government, local universities, and the community college. And in a series of prescient moves, Cleveland Tomorrow established NorTech to help existing companies enhance their use of technology and accelerate innovation in products and processes, Team NEO to target business retention and attraction, and Neighborhood Progress Inc. to coordinate the activities of community development corporations in low-income neighborhoods.[53]

Cleveland Tomorrow, like the CICP, benefited from membership exclusivity. As one study observed, "[The CEOs] were comfortable making decisions and they were comfortable with one another."[54]

Cleveland Tomorrow also benefited from exceptional leadership. Richard Shatten, who became the second executive director of the organization in 1985 at age twenty-eight, had a quiet way of making things happen.[55] Shatten built a regional and national reputation as someone who could not only put forward transformative ideas but then doggedly build multisectoral coalitions and vehicles for implementing those ideas. At a Brookings Institution forum in 2000, Shatten stated that, "being right is irrelevant to the growth of cities and metropolitan areas. Good ideas are critical, but they have impact only when they are implemented thoughtfully and effectively. And sound implementation only happens when a community develops a civic, corporate, and political culture that can translate good ideas into action and execute with discipline and imagination."[56]

Although Cleveland Tomorrow merged in 2004 into a broader metropolitan-wide business organization, the Greater Cleveland Partnership, the legacy of the organization, continues to this day.[57]

SCALING DOWN: 3CDC AND CORTEX

While the Indianapolis and Cleveland examples demonstrate what might be called general-purpose leadership institutions, some cities have created the private-civic leadership model for a special, narrowly drawn purpose or task. Two examples highlight the importance of market-savvy economic impact and potential replicability.

In 2003 the Cincinnati Center City Development Corporation (3CDC) was formed to spur redevelopment in the greater downtown area, including the long-distressed Over-the-Rhine community.[58] The incorporation of 3CDC as a 501(c)(3) nonprofit corporation implemented a major recommendation of an economic development task force that had been convened by Mayor Charles Luken in the aftermath of the 2001 riots that followed the police killing of an unarmed African American teenager. As a catalyst for development, 3CDC has established four strategic goals: create great civic spaces, create high-density mixed-used development, preserve historic structures and streetscapes, and build diverse mixed-income communities supported by local businesses.[59] Although the mayor helped spur the establishment of the organization, 3CDC's board is exclusively composed of corporate CEOs.

3CDC stands out for its market sophistication. Operations are funded privately through a combination of corporate contributions, management fees, and below-market developer fees. The corporation manages over $250 million in investment funds through the Cincinnati New Markets Fund and the Cincinnati Equity Fund. Like the CICP, 3CDC has become a conduit for smart, market-oriented investment by companies, philanthropies, and individuals throughout the Cincinnati region.

St. Louis has pursued a different but extremely effective model. In 2002 a group of anchor institutions there—Washington University, Saint Louis

University, the University of Missouri–St. Louis, BJC HealthCare, and the Missouri Botanical Garden—collectively established a 501(c)(3) corporation to oversee the development of a 200-acre innovation district in the heart of St. Louis. The district is known as the Cortex Innovation Community (Cortex is an acronym for the Center of Research, Technology and Entrepreneurial Exchange). The state and the city granted the corporation several critical powers: the power of eminent domain, the power to abate taxes, and the power to approve or reject building plans.[60]

In fifteen years, Cortex has become the St. Louis area's largest innovation hub, generating 4,200 tech-related jobs and more than $550 million in investment. Taking advantage of the proximity of major research universities, Cortex has leveraged the creative mix of university talent, mature companies, startup firms, and research labs. In particular, Cortex has created six innovation centers, each with its own community and programming; in several cases, Cortex has attracted nationally known intermediaries such as TechShop and Cambridge Innovation Center to base facilities in the district. Cortex has also created a magnet high school in the St. Louis Public Schools District, the Collegiate School of Medicine and Bioscience. The students come from all over the region, representing the largest spread of Zip Codes of any regional public school.[61]

The rise of CEO-led general-purpose and special-purpose corporations represents a structural shift in the role of business and civic leaders in U.S. cities. New models are being tested that enable these leaders to enhance the prosperity of the city and the broader metropolis in direct and concrete ways. This goes beyond conventional constituency organizations, which represent the interests of members before those of local and state governments or propose a regional agenda through evidence-driven reports and task forces.

PUBLIC SPACE, PRIVATE MANAGEMENT

Beyond these CEO-led efforts, many cities have been embracing other network governance models over the past several decades. The prime examples involve nonprofit organizations that have been deputized by local government to be civic managers of public spaces. Conservancies, for example, have become a popular vehicle for delegated authority in recent years. Conservancies offer a win-win solution: they raise substantial private and civic resources for the management of public spaces. The calculus is quite simple and mutually beneficial. Competition over scarce public resources in cities is fierce and the hierarchy of needs understandably puts urgent human needs ahead of the stewardship of parks and riverfronts. "In the era of shrinking budgets, cities see private operators as key partners in the management of spaces."[62] Conservancies, however, help ensure that iconic parks (such as the Golden Gate Bridge Park Conservancy in San Francisco), riverfronts (the Detroit Riverfront Conservancy), waterways (The High Line Canal Conservancy in Denver), and abandoned rail lines (Friends of the High Line in New York) are available to meet their cities' needs for recreation and the protection of green spaces.

BIDs have become the most prevalent form of networked governance at the microscale. BIDs emerged in the United States after a period of severe urban decline and disinvestment that left downtowns dirty and dangerous. As Goktug Morcol, a scholar of public administration, has observed, "BIDs were a response to this decline, an effort to revitalize urban areas through self-taxation and self-governance by the owners of business properties."[63]

The assessment mechanism is fairly straightforward. A surcharge is applied to the real estate tax bills of office, retail, hotel, and residential properties and paid directly to the BID organization. These funds are allocated toward services in the business district such as cleaning, security, and construction. The BID is given the authority to file municipal liens and judgments against property owners who fail to pay. Nonprofit organizations such as universities (which do not pay local property taxes) generally provide voluntary contributions.

In many respects, BIDs represent an effort to replicate the cohesive focus and common assessment model of the suburban mall. As Patrick Kerkstra has written in *Philadelphia* magazine:

The [suburban malls] were safe. They were clean. And they were run by a single management agency. Center City's shopping district, meanwhile, was balkanized amongst dozens of property owners, while the public spaces were the responsibility of a confusing array of often inept and perpetually underfunded city departments and agencies.[64]

BIDs brought institutional order to this chaos, enabling such issues as litter, graffiti, and crime to be dealt with in a professional and efficient manner. Today there are more than 1,000 BIDs in the United States. Many deploy uniformed sidewalk cleaners and safety ambassadors who coordinate closely with local police. Many have moved beyond "clean and safe" to enliven public spaces with programming, food offerings, and festivals.[65]

The relationship with the public sector is intricate and multilayered. Beyond public safety, some entities, such as the DowntownDC BID, work closely with government agencies to help homeless individuals get mental, housing and additional services; others, such as the University City District in Philadelphia, design and deliver skills initiatives that are customized to the needs of district institutions, particularly large employers such as hospitals and universities; still others, such as Central Houston Progress, are delegated authority to raise capital for infrastructure projects through tax increment financing.

The Center City District (CCD) in downtown Philadelphia is a standout. A city ordinance incorporated the Special Services District of Central Philadelphia (SSDCP) on March 21, 1990, as a private sector–directed municipal authority under state law. The initial ordinance was quite limited in scope, enabling the new district to provide security, cleaning, and promotional services. Subsequent ordinances expanded the remit of the BID to include the maintenance, improvement, and expansion of streetscapes, parks, and plazas.

Paul Levy, the president and CEO of CCD since its inception, describes the large effects of small interventions:

Each year for the last 15 years, the CCD has made improvements that steadily add up: 1,000 street trees, 2,200 pedestrian-scale, light fixtures, 683 maps and directional signs for pedestrians and 233 for motorists; there are also maps and historic information on transit shelters and graphics and illuminated signs for 100 entrances to underground transit. . . . On the Avenue of the Arts, there are synchronized color-changing LED lights on the facades of eight different buildings. All are visible signs of transformation, giving confidence to investors, developers, businesses and residents.[66]

These actions—"lighter, quicker, cheaper," in the parlance of Fred Kent of the Project for Public Spaces—gave CCD the legitimacy to take on larger, more ambitious projects. *Philadelphia* magazine described the progression: "First you lay the foundation, clean and safe. Then you market it. Then you make modest improvements to the streetscape: lights, planters, signage and so on. Then you dabble in some small scale development work, like the café on the southeastern tip of the Parkway. Then the projects get bigger: Aviator Park in Logan Square, Dilworth Plaza, the [Reading] Viaduct."[67]

The *2017 State of Center City* report offers these remarkable statistics, the product of almost thirty years of unrelenting activity:

> Center City is the largest employer in the region, boasting 292,746 wage and salaried jobs in addition to 8,500 who are self-employed, freelancers, or partners. Greater Center City is the fastest growing place to live in the Philadelphia region, with a 2016 estimate of 188,000 residents. Downtown comprises 5.7% of land area in the city, but generates 32% of property tax revenue, 42% of jobs, and 43% of the wage tax generated in Philadelphia. Jobs are concentrated at 59 per acre in Center City, contrasted with 4 per acre in Philadelphia and 1 per acre in the suburbs.[68]

WHO'S IN CHARGE?

The essence of New Localism is that cities have more power than they think and more problem-solving capacity than they know *if* they organize differently. The stories in this chapter show how cities unveil and tap hidden strengths by aggregating public, corporate, philanthropic, and university stakeholders into networks that work together to tackle hard challenges and leverage distinctive opportunities. The best networks have a smart recipe: *Build from strength to address needs rather than build from needs to address strength.* This enables cities to realize the full value of latent assets, whether they are sector-based (as in Indianapolis and St. Louis) or geographic (as in Cincinnati and Philadelphia).

The rise of governance networks as primary actors in cities and metropolitan areas is not without controversy or conflict. As Peter Bogason and Juliet Musso have observed, "Although network governance has the potential to promote deliberation and to improve flexibility and responsiveness in service provision, it also raises serious issues regarding equity, accountability, and democratic legitimacy."[69]

The examples highlighted in this chapter illustrate the fundamental tensions of democracy and diversity. To a large extent, these networks are organized and governed by "elite" businesses and philanthropies. The racial, ethnic, and even gender makeup of these organizations rarely resembles that of the communities they serve. And, because of their market power, they often act at a speed that outpaces the traditional timeline for community deliberation.

As a result, they are often the targets of attack and vitriol. In New York City in 2013, resentment that the grandest parks—Central Park, High Line, the Battery, and Prospect Park—were in the hands of privately held conservancies led community activists to propose—unsuccessfully—that these conservancies tithe 20 percent of the dollars they raised for less well-endowed parks.[70] Business improvement districts are often attacked for deepening the divide between urban haves and have-nots. As Kerkstra wrote in *Philadelphia* magazine, "Those neighborhoods with the means to pay a bit extra get sidewalk cleaning, lighting, lovely parks and constant programming. Those that can't afford it get only the ever diminishing services provided by City Hall."[71] A 2016 *New Republic* article on BIDs, under the provocative title "Business Improvement Districts Ruin Neighborhoods," ominously warned: "If the BID model continues to proliferate, the commons that make a city great could be completely at the disposal of a single class, one that's inherently opposed to discourse and organizing."[72]

Yet it is simplistic to view network governance as an assault on the broader governance of a city. At a time of increasing demands and diminishing help from higher levels of government, network governance represents an opportunity to ensure that a city fulfills its broader social and economic purpose. Maximizing the employment and residential potential of downtown and midtown areas creates economic opportunities for city residents and generates tax revenues that can be used to fund needed services for the broader population. And regular participation in cross-sectoral networks can help increase the transparency and responsiveness of government. As Stroker says, "The appeal that lies behind networked governance is that it provides a framework for a more expansive vision of democracy to operate. The conception of democracy that underlies the idea of networked governance is that democracy is a process of continuous exchange between governors and governed."[73]

Networked governance, in our view, holds the potential not just for more beneficial economic and social ends but also for more democratic and participatory means. The ability of the stakeholders involved in networked governance models to build on the strengths of existing assets, to merge public, private, and civic interests, to break down the barriers of existing silos, and to establish fresh voices of city leadership serve as building blocks for new localism. Structured collaborations within and across cities facilitate governance that is geared toward solving today's problems while also preparing for tomorrow's challenges.

The Indianapolis story highlighted in this chapter shows how a unified public sector can provide a platform for the development of effective leadership from the private and civic sectors. The Cincinnati, Philadelphia, and St. Louis stories show how a smart public sector can delegate responsibilities to nonprofit entities and, in the process, achieve public goals and raise private and civic capital.

In the end, however, networked governance is a complement to functioning government, not a substitute. As responsibilities shift downward in societies, capable local governments become a necessary component of problem solving and leadership. The next chapter shows how strong local government can unlock the hidden wealth of public assets, leverage private sector investment, and shape the city through transformative investments. For that we need to travel to Copenhagen, Denmark, to understand the power and potential of a twenty-first-century public asset corporation.

SIX

Reclaiming Public Wealth
COPENHAGEN CASE STUDY

We are not here for a quick fix: we are here for the long haul.
—Jens Kramer Mikkelsen, CEO,
Copenhagen City and Port Development

To be most effective, New Localism requires robust sources of local revenue that can be reinvested in local priorities. Cities across the United States struggle with their fiscal capacity, but many are leaving significant assets on the table. Copenhagen, Denmark shows how a city can reclaim public assets within its border and capture their value appreciation to create new public-purpose revenue. Adapting this model to the United States presents challenges, but promises to revive urban finances and ensure longer-term stability.

Like Pittsburgh's and Indianapolis's, Copenhagen's story began in crisis.

In the mid- to late 1980s, the city was experiencing a 17.5 percent un-employment rate, a loss of taxing capacity, and an annual budget deficit of $750 million. For decades, government policies had subsidized the out-migration of families to the outskirts of Copenhagen, leaving a city over-represented by pensioners and college students, neither of whom contributed greatly to the city's tax revenue. With a stagnant economy and the traditional manufacturing industry moving out, the city government had to do something radical to spur economic growth and attract a strong tax base.[1]

And so it did.

Beginning in 1990, an alliance formed between the Social Democratic mayor of Copenhagen, Jens Kramer Mikkelsen, Prime Minister Poul Schlüter of the Conservative People's Party, and Social Democratic Party leader Svend Auken. These three leaders agreed to transform Denmark's capital city by catalyzing investment in housing and state-of-the-art infrastructure, making it attractive to new citizens and strengthening the city's tax base. Undertaking these improvements without increasing local taxes posed a challenge, so the trio decided to focus on developing public land within the city's borders that had been left idle and unused.[2]

As Jens Kramer Mikkelsen recalled,

> While discussing how to improve Copenhagen's infrastructure, a small group of people from the city administration and the [national] Ministry of Finance went to the corner of the room to discuss the broader implications and opportunities of large-scale infrastructure investments in Copenhagen. We knew the city was in a desperate situation and we needed to come up with something to address this situation. However, to pay for the grand infrastructure project we needed serious money. We could not raise taxes. Also, we needed agility and flexibility to operate.

The solution: a new publicly owned, privately managed corporate vehicle that could regenerate large areas in the city's core, maximize the value of underutilized public land, and use the revenues generated by smart zoning and asset management to finance transit and other infrastructure. The aspiration was to combine the efficiency of market discipline and mechanisms with the benefits of public direction, legitimacy, and low-cost finance.

And so began the remarkable transformation of Copenhagen over the past twenty-five years from an ailing, depopulating manufacturing city to one of the wealthiest cities in the world. Through this process, Copenhagen established itself as a preeminent leader of New Localism, demonstrating that market power, innovative thinking, and solid leadership can be used for public benefit.

The intervention proceeded in three discrete phases.

The first phase involved creating the Ørestad Development Corporation in 1992. The corporation was charged with redeveloping Ørestad—an area about 1.2 square miles in total located between the city of Copenhagen and the Copenhagen airport and the bridge connecting Denmark to Sweden—and using the revenues generated by redevelopment to finance the construction of a transit system for portions of the city. The land, owned by the national government, had traditionally been reserved for use by the military.

The Ørestad Development Corporation pioneered a close partnership between the national government and the city government of Copenhagen; the corporation was co-owned by Copenhagen Municipality (55 percent) and the National Ministry of Finance (45 percent). While the State of

Denmark provided the land, the city government set the zoning, altering the permitted uses from protected heathland to commercial, educational, retail, and, ultimately, residential.

The catalytic move to spur development of this area was the construction of a metro transit line connecting the Copenhagen city center to the Copenhagen airport. National law explicitly tasked the Ørestad Development Corporation with developing the area to raise capital for the construction of the first two stages of the Copenhagen metro (the M1 and M2 lines). To sequence the buildout of the metro system before the full development of the land, the Ørestad Development Corporation took out a loan against the value of its land assets to fund the construction.

The full development of Ørestad is expected to take twenty to thirty years, at which point an estimated 25,000 people will live in the area, along with a daytime population of 20,000 students and 60,000 workers. The first office building was constructed in 2001 and the first residential buildings were completed three years later. As of December 2016 the residential population had reached 10,000 and the worker population totaled 17,000.

The second phase of development involved the revisioning of the Copenhagen port and the restructuring of its management. Historically, the Port of Copenhagen was run largely as an industrial harbor. The port was managed inefficiently and ran continuous annual deficits. To balance these deficits, the port's management would generally sell unused land to developers. The opening of the Øresund Bridge in 2000, connecting Copenhagen with Malmö in Sweden, dramatically reduced harbor traffic in the ports of both Copenhagen and Malmö, opening up opportunities for the redevelopment of inner-harbor areas for residential and commercial purposes.

To take advantage of these possibilities, the Port of Copenhagen Ltd. was put in charge of both the land management and urban redevelopment of the commercial harbour. The company operating the port functions, the Copenhagen Malmö Port AB (CMP), thus became an entity with a narrow remit. As a result, for the first time in a century, the port realized profits by operating in a more efficient and cost-conscious manner.

The final phase of development involved consolidating the Ørestad Development Corporation and the Port of Copenhagen Ltd. under one entity—The Copenhagen (CHP) City & Port Development. As with the

Ørestad Development Corporation, the city of Copenhagen initially owned 55 percent of the CPH City & Port Development, with the remaining 45 percent owned by the Danish national government. A transit construction company was split off from the merged company to take full responsibility for building the expansion of the metro system. Jens Kramer Mikkelsen, who by then was heading the Ørestad Development Corporation, took the helm of the new merged corporation.

Over the past decade, CPH City & Port Development has transformed various areas of Copenhagen. They include the Ørestad area, the formerly industrial South Harbor area, the North Harbor, and an industrial area known locally as Paper Island. CPH City & Port Development has deployed the same innovative model of governance, finance, and operations used by both the Ørestad Development Corporation and the Port of Copenhagen. Since its formation in 2007, CPH City & Port Development has managed about half of all the redevelopment projects undertaken in Copenhagen. Eleven of its sites are landfill sites reclaimed from the sea.

The impact of CPH City Port & Development has been transformative at the city scale as well as at the district and project scales.

A revitalized economy, a stronger tax base, and an expanded transit system have recharged the city. By 2013 the daily ridership on the Copenhagen metro amounted to 460,000, with an annual ridership of 55 million passengers. Like the Ørestad Development Corporation, CPH City Port & Development was established with the explicit purpose of using the revenues of redevelopment to finance the construction of infrastructure (specifically the City Circle metro line). The financing of this major transit expansion, as well as of metro connections to North Harbor itself, involved sophisticated management of public assets.

The sequence, simple and effective, generally works as follows:

> National and local government transfer assets to CPH City & Port Development;
>
> Local government rezones the land for residential and commercial use;
>
> The land increases in value;

CPH City & Port Development borrows (generally with loans on favorable terms from the Denmark National Bank) based on the (increased) value of the land;

CPH City & Port Development either transfers the capital to the metro construction company for broader transit investments or uses it to pay for local infrastructure that enables the development of the land;

CPH City & Port Development facilitates development through a variety of mechanisms, including land sales to or lease agreements with developers and, in a limited number of cases, development by the corporation itself; and

The newly generated revenue services the debt.

This process results in a virtuous cycle. CPH City & Port Development invests funds from the sale of public land and assets under its control in a broad range of infrastructure projects, including public transit, roads, and recreational and other public amenities. These infrastructure improvements in turn increase the value of CPH City & Port Development's remaining land and assets, which in turn enables the corporation to invest and expand further.

The ongoing transformation of North Harbor best illustrates the impact of these investments at the district and project scale. North Harbor is the corporation's most recent redevelopment project and, together with Ørestad, the largest urban development project in Denmark. The project was showcased as "The Sustainable City of the Future" at the COP 15 UN climate summit, hosted by Copenhagen in 2009, and at the Architecture Biennale in Venice.

There are multiple reasons for these accolades.

The North Harbor project is essentially building a new city within the city in a dense, sustainable, transit-connected environment. Eventually the entire North Harbor area will include residential, commercial, and office space and the capacity to accommodate 40,000 inhabitants and 40,000 workers.[3]

The North Harbor district is partly built on surplus soil pulled up from the underground during the metro construction. The amount of soil deposited has been so substantial that it has actually raised the level of the new land by a meter to better prepare North Harbor for climate change and rising sea levels and to offer businesses and residents an assurance of climate resiliency.

National and local law require that new construction in the North Harbor must conform to Copenhagen's larger ambition of becoming the first capital city to be carbon neutral by 2025. Developers must adhere not only to national and local standards for energy consumption but also ensure that materials are sourced locally, building insulation is adequate, the construction process is conducted properly in terms of reduced accidents and suitable working conditions (lighting, temperature, and the like), and employee satisfaction is high. Local law also requires that at least 25 percent of the housing in new city districts is set aside as social housing for lower-income residents.

The North Harbor project finances both the redevelopment of the North Harbor itself and the continued expansion of the city's metro system. To support this, CPH City & Port Development has created a smart profit-sharing mechanism: the corporation receives part of the property value increase generated by the introduction of a metro station.

The mechanism works as follows. CPH City & Port Development includes a clause in all sales agreements requiring the purchaser to pay a supplement to the purchasing price if and when a metro station is established in close proximity to the property. Agreements specifically require the purchasers to pay an additional $11.41 per square meter for office buildings or $5.71 per square meter for residential properties annually for a period of sixty years after the establishment of the metro station within a fifty-meter radius of the property. In this way the public realizes a portion of the value that it creates through the introduction of a transit system rather than allow it to be realized exclusively by private owners.

WHAT COPENHAGEN TEACHES OTHER CITIES

The Copenhagen story is an example of how the public sector can realize the full potential of public assets to spur large-scale regeneration, finance critical infrastructure or other needs, and participate in the value appreciation that naturally comes with urban prosperity. The public asset corporation model has made the city's industrial harbor a vibrant, multipurpose waterfront while channeling the proceeds of land disposition, revaluation, and development to finance new infrastructure.

CPH City & Port Development is one of the most seasoned examples of the public asset management approach popularized by Dag Detter and Stefan Fölster, two Swedish experts in public finance. First in *The Public Wealth of Nations* and more recently in *The Public Wealth of Cities*, Detter and Fölster have promoted a third alternative to the conventional choice between political management and full privatization: public ownership that uses private sector techniques and talent and, while protected from cronyism and interference, retains its status as public and hence contributes to public fiscal well-being.[4] Their core argument is a disruptive idea in public policy that links management systems, global public asset value, and the proper role of politicians in a democracy.

The Copenhagen model, of course, is deeply rooted in the Danish governance structure and collaborative culture, which makes exact replication difficult. Governance in Denmark is carried out through a decentralized system that provides municipalities with enormous powers and the ability to operate with considerable independence from the national government. Local governments in Denmark account for over 60 percent of government spending, the highest level among advanced nations in the OECD.[5] And as Bruce Katz and Luise Noring have observed, "Along with strong local power comes strong local capacity. The knowledge and decision-making capacity of the public sector is robust, with a steady supply of highly educated public servants across technical, environmental, social and business fields."[6]

But Copenhagen offers multiple lessons for cities that transcend differences in society, culture, and governmental structure.

First, *cities need to know what they own as well as what they owe.*

A key element of the success of CPH City & Port Development is market knowledge. Few nations or cities are able to do a proper accounting of their collective assets and hence cannot detail to citizen shareholders the ownership value, the return on that value, and how it could potentially be restructured to be more productive.

Many U.S. cities are, in essence, a "fact-free" zone when it comes to public assets. They have little knowledge of the assets they own and the market value of those assets, either under current or altered zoning regimes. Ironically, U.S. cities know what they owe (such as pension liabilities) but not what they own. Rectifying that disconnect is the first step toward sane and sensible public finance.

Inventorying land assets is not a new idea. The use of cadastral surveys or maps to provide a register of land ownership dates back to the Roman Empire. In the age of such innovations as geospatial mapping, big data analytics, and block chain technology, it is likely that this information deficit will ultimately be filled by local government acting in close concert with tech entrepreneurs. These efforts will transform public record keeping, enable transparency, and provide a foundation for a new system of public finance.

Second, *cities need to know the value of what they own and leverage that value for public good.*

In a world in which we regularly are in awe of the financial power of private assets and capital markets, the public sector is still among the largest holders of wealth through real estate holdings, transportation systems, utilities, government-owned corporations, and sovereign wealth funds. As Detter and Fölster argue, a relatively small increase in the return on public assets would contribute significantly to revenue that supports the public sector and hence lessens the need to raise taxes, while increasing the likelihood of new investments in things such as infrastructure.

Copenhagen's experience shows us the transformative impact of this basic insight. CPH City & Port Development has unleashed the market potential of land that was used for industrial or other purposes in the past and has now been repurposed for a restructured economy. The effort has benefited from the smart valuation and disposition of nationally and locally owned land. Mads Lebech, CEO of the Danish Industry Foundation and a member of CPH City & Port Development's board, explains the mix of land transfers and strategic rezoning: "The national government owned the Port of Copenhagen, but they could not develop it without local government that regulates building permissions, land zoning, and conducts urban development. Together they could do a lot. Alone they could do nothing!"[7]

A common refrain in the United States is that cities are broke and encumbered with public liabilities. Detter and Fölster persuasively argue otherwise, using Cleveland as a test case. As they recount, the city reported a total assets value of $6 billion in 2014. While this amount exceeds the city's liabilities, it still largely underestimates the true value of the public assets.[8] Like most U.S. cities, Cleveland reports its assets at book value, valued at historical costs. If reported using the International Financial Reporting Standards (IFRS), which require the use of market value for assets, the assets' worth would be significantly higher than what is currently reported.[9]

Detter and Fölster conservatively assume a price-to-book ratio (the multiple of the market value over the account's book value) of about 5. Under that assumption, Cleveland's assets would be worth U.S. $30 billion, a figure that still does not include the many assets that are unaccounted for. They also cautiously assume that the city could earn a 3 percent yield on its commercial assets with better asset management—specifically, with more professional and politically independent asset governance. A modest 3 percent yield on a portfolio worth $30 billion would add up to an income of $900 million a year, more than Cleveland's current $700 million annual net investments, the authors claim, "In other words, even with a modest yield, Cleveland could double its investments."[10]

Cleveland is by no means exceptional. It represents a common scenario across U.S. cities, and in fact internationally, of public wealth trapped in real estate and other commercial assets that are not optimized.

Third, *cities need to unify or, at a minimum, align the management of public assets.*

CPH City & Port Development evolved after several mergers of public entities. Lars Rohde, chairman of the board of governors of the Nationalbank, states that before the bundling of public assets and the merging of public companies in Copenhagen, ownership of public assets was highly fragmented. With fragmentation, local government loses sight of its assets and makes decisions in a piecemeal fashion. This had a negative impact on the city's ability to raise capital for transformative urban development. Rohde points out that, through this fragmentation, large-scale infrastructure investments benefit only individual property owners and in a random way, as people living in close proximity to the metro stations see their property appreciate in value.[11] Copenhagen's innovation was unifying public ownership of the land prior to infrastructure development, which ensured that the public as a whole benefited from the resultant appreciation in value.

Many U.S. cities and counties, by contrast, have multiple, often independent institutions that own public assets and are solely responsible for their disposition. The list of these institutions—airport authorities, port authorities, water and sewer authorities, convention center authorities, stadium authorities, redevelopment authorities, public housing authorities, land banks, school boards—is long and varies across places. And the levels of government that direct these entities (and the laws and regulations that govern them) is also complex. Many of these entities emerged over the past century in hopes of preventing corruption, enabling greater efficiency and, in some outrageous cases, diminishing the power of certain racial and ethnic groups. Viewed against the highly fragmented reality of public ownership in the United States, adapting the Copenhagen model, in part or in full, will be an exercise in putting Humpty Dumpty back together again. It will, however, be highly profitable for the regions that do.

Fourth, *cities need to insulate the management of public assets from political interference.*

CPH City & Port Development operates with remarkable insulation from political interference; the operations of the company are public but not political. Operating with minimal interference from national and local governments enables the corporation to take advantage of public assets, legislative powers, and local market economy to finance major infrastructure investments and the sustainable redevelopment of underutilized assets, including the industrial harbor. The corporation, in other words, keeps its eyes on the prize—long-term public gains—rather than on short-term political considerations such as the reelection of a particular individual or party.

Carsten Koch, the director of the board of CPH City & Port Development, argues that depoliticization has been achieved by having CPH City & Port Development governed by national law.[12] One critical statutory requirement: the mandate to optimize commercial gains in order to generate profit for the city of Copenhagen and thereby enable the construction of the metro system. A clear mandate for corporate profits to be designated for metro construction creates transparency and eliminates the potential for funds to be directed toward political issues or uses.

Similarly, the central role played by Jens Kramer Mikkelsen, a former politician, helps explain the depoliticization of corporate decisions. Kramer has successfully acted as a buffer between the company and local and national political leaders. His prior experience as an elected official has enabled him to be politically savvy and to shield the company from political interference so that it can operate as an independent, privately run corporation.

In the United States, many public authorities that were initially established to ensure political insulation are riddled with political interference, the Port Authority of New York & New Jersey being only the most well-known example. Changing the culture and behavior of public authorities is as important as are corporate or statutory issues of institutional mergers and powers. The success of this model depends on its ability to operate with agility and adapt to shifting market demands. The removal of the political class from public asset management has a salutary effect on democracy by transitioning politicians from asset gatekeepers to consumer and citizen advocates on behalf of public asset productivity and quality.

Fifth, *cities need to engender a culture of collaboration across the public, private, and civic sectors.*

Much of the success of the Copenhagen model is rooted in the cooperation between national and local government and alliances across political parties. These broad coalitions ensure political stability and policy continuity. In Denmark, the penchant for collaborative governance extends well beyond government: as Peter Damgaard Jensen, CEO of PKA Pensions, says, "Because we are a small country, CPH City & Port Development can have collaboration with all actors, both public and private. If you know the property investors in the ten largest pension funds, you can put together a strategy that works. You can round up everybody with a decision-making capacity in one room. The network of people that can make this happen is small and accessible."[13]

Collaboration sounds like a soft concept, but it has a hard market effect. The co-ownership of Copenhagen City & Port Development ensured that the corporation could borrow at low interest rates, thanks to the credit ratings of the national government and the city. Board director Carsten Koch noted, "The access to cheap loans and the ability to keep operating despite massive debts is the single most important feature of CPH City & Port Development. . . . Without that, we would have shared the destiny of other property developers during the recent recession, as we are just as vulnerable to market dynamics as other property developers." Koch pointed out that, despite being somewhat sheltered by the high credit standing of its owners, CPH City & Port Development is nevertheless subject to international rules of accounting that require it to list both assets and debts at market value.[14]

The evolution and management of CPH City & Port Development represents a triumph of collaboration. Many U.S. cities have hostile relationships with their state governments either because of partisan differences or because of more basic issues of power and control. Yet several dynamics—a municipal fiscal crisis, a radical scaleback of the federal government, a unified vision of urban growth across key public, private, and civic stakeholders—could provide the impetus to experiment with new institutional models and forms of collaboration. To this end, it is helpful to remember that the Copenhagen model was devised and designed during a period of fiscal and economic distress.

Sixth, *cities should maximize the benefit of public ownership and private management.*

The Copenhagen model empowers public and private sectors to do what each does well and to leverage their core competencies. The creation of a hybrid corporation was intended to combine the efficiency of market discipline with the benefits of public direction and legitimacy.

The public sector sets the basic rules of the game for sustainability and social inclusion. In fact, Michael Nielsen, CEO of ATP Properties, says that close collaboration with the local municipality on planning and permits is a prerequisite for conducting the kind of large-scale urban development that CPH City & Port Development undertakes. "Copenhagen municipality and CPH City and Port Development have a solid collaboration. The local municipality gives sufficient freedom of operations to CPH City and Port Development. If CPH City and Port Development had to ask for permission the whole time, nothing would ever happen. On the other hand, CPH City and Port Development justifies its existence by funding the [transit system] and that is how CPH City and Port Development has gained the public's goodwill," he said.[15]

At the same time, a corporate model allows several elements of large-scale regeneration—site selection and sequencing, building design, procurement of goods and services, joint ventures with private companies, circular economy techniques—to be conducted in a more efficient and streamlined manner. Governments are usually hamstrung by a multitude of formal rules and regulations and informal modes of operation when trying to innovate; corporations have much greater latitude.

Because CPH City & Port Development is a corporation, its annual board meetings are not subject to public disclosure and scrutiny. Making the internal deliberations and plans of the corporation publicly available might jeopardize its ability to negotiate partnerships with private sector actors. However, CPH City & Port Development makes other reports and documents available on demand to the public and the news media.

Copenhagen has found that by managing transactions through a publicly owned, privately driven corporation, operations run faster and more efficiently in comparison to how local government traditionally tackled public development projects. This allows the city and state to set ambitious targets to meet the growing demand for resources and infrastructure.

Finally, *cities need to think and act for the long term.*

Copenhagen is a remarkable example of long-termism, pursued by both the corporation and many of its private financial and development partners. CPH City & Port Development reflects the salutary benefits of sustaining efforts in a focused, disciplined, almost maniacal way. The Ørestad Development Corporation (the predecessor of CPH City & Port Development) was authorized in 1992. The corporation is not an overnight success story; it has been plying its trade for decades.[16]

Focusing with such intensity is unusual in an era when technology and information overload present constant distractions. Acting for the long term defies the short-term thinking that permeates the political and business class. Yet there is no choice. Urban transformation does not happen by press release or tweet, nor does it neatly follow the timetable of election cycles. City building that is meant to last depends on institutions that are empowered to act for long-term market and social returns rather than short-term political or economic gain.

The United States lacks this kind of institutional infrastructure. Politically directed authorities use the disposition of public assets to fill short-term budget deficits on a project-by-project basis. The immediate budget needs of local government are exacerbated by the similar short-term orientation of financial institutions such as commercial banks and pension funds.

RETHINKING PUBLIC BALANCE SHEETS

The Copenhagen story compels us to think anew about public finance. Traditional public finance prioritizes attention on revenue and expense statements (the budget) and liabilities but is largely disinterested in the asset side of the public balance sheet. Revenue statements tell us what the government receives in taxes, fees, and intergovernmental transfers, and expense statements tell us what the government pays in personnel, service costs, and debt service (including pensions and health care liabilities). Politicians, taxpayers, and the financial markets pay attention to the liability side of the balance sheet as it relates to how debt service, pension costs, and other obligations drive the need for new revenue or cause a reduction in services.

The asset side of the balance sheet, what government owns, gets much less attention; except occasionally as part of a political campaign for government to do more with less and increase efficiency. But those pledges are largely disconnected from the substantive issues of public asset management: what government should own or sell, how to manage ownership, and how returns on better management can add value to future budgets. In times of extreme fiscal crisis governments sell off real assets to fill budget holes, as has happened in many large city school districts over the past decade. But asset ownership and the return on those assets are not a significant part of most public budget deliberations; in large part because government management has been disconnected from basic economic thinking regarding the need to increase value over time.

Private firms think about asset management and revenue in ways that the public sector too often does not: how what you own (not just what you owe) can change a budget calculation. Increasing the productivity of public assets (the return on those assets) may be critical to funding public budgets without always raising taxes and fees or cutting services. Yet surprisingly limited attention has been paid to this matter outside the extensive literature on the advantages or disadvantages of privatization and the government outsourcing of services to private firms. But with respect to the major domains of public ownership—commercially valuable land, public transit systems, including airports and ports, and publicly owned companies— much less attention is paid.

The revenue from increasing public asset productivity is the optimistic side of the public balance sheet discussion: it asks how we can use assets to generate more revenue, increase public wealth, and be better able to meet present and future obligations. The paucity of attention paid to the quality and productivity of public asset management has come about in large part because the nation has been held hostage to partisan battles that rarely allow the conversation to take place in a substantive way. We are caught in an intellectual dead-end as it relates to alternatives: a public ownership status quo with limited incentives to exercise better financial outcomes versus a privatization mentality that prefers to fully outsource or sell public assets.

The public ownership status quo (identified generally with the political left) is based on support for the extensive role of the public sector, including an assumption that government management of publicly funded goods is largely sacrosanct. This perspective fits the self-interest of politicians, who, once elected, become the gatekeeper of access to public goods. But the conflation of universal citizen use and direct government management is an anachronism, both practically and intellectually. Moreover, it places the political left in a problematic position, one that too often downplays or excuses government mismanagement because it assumes that is the only way to protect public ownership and wealth—in keeping with their values.

A privatization perspective (identified generally with the political right) holds that government should own and manage only what is necessary to collective well-being and security and, in addition, cannot be operated as a private concern. For economists, true public goods cannot be private because they are nonrivalrous (everyone gets access) and nonexcludable (use by one person does not diminish others' use). But there are a range of services and assets that are not public goods in the strict sense and about which there is significant disagreement over privatization versus keeping them public; some examples are public housing and public transit. The assumption that profit maximization will always result in better social outcomes or that full community access can be assured without any public purpose guardrails or regulation is where the fallacy of the right matches that of the left. The left valorizes government; the right valorizes markets.

The battle between these two choices in public asset management has contributed to political partisanship by posing a false choice between management mediocrity and the loss of ownership rights. These choices, driven by fallacies that are supported by old ideologies, contribute to political dysfunction. If you suggest to those on the left that public assets are better managed through private sector principles and incentives, you are accused of neoliberal apostasy. If you suggest to those on the right that the public has a significant economic development role that can be exercised through assets it owns, many will view you as a hopeless socialist.

Indeed, poor management of public assets by governments leads to inefficiency and often cronyism, which ultimately degrades public wealth and the capacity to deliver quality goods to citizens. At the same time, the wrong kind of profit seeking associated with critical goods and services exacerbates problems of equity and access and limits longer-term public sustainability. It also denies the public sector the capacity to use what it owns to generate needed revenue. In a world where private enterprise is so valuable, why shouldn't public wealth be managed in ways that increase its own value and economic power, and hence ultimately deliver stronger public returns?

Luckily, the world is not yet being run from either a graduate school seminar on neoliberalism, where market fundamentalism and virtually any public-private venture are viewed as the same, or from those right-wing think tanks that assume markets solve all problems. Between these two extremes are pragmatic and significant examples of the delegation of public goods management to civic and private sector actors where public access is protected. Whether this occurs through special service districts, charter schools, quasi-public development agencies, or the simple outsourcing of social service and government systems management, there is a growing number of examples of hybrid systems and partnerships that blend public control and private enterprise. Many of the placemaking efforts mentioned in previous chapters are rooted in pragmatic hybrid arrangements of this sort.

But these hybrid partnerships do not extend significantly enough to the major public assets that could be game-changers in terms of productivity revenue and public wealth, as happened in Copenhagen. Americans who travel abroad sometimes wonder why many of our airports fall short of the standards of the best international airports, or why other nations seem to do a better job with public transit and the management of other public assets, from ports to parks. The answer we are tempted to give is that the United States do not invest as heavily in public infrastructure as many other nations and that a market-oriented American ethos with an entrepreneurial culture prefers private solutions (cars versus trains) to public management. That answer is certainly part of the story.

But there is another answer. In the United States, government has more control of public assets than it does in other nations. Airports are a good example. A recent survey of European airports showed a dramatic increase in private investment and public-private ownership arrangements among the 500 airports on the continent. Today 126 of the 500 European airports are a mixture of public and private ownership, with seventy-nine being fully private.[17] The largest airports, in particular, are open to private investors and a range of public-private partnerships. Some of the largest are corporatized entities that act as independent enterprises and follow basic commercial strategies but are still owned by public authorities. These arrangements starkly contrast with those for American airports, where government entities dominate airport ownership and management, with the exception of small private aviation fields.

The United States actually has less political space for building models that allow for private management and innovation while remaining partially or fully public in ownership and regulated use. This is particularly true when compared with some Northern European and Asian city-states. This comes as a surprise to Americans, who think of the United States as a leader in business and management innovation. That may true of capital markets and technology firms, but it is less true with respect to public sector management, particularly of major public assets. In those areas the United States lags other nations in everything from financing infrastructure through public-private partnerships, to selling off legacy functions upended by new technologies (such as the postal system in Germany), to managing the transportation of people and goods.

Rethinking the asset side of the public balance sheet cannot happen unless there is transparent analysis whose data can facilitate a strategy that includes the development of privately run companies owned by the public. To do so, we need to know what a municipality, county, or state owns; how much it is valued in market terms, what its best uses are in terms of overall private and public strategy, and what its present returns are in today's management system. We also have to separate out commercially valuable assets with public goods that cannot and should not be monetized, from government buildings to streets and public spaces. Commercial real estate assets owned by the public that are underperforming in terms of both use and returns hold promise for rethinking their management.

The United States stands to benefit from adopting the European model of extracting public value from the value created by the public. This method of dealing with fiscal pressures—the New Localism method—will better position communities across the country to generate capital for projects that will most benefit citizens.

ADAPTING THE COPENHAGEN MODEL
TO THE UNITED STATES

The United States, of course, is not without its own innovations in local finance and development. While no place has developed a model as efficient as Copenhagen's, cities are discovering ways to better convert market momentum into fiscal flexibility. Tax increment financing (TIF) districts, for example, have been used to great effect in places such as Washington, D.C., to better capture and socialize the value appreciation of large-scale infrastructure. TIFs are a means by which revenue increases from future property taxes are diverted toward a community's development projects. Additionally, while many single-purpose public corporations and authorities in the United States have been rightly maligned, there are examples to build from such as Philadelphia's Industrial Development Corporation.

A drive down Broad Street in South Philadelphia past the stadium district with its vast parking lots leads directly into the old Philadelphia Navy Yard, a 1,200-acre site that was one of the prime bases of the U.S. Navy since 1871. North of that site was once a smaller naval base that was the first American naval base, founded in 1776, when the nation declared independence. Philadelphia's past is well defined, but it is now working more diligently on its future.

The remarkable thing about the Navy Yard today is that it represents one of the best business renewal stories in America, and it happened just over the past fifteen years. In the early 1990s the base was closed as a result of the Defense Base Closure and Realignment Commission (or BRAC) report, which mandated which American bases be closed in the post–Cold War years as the percentage of GDP dedicated to the military declined significantly. The navy base had already lost a good deal of its shipbuilding contracts, but the closure announcement sounded like its death knell.

Throughout the early 1990s there were attempts first to save the base through political action and then finally to recruit a new shipbuilder through expenditures of public subsidy. Eventually a Swedish firm was recruited, which was eventually taken over by a Norwegian firm, which is still in business but at a scale far below what many imagined when they were trying to save the base. The political machinations of saving the base are mentioned in Buzz Bissinger's *Prayer for the City* and has been used as a story prop in Netflix's *House of Cards*.[18]

At the same time this was happening the entire site was slowly being acquired by the city's economic development agency, the Philadelphia Industrial Development Corporation (PIDC), from the U.S. Navy. At the time nobody understood that the best thing that happened was that people were unable to stop the closure or recruit more shipbuilding. What they had was a unique site that, though empty, had beautiful architecture in its remaining buildings and an extraordinary location in the city, close to the airport and major highways. Moreover, it was situated at the confluence of two rivers, with dozens of impressive battleships mothballed along its docks. It was an urban icon that could be reinvented; but only a few people recognized it as such.

With a well-crafted master plan that was flexible but with very strong design guidelines, the PIDC began to market the Navy Yard as the future and not the past, and incredibly, the future won out. Today there are 150 businesses at the Navy Yard, many occupying newly constructed offices, including the headquarters of GlaxoSmithKline and Urban Outfitters. There is a technology cluster of energy-related innovations that has attracted federal and state research funding and is supported by Ben Franklin Technology Partners. More than $1 billion in public and private investments have been made at the Navy Yard, and currently there are more than 12,000 full-time employees, working in 7.5 million square feet of commercial space. The site is an experience as well as a business campus, with curated open spaces, restaurants, a new hotel, bike and running paths, and a constant flow of new companies onto the campus.

The transformation of the Navy Yard was driven by the PIDC and the development partnerships it forged with private real estate developers. The PIDC has a long history of managing and repurposing real estate, using the bond market when needed and managing tax credit incentives (which the Navy Yard received from the State of Pennsylvania). It has been in that business since its founding in 1958, and it would be hard to identify a major project, from the city's convention center to its new stadia, from major hotels to industrial parks, in which the PIDC has not played a role.

The agency was created with a board structure that eschewed full public governance control. Appointments to the board are shared by the Philadelphia Chamber of Commerce and the City of Philadelphia, with the chamber getting one more board appointment than the city. Many mayors come into office resenting the PIDC just as they do with the downtown special services district, the Center City District. The resentment is based on the fact that they do not fully control either of those agencies, although they can significantly influence them, particularly the PIDC. But soon the mayors learn how much they need them to get things done, and so they adjust.

The PIDC is effective because it is a hybrid, able to blend public and private tools and credibility in a singular organization. It has a balance sheet to buy properties and land and bank them as needed. It can allocate tax credits from the state, and it manages TIF financing. It can issue tax-exempt bonds as needed. And it has the credibility to work with developers and entrepreneurs, planners and architects, politicians and bankers. It can allocate public capital and leverage private capital by taking subordinate security positions that derisk private capital or by setting the table during the early and riskier stages of a project.

Every city and state has agencies with some or all of the capabilities of the PIDC, although many are not as deep in terms of capacity. The present director, John Grady, drove the Navy Yard development and is as good a finance agency head as can be found anywhere in America. Publicly created development agencies and special-purpose authorities are how much of development finance gets done in the United States in housing, economic development, and infrastructure development, including the cleanup of brownfield sites. The work of those agencies, besides gaining capital access through tax incentives and bonds, is to remove barriers to getting projects financed and completed. They do so by standing in the middle of public and private realms and functioning as advocates for both sides.

But bigger breakthroughs are needed. In many regions we need organizations like the PIDC with their public tools and credibility but with a significantly more robust balance sheet and the ability to act in a more private sector manner by capitalizing private funds and making greater profits from the value they create. In contrast to the Copenhagen example, most American public finance agencies have a project-by-project focus rather than a long-term balance sheet focus. They are not able to take the long view because they are too captive politically even if well managed, as with the PIDC. They view themselves as catalytic for private investment, which is an important role, but in doing so they often do not share enough in the equity being created through their work and risk. When this happens, the public loses out.

The PIDC has sparked the revival of the Navy Yard and will make money for its balance sheet as the yard's manager and as the seller of the land. It also will play a role in the creation of a special services district for the Yard. But the scale of these transactions are such that the PIDC could have come out of it with a stronger position for its balance sheet and hence for the potential targeting of more infrastructure development in the area.

Agencies like the PIDC and hundreds of other authorities across the nation do great work. But New Localism and crushing fiscal and infrastructure pressures demand that in the future, public finance agencies must be reinvented along the lines of the Copenhagen model.

NEW LOCALISM AND PUBLIC WEALTH

CPH City & Port Development is a model of New Localism in action, having a long-term perspective for urban growth, governed with a private sector mentality while retaining public accountability, and generating robust local revenue to be reinvested in the city.

The most important thing to learn from Copenhagen or many of the examples that Detter and Fölster examine is to put market power in the hands of public wealth holders: citizens. But that cannot be done if there is a lack of transparency about what we own and what it produces, a genetic fragmentation of public asset management, and an unwillingness to create a wall between the commercial management of assets and political interference. We have emerging examples in the United States of overcoming some of these obstacles, but they are not bold enough, well capitalized enough, or independent enough to move the needle. In contrast to many economic development finance authorities in the United States that provide bond financing, catalyze development projects, and manage major transportation and port operations, the Copenhagen model has several distinguishing features: it rationalizes the assets of preexisting public authorities, functions through explicit and ongoing collaboration between local and national government, is fully depoliticized, and embodies long-term thinking. Adapting Copenhagen's success to the United States will necessitate replicating those features and overcoming a series of structural hurdles.

The United States also has to come to terms with the fact that public assets can be effectively managed by the same private systems and principles that build private wealth and productivity, but with a public purpose mandate. This assumes an integration of public ownership and commercial operating principles, including the ability to utilize governance and management that can align commercial operating outcomes with public wealth.

The inability to identify a more dramatic integration of public purpose and commercial management in the United States keeps us in a fiscal and intellectual straitjacket that is less and less productive over time; it keeps us arguing against cronyism and inefficiency with the political left and against rent seeking and the loss of public wealth with the political right.

As we discuss in subsequent chapters, the public asset corporation model could be a major vehicle for helping cities in the United States finance the future through a series of transformative investments. The next chapter begins this conversation with a deep and extended overview of the strategies cities use to advance economic inclusivity.

SEVEN

New Localism and Economic Inclusion

The future is already here; it's just not evenly distributed.
—William Gibson, NPR interview

Integrating economic growth and economic inclusion is a central challenge for New Localism. Urban economic growth efforts will not succeed over the long term without strategies that provide more opportunities for lower-income residents or those displaced by a rapidly changing job market. We explore strategies for local economic inclusion, including workforce connections, K–12 innovation, life-cycle approaches to learning, and expansion of social capital. Such local inclusion initiatives are critical but are also limited in the absence of national efforts to address health care, pensions, and income supports during periods of economic dislocation.

The experiences of Pittsburgh, Indianapolis, and Copenhagen exemplify ways in which New Localism can drive economic prosperity. New Localism must also incorporate economic inclusion into its work at every possible stage. We define economic inclusion as bringing people into the economic mainstream: as employees, consumers, and citizens. The most important challenge for American cities is how new types of economic growth can advantage people with limited incomes and work force skills.

Local inclusion strategies must emphasize providing job opportunities, education and training, and a variety of related supports. At the same time, federal entitlements such as social security and health care also need to be extensive and stable enough to support participation in an economy in which individuals move in and out of jobs and skill requirements change quickly. A national system that provides adequate health care, pensions, and income supports during periods of social dislocation is a complement to a strong market economy.

Economic policy can be generative or redistributive. The former focuses on catalyzing growth in the economy as a whole, while the latter focuses on redistributing income or social benefits. Redistributive policies are either people-based, directed toward household or labor market interventions, or place-based, intended to address specific geographies due to high levels of poverty, obsolete infrastructure, or disruptive economic change.

Major redistributive policies, such as the earned income tax credit, are best pursued at the federal level. Federal redistribution is more effective than more local efforts because the federal government has a larger pool of income from which to draw and there is less capacity to opt out. Federal redistribution is largely people-based. State redistribution is generally linked to providing support for public goods in jurisdictions with taxing capacity disadvantages.

High levels of poverty in cities give rise to political pressure with respect to local redistribution, often through local labor market interventions. While this may work politically, the wrong strategies can backfire. When cities and counties take the lead in advocating for higher minimum wages, for example, there is some danger that businesses will move to jurisdictions where wages are lower. It is more effective if minimum wage rates are standardized regionally or based on state and federal rules and if significant changes are transitioned over time, to allow businesses time to adjust. Early results from a recent study in Seattle, where an increase in the minimum wage went into effect, tentatively demonstrate a loss of low-wage jobs.[1]

A major complaint about local redistribution is that it drives up costs and makes the community less competitive for overall growth. That is sometimes true, although costs are not the only factor driving business location. If a higher-cost jurisdiction remains pivotal to a firm's profitability or if the value of local public goods and market opportunities compensates for those costs, the overall value proposition may keep a firm in place. Or, as in the case of certain small businesses, firms may have no choice but to stay and absorb the cost. Firms and individuals make calculations on what they receive, not only on what they pay. Businesses and individuals will sometimes pay more taxes willingly if taxes produce tangible benefits and if they believe in the area's future market growth.

But in a world of increasing choices, higher costs can be counterproductive if they choke off economic growth and capital investment. This is increasingly a problem even for the federal government, for significant capital earned by firms domiciled in the United States but made overseas remains offshore so that firms can avoid paying the higher U.S. corporate tax rates. A global economy with national tax systems may prove to be unwieldy for certain industries or for transnational compliance, in general.

Cities emerging from prolonged periods of population and job loss can be hard-pressed to pursue local redistribution. Many such cities are challenged by regulatory systems that inhibit entrepreneurship and real estate growth, legacy liabilities that make it hard to fund public budgets, and old governance systems that need to be revamped with better management. They generally have to prioritize the basics of public goods management and political reform to ensure sustained growth. You cannot redistribute what you cannot create.

In this chapter we explore local economic inclusion strategies, that is, the actions that New Localism can take to generate a more inclusive level of local prosperity. Such strategies can result in poverty alleviation impacts but should not be viewed as an anti-poverty strategy in the broadest sense. A more substantive national anti-poverty strategy requires the right combination of federal redistribution and local economic inclusion.

The strategies that we review fall into four categories:

- *Connection strategies* that link people to opportunity through information, skill building, and related support;

- *Innovation strategies* that improve the existing K–12 system through best practices and smart investments in training and technology;

- *Extension strategies* that extend the learning potential of K–12 by investing in early childhood education and the school-to-career pipeline; and

- *Organizing strategies* that elevate the social capital of place to increase access to public and private investment.

There are many other poverty alleviation strategies that could also be discussed, from family structure to consumer finance to the cost of housing. They are clearly all critical, particularly affordable housing. But housing policy in America is largely federal and despite the important work of local housing inclusion strategies, federal investments remain determinative. We chose these four strategies because they reflect a New Localism perspective with respect to systems building across local sectors.

CONNECTING GROWTH AND POVERTY

The colocation of poverty and growth is common to most American cities, including those that have emerged from years of decline. Philadelphia is a case in point. Philadelphia's downtown is the most important residential growth hub of the city, with more than 180,000 residents, and represents the largest single concentration of employment in the region. It accounts for 42 percent of city jobs and 32 percent of all property taxes in a land area that constitutes less than 6 percent of the city. Philadelphia's tax base would disappear without it. The central core also has the most educated population in the city, with 59 percent of its adults having a college degree or higher. The rate is much higher for those between twenty-five and thirty-four years old, the largest age cohort moving into the downtown area or neighborhoods proximate to it.[2]

Just west of the downtown area is the city's second growth hub, the University City area, where the University of Pennsylvania, Drexel University, the University Science Center, University of the Sciences, and a complex of medical centers and research facilities have generated millions of square feet of commercial real estate over the past decade, as well as new residential, retail, and cultural amenities.

The 2.5-square-mile University City area in West Philadelphia employs 77,000 persons, making it the second largest employment center after the downtown area, and has 44,000 students enrolled in its universities. This second growth node is moving steadily east to connect to the downtown area, as well as south along one of the city's riverfronts. As with Center City, its population is growing. The University City area also has a significantly greater share of educated residents than the city at large and is among the most important research centers in the state.[3]

These growth hubs occur in the middle of a very poor city. Philadelphia has the highest level of poverty among the ten largest cities in the nation.

About 26 percent of Philadelphians live below the poverty line, including almost half of that number living in deep poverty, defined as below 50 percent of the federal poverty line.[4] The result is an uneasy coexistence of dramatic contrasts: young newcomers focused on the future economy, others with limited workforce skills and seemingly limited chances for economic advancement.

How do university research and medical centers link to high-poverty neighborhoods on their periphery? The answer is especially complex because of the history of strained relationships between many universities and their neighbors. In Philadelphia those tensions go back to large-scale urban renewal in West Philadelphia more than half a century ago when Penn, Drexel, the Urban Science Center, and the city government used eminent domain to partially displace a predominantly African American community in the way of expansion.[5]

Three factors heralded a new phase in university-community partnerships in the 1980s and 1990s: (1) changes in political power in a city that had become majority African American, (2) the real estate self-interest of the universities, which needed to expand, and (3) a different type of leadership both at the universities and among local civic groups.

Partnership or compromise became the only alternative in an era of shifting power dynamics when politicians were less likely to give the universities a blank check. University leaders understood they could no longer bulldoze a neighborhood. They had to engage differently. Universities began to build linkages with neighborhood organizations based on common or intersecting community development objectives.

The University of Pennsylvania became a national leader in rebuilding relationships to its proximate communities during the presidency of Judith Rodin, who grew up in West Philadelphia. During her tenure from 1994 until 2002, the tide turned from reciprocal suspicion to active partnership. Much has been written about this transformation, including a book Rodin authored.[6] The changes and challenges are a case study in how universities wrestle with self-interest and public interest in everything from crime and safety to housing, small business development, employment, and the remaking of public spaces to encourage connections between institutions and neighbors.

The University of Pennsylvania and Drexel University have used four methods to link universities and neighborhoods during the past several decades: (1) employer-assisted housing, (2) public education, (3) elevated use of local, minority-, and women-owned companies in procurement, and (4) direct employment linkages. There have also been other service and technical assistance programs, but those four are the primary drivers of reengagement.

Both universities utilize employer-assisted housing programs to encourage homeownership close to their campuses. They use credit counseling, grants, second mortgage loans, and mortgage guarantees. The programs have been available to workers on every step of the income scale. The schools also built additional on-campus student housing to discourage rental speculation by landlords who rent to students and overheat the market. But student housing cannot be fully controlled, and tension between town and gown over student rentals in traditionally nonstudent communities continues.

Both universities have adopted a public school. The Penn Alexander School receives a subsidy from the University of Pennsylvania that helps keep the student-teacher ratio as low as 18:1, far lower than in other city schools.[7] The academic record has been strong and the impact of the school on neighborhood housing values significant. Drexel University recently sponsored a new middle school in the neighborhood managed by the Science Leadership Academy, a member of the school district's innovation schools program.[8]

Both universities have active procurement goals regarding minority- and women-owned businesses, and are participating in apprenticeship programs to increase the number of nonwhite workers in the building trade unions. Other research centers and civic groups in the community are playing roles in training and linking neighborhood residents to employment. The Wistar Institute, the oldest independent medical research center in the nation, manages a successful biomedical technician training program in partnership with the city's community college. The University Science Center uses its laboratory spaces to provide science training for public school students. And the University City District (UCD), the special services district for the area, plays an active role in work force development.

UCD is now a workforce intermediary that collaborates with the human resources departments of the local institutions to get information on future employer needs, bringing in potential applicants for skills training and then helping them apply for the positions. The program concentrates on the soft skills of customer service, employee-employer relationships, and basic work discipline. It places about 200 workers a year and has the potential to expand. Matt Bergheiser, the executive director of UCD, is taking the workforce role a step further by creating businesses to contract directly with the institutions. The first one is a successful landscaping business whose profits help pay the costs of UCD's other workforce training programs.

How far can these partnerships go? The next phase of development by Drexel University will be an indication. John Fry, the current president of Drexel University, wants to more fully integrate university-led innovation and economic inclusion. He is vocal about the merger of those efforts. A former executive vice president at the University of Pennsylvania under Judith Rodin, he went on to become president of Franklin and Marshall, where on a smaller scale he continued the Penn playbook to reconnect place and university.[9]

Fry returned to Philadelphia in 2010 to take the helm at Drexel, a school best known for engineering, design, and a cooperative program whereby undergraduates take up to five years to earn degrees. They are required to take a year of full-time paid internships. Fry wants to use the historical platform of Drexel—business partnerships, technical skills, and applied research—along with proximity to the downtown area to put innovation and inclusion into reciprocal balance.

Drexel sits at the center of entrenched poverty and future economic growth. It is bounded on the south by the University of Pennsylvania, on the east by the downtown area, and on the north and west by neighborhoods some of which have unemployment rates above 15 percent, poverty rates above 40 percent, median incomes of around $21,000, and a large share, 26 percent, of adults without a high school diploma.[10]

Currently, Drexel is building east toward the downtown and away from the neighborhoods, proposing a new mixed-use community, Schuylkill Yards, that over the next twenty years could generate 6 million square feet of new office and retail space, as well as spaces for startup companies and research labs.[11]

As Drexel builds Schuylkill Yards, the University Science Center may build another 4 million square feet close to its existing campus over the next decade. Along with Penn's continuing medical and research lab expansions to the south, these efforts could reshape the city's center of gravity in terms of job location. This is Philadelphia's innovation district, within walking distance of the third busiest rail station in America and a vibrant downtown.[12]

Fry wants to build education and workforce ladders from the neighborhoods into Schuylkill Yards in ways that exceed current efforts. To this end, Drexel has embarked on an effort to improve early childhood centers and all the schools in the neighborhood, as well as developing student recruitment programs in those neighborhoods. This is a deeper and longer-term perspective than more immediate transactions for procurement and construction jobs. The challenges are greater: it will be harder to manage and measure and, when completed, there will be few ribbon cuttings or newspaper headlines.

Will it work? The intent and commitment are admirable, but there is reason to be cautious. Managing university constituencies with regard to budgets and incentives while delivering on promises to local communities is a difficult balancing act. Moreover, even the best efforts cannot control public schools, neighborhood conditions, and changes in the job market. The deeper the commitment to effecting long-term changes in poverty areas, the more complex the issues become, from family life to the range of institutions in which those families participate or with which they transact. But efforts like Drexel's must be pursued, tested, refined, and replicated.

Connecting hubs of growth and neighborhoods of poverty is based on three organizing principles: building civic engagement, developing immediate connections, and pursuing longer-term strategies. Civic engagement is the basis for trust and common purpose. It sets the stage. The immediate connections—job contacts, contract procurements, placemaking activities—are tangible outcomes that emerge from civic engagement and reinforce the efforts. They often require specialized intermediaries such as the UCD to work with local businesses and service groups.

The deeper connections emerge from long-term strategies rooted in reshaping schools, elevating the capacity of neighborhood institutions, and making the case to the university community. If they succeed, the result is structured opportunity ladders from neighborhood to career. We have great examples of the first and second organizing principles in action, building civic engagement and developing immediate connections. The deeper engagements are the hardest parts of the enterprise to craft, but civic and neighborhood leaders are now prioritizing those as well.

INNOVATIONS IN K–12 SCHOOLING

A major determinant of economic inclusion is skills. In this regard the public sector focuses on what it directly controls, the K–12 education system. But over the past twenty years there have been numerous civic and private sector interventions and partnerships that have sought to elevate the performance of public school and K–12 performance more generally. And as a result, K–12 schooling stopped being a purely public sector enterprise.

Few institutions in America are more politically contested than schools, particularly those that serve low-income and minority children. Schools are where issues of race, class, political power, and social legitimacy collide with the realities of raising children and building tomorrow's workforce.[13] New problem solvers are entering the political fray, adding new options and strategies. Some have worked; others have failed.

Countless reports show American children falling behind in global comparisons, particularly in mathematics and science.[14] America's competitive advantage throughout much of the late nineteenth and early twentieth centuries was attributable to K–12 schooling and a growing infrastructure of universities. An early adopter of universal elementary and high school education, America also took a more democratic perspective on college entrance than other nations, where universities were overwhelmingly for elites.

Major advances in national growth followed the development of universal public schooling, the creation of land grant universities, the development of the national community college system, and the provision of federal research investments. By the 1970s, however, the U.S. advantage had begun to slide, and that slide has continued.[15] The depth of the decline in American K–12 education differs according to how the data are viewed. When low-income public schools are dropped from the comparison and only data from urban magnet, private, and suburban schools are used, Americans match up well.[16] We are still behind the top leaders, but competitive.

But schools that serve low-income students, particularly those with large numbers of African American and Hispanic students, perform far below where they must to increase the life chances of their students. Disaggregating the data might yield temporary comfort on global comparisons but does not get at the problem of social divisions and long-term competitiveness, particularly as the demography of the nation changes and income divergence widens.

The reasons schools are not working for low-income children are hotly debated but generally include insufficient school funding, poor management, poor teacher preparation, lack of early childhood and home support, poorly compensated teachers, lax curriculum standards, elevated teacher to student ratios, lack of economic integration, lack of teacher diversity, the loss of learning attributable to long summer breaks, overly rigid curricular and testing standards, inflexibility in union contracts with respect to hiring and firing, and the difficulty of introducing innovation in rigid administrative systems.[17]

And there is another major explanation. The more income a family has, the greater is its ability to compensate for school inadequacies through the use of tutors, after-school enrichment programs, educational summer camps, social networks, and other aids.[18]

Over the past two decades an uneven patchwork of reforms has transformed most big city school districts from vertical command-and-control authorities to networks with more decentralized management. The innovations in school management were largely driven by discontent on the part of parents, politicians, and businesses and by reactions to federal testing standards, especially during the many years of No Child Left Behind legislation.[19]

The typical large urban school district today has traditional schools, magnet schools with citywide reach and admissions standards; charter schools that are publicly funded but managed largely by private nonprofit organizations, and a variety of other contract-based alternative schools linked to behavioral learning issues. Charter schools are growing more rapidly than other alternative public school forms and are also the most controversial among teachers unions and school administrators.[20] To some school officials, charter schools represent unwelcome forms of privatization, while to many parents they are a welcome public school choice.

Currently about 6 percent of all public schools in America are charter schools, educating over 3 million students in 6,800 schools, with as many as 1 million students on waiting lists.[21] The waiting list data are not always a reliable indicator of demand because they are not systematically sorted, contain names in duplicate, and often include children from other charter schools seeking better charter schools. That said, there are examples of charter schools with thousands of applications for a very small number of slots.[22]

In some American cities charters make up an increasingly large percentage of total enrollment, with fourteen districts having more than 30 percent of students enrolled in charter schools.[23] Large-scale charter cities include Washington, D.C., Cleveland, Detroit, San Antonio, Philadelphia, and New Orleans (where, post-Katrina, virtually all schools were chartered).

Charter school performance is uneven but with some promising signs, particularly in states that do a better job of authorizing charters and in communities where some of the high-functioning charter networks play a substantial role. There is some evidence that charter schools do better than traditional schools in test scores of low-income African American and Latino students. The Center for Research on Educational Outcomes (CREDO) at Stanford has conducted an in-depth study of charter schools in forty-one cities that shows math and reading growth gains in comparison to traditional public schools with the same demographic profile.[24] Likewise, an independent study of the KIPP (Knowledge Is Power Program) charter network by the econometric group Mathematica has shown statistically significant advancement by KIPP students.[25]

But other studies show much less promise by charters, and the CREDO studies also post poor results for many charters. Moreover, charter-funding formulas in many states do not compensate districts for a loss in revenue. Even while charters receive less funding per pupil than traditional public schools in the same district, the districts are short-changed if they are not able to manage the stranded costs.[26] This is perhaps the greatest source of tension in the school district-charter school debate.

Some of the largest networks of charter schools now function as mini-districts run by charter management organizations either in a single city or as regional and even nationwide systems. Networks such as Success Academies, KIPP, Yes-Prep, Mastery, Uncommon Schools, Green Dot, Aspire, and others have created distinct approaches to building and managing school culture, utilizing data, training teachers, and organizing classroom instruction. While publicly funded, they have also been supported by private philanthropy, businesses, and civic groups of various kinds. But mostly they have been driven by bottom-up customer demand for schools that are safe and seem to perform.

Like magnet schools that specialize in science or art, charter schools are an example of an organizational innovation, and the innovation has been largely (parent) demand-driven. The number one job for all school districts is to fund what works, whether traditional district schools, charter schools, magnet schools, or other hybrid models. The first rule of innovation is to remain agnostic about organizational form but concentrated on outcomes. Fund what works.

Innovations coming from other directions include the increased use of technology and blended learning techniques. It may be that the large investments being made today in educational technology startups and growth companies will pay off in terms of both cost and performance for districts educating low-income children, but it is too early to evaluate impact.[27]

Along with new technologies, better use of value-added data assessment systems, the application of new cognitive psychology techniques to assist with social and emotional learning, high school internships and early college enrollment, summer and after-school initiatives designed to prevent learning loss, and new teacher training methods that emphasize master-apprentice models are all becoming more commonplace.[28]

The diffusion and replication of innovations within education remain relatively slow-paced, a result of the grip of large school districts, university teacher training systems, and partisan battles between statehouses

and city halls over policy and funding. But if there is one thing that contentious school reform debates can agree to, it is the value of having high-
quality teachers. Outstanding questions in this respect are how to create
healthy school environments where teachers thrive, how to scale the best
teacher training methods, and how to sustain a profession with relatively
low compensation.

In several cities civic and business interventions are also being applied
to the reinvention of Catholic school systems. Catholic schools played a
huge role in educating generations of immigrants in American cities and
often outpaced district schools in their educational success with inner-city
residents. The collapse of urban Catholic schools, which in their heyday
could educate 20 to 30 percent of students in some cities, occurred because
of the changing demography of where Catholics lived and the absence of
the teacher subsidy that came from priests, nuns, and male religious orders.
Fifty years ago almost 60 percent of teachers in Catholic schools came from
the Church; today that figure is much lower.[29]

While the closure of many urban Catholic schools was also affected by
the financial and social crisis within Catholic archdioceses linked to sex
abuse scandals, Catholic schools may have escaped the worst of the Church's
brand problem. There is still wide support for Catholic education among
Catholics and support among many non-Catholics.

Many public school districts never understood the significant fiscal
contribution that came from a parallel private system built from archdiocese and Catholic religious orders. Millions of Catholic households paid
taxes to support public schools but sent children to Catholic schools, thus
eliminating the need for public support. As that parallel system declined,
it had an impact on public fiscal capacity.

Some of the same social groups—business, civic, philanthropic—that
support the charter movement are trying to revive Catholic education. And
in some instances the format for change has been similar: a decentralized
nonprofit outside the archdiocese is formed to run multiple schools. This
is a huge departure from how business used to be done in the typical archdiocese. As some of these schools are being renewed, the extent to which
they were burdened with aging infrastructure, limited technology, and
outdated human resource development is becoming clear.

In the Bronx and Harlem a nonprofit network, the Partnership for Inner City Education, has emerged to run multiple Catholic schools after recent closures. The same is true for Independence Mission schools in Philadelphia and the Catholic Partnership Schools in Camden. Those networks were all a response to archdiocese shutdowns, with parents, civic groups, and businesses coming to the rescue. Whether they will create a long-term sustainable growth model in the inner city is still an open question.

New national Catholic networks such as Cristo Rey and the Nativity-Miguel Coalition are also emerging and sharing methods for teaching and management across their system. Their efforts are nascent and fragile, and it is far too early to know the extent to which they will contribute to the long-term revival of Catholic urban education. But the shift from vertically controlled organizations that had limited capacity or incentive to adapt to change to collaborative networks more willing to rethink strategy gives them more of a fighting chance.

The strategies of New Localism are increasingly important to school reform. Civic and private concerns must continue to knock on public and parochial school system doors, looking to unlock higher levels of achievement in systems that are often slow to adapt to change. To succeed over the long term, business and civic leaders will have to strengthen partnerships with public districts and teachers unions wherever possible.

We need broad agreement that we have a crisis and that we understand some of the attributes for success. These attributes include a strong achievement culture, high-quality management, the constructive use of data, an emphasis on teacher development, attention to noncognitive learning as well as cognitive pursuits, the financial ability to serve students with widely different learning styles and social needs, and the latitude to problem solve as roadblocks emerge. The framework and examples for success exist in a variety of private, district, and charter efforts. The will to replicate that success is what must exist as well. Otherwise we are giving up on too many young people, and the economic and social consequences will be significant for us all.

EXTENDING LEARNING BEFORE AND AFTER K–12

The most forward-thinking policy and educational leaders conceptualize communities as learning environments that extend from early childhood into careers. However, local public jurisdictions generally focus on student achievement primarily through K–12 education. Just as a New Localism perspective on K–12 schools has to replicate the best innovations, there is an emerging practice throughout the nation of extending learning investments prior to kindergarten and after high school. This requires the kind of cross-system perspective that is native to New Localism.

The transition periods in early childhood and adolescence, as well as the post–high school transition, can be determinative. And for many low-income children and young adults there is inadequate support or guidance to move through these transitions. This is particularly true, for example, for large numbers of foster children who age out of foster care at age eighteen (sometimes before they graduate from high school) and often drop off the radar screen of support systems.[30]

The Center on Children and Families at Brookings has developed a life-cycle model it calls the Social Genome Model.[31] This was a joint effort of the Brookings Institution, the Urban Institute, and Child Trends. It demonstrates the pervasive achievement gap between advantaged and disadvantaged children and shows the effectiveness of various interventions in promoting higher levels of social mobility.

The Social Genome Model shows that children born to families making less than 200 percent of the poverty line have a 44 percent chance of reaching the middle class or higher, while children from families making over 200 percent of the poverty line have a 64 percent chance. The odds are significantly worse for children born into families with incomes in the bottom quintile, who have only a 30 percent chance of reaching the middle class or higher over the course of their lives.

The model also shows that just one intervention in early life—access to preschool education—can close the gap in school readiness and improve low-income children's cognitive and behavioral outcomes to nearly the success rates of their higher-income peers. With multiple targeted interventions in early childhood, middle childhood, and adolescence, the achievement gap—that is, the gap between the percentage of children from low- versus higher-income families reaching middle class by middle age—is reduced by a full 70 percent for low-income children.[32]

As the Social Genome Model confirms and anyone involved in trying to win the battle against poverty knows, placing emphasis on the early childhood years is critical. The data on the impact of high-quality early childhood education are compelling. When the Nobel Prize economist James Heckman analyzed the cost and benefits of tackling poverty, quality early childhood care emerged as the most important factor. His research methods are econometric but draw on work from neuroscience and developmental psychology. He studied not only cognitive outcomes but also a wide range of social and emotional outcomes that matter in subsequent years.[33]

The research on early childhood learning tells us much about the broader ecosystem of parental support and adult-child interactions. The amount of learning that happens between infancy and age five years is remarkable: language acquisition, cognition, emotional capacity, and moral judgment. Nearly two decades ago the National Academy of Sciences issued a landmark report on early childhood learning titled *From Neurons to Neighborhoods: The Science of Early Childhood Development*. It covered a massive amount of information and research and began to make the link between child care and neighborhoods or social context in important ways.[34] The implications of these connections have not penetrated public policy to the extent necessary.

More and more cities are making universal prekindergarten programs a civic cause. This is happening in cities as diverse as Washington, D.C., New York City, Tulsa, San Antonio, and Philadelphia. Some of it is funded through special taxes, as with Philadelphia's tax on sugary beverages and Seattle's recent property tax levy.[35] We need an even more robust social movement, and this is where New Localism is critical. The universal K–12 movement that emerged in the nineteenth and early twentieth centuries has to be replicated as a twenty-first-century movement in support of quality early childhood learning.

At the other side of the youth life cycle, a great many cities and counties have also reduced escalating high school dropout rates by paying greater attention to the crisis points that can be identified in sixth, seventh, and eighth grades that may lead to eventual dropping out. School districts have supported or created alternative schools to help students drop back in and build competencies that lead to graduation and career opportunities.[36]

Chicago is making substantive progress in reducing high school dropout rates without a reduction in overall competencies, as evidenced by test scores. This is a critical distinction because the certificate has to signal competencies. In fifteen years the graduation rates in Chicago have gone from 47 percent to close to 70 percent, a long way from where they need to be but moving in the right direction.[37]

Chicago is also a city where the system of community colleges excels, making it easier to transition many high school graduates into careers. Since 2011, under Mayor Rahm Emmanuel, the seven community colleges have undergone a major reinvention to better align their curricula with employer needs through partnerships with more than 150 businesses. The schools specialize in different areas (such as health care or information technology), and recently the city instituted an incentive tuition system for all students who graduate from high school with a 3.0 grade point average.[38]

If there are institutions in America that are underleveraged in the fight for economic inclusion, it is the 1,100 community colleges that can provide young people and adults with an opportunity to gain skills in the rapidly changing workforce of the global economy. Community colleges are the closest institution America has to a sustainable employer-employee apprenticeship system, and in many places, businesses in collaboration with community colleges have created structured career pathways. They have not been elevated within public policy and public budget decisions to the extent these schools deserve, and unlike most universities, few community colleges can build endowments or carry out significant private fundraising.

A life-cycle learning perspective requires cross-system collaboration. New Localism governance encourages collaboration across systems more than the management of any singular system. One mayor who understands this is Greg Fischer of Louisville. Fischer launched Cradle to Career, an integrated effort of disparate organizations focused on kindergarten readiness, elementary and secondary education, college completion, and workforce-oriented skills training.[39]

While not in control of all these systems, Fischer could take the big-picture view and consider the life trajectory of a child as a whole rather than as a series of disconnected, compartmentalized schooling events. His contribution was to pull together key community institutions and get them working together, assigning responsibilities for specific efforts and asking for tangible results by 2020.

The Louisville Metro United Way took responsibility for early care and kindergarten readiness, aiming for 77 percent of entering kindergarteners to be prepared for school. Jefferson County Public Schools district is leading the K–12 success effort, aiming for 70 percent of graduates being college or career ready. 55K, a local nonprofit organization, is leading the initiative to increase the percentage of working-age adults with bachelor's or associate degrees to 40 percent and 10 percent, respectively. And the Louisville Metro Office of Civic Innovation is leading the effort to tighten the talent pipeline between students and employers.[40]

The co-founder and former CEO of a global mid-sized family manufacturing business, Fischer has also worked with business leaders, the state government, and the nearby city of Lexington to create the Bluegrass Economic Advancement Movement (BEAM). Its ambitious goal is to bolster the region's prowess in advanced manufacturing, exports, and foreign direct investment, building on the distinctive competitive assets and advantages of the region. To achieve this goal, the two cities and their partners have offered targeted company outreach programs, small export grants, and a regionwide export strategy. The result has been impressive: BEAM's five-year goal to increase export successes for small businesses by 50 percent was reached in three years.[41]

The Cradle to Career and BEAM initiatives draw on leadership traits in mayors that are qualitatively different from the more conventional ones useful for running a hierarchical government where command-and-control lines of authority are in place. Soft power requires the ability to convene, cajole, and even shame private, civic, university, and community leaders to come together and collaborate. This is community organizing at a high level.

COMMUNITY ORGANIZING

The concept of social capital may be somewhat overused, but it is a significant factor in discussions of economic inclusion. The informal ties that
generate trust, reciprocity, and meaningful association are important to
the development of market economies, the maintenance of local cultures,
the creation of political power, and the ability to extend outward to find
opportunity. Strong social capital can insulate groups and also expand the
reach from one group or one individual to an outside group or individual.
Social capital, as Robert Putnam notes in Bowling Alone, comes in both
bonding and *bridging* forms: some linkages that inwardly cohere and others
that connect outward.[42]

Many low-income communities exhibit strong social capital layered
with high levels of internal and external distrust. The social capital emerges
from overlapping relationships of households and kinship connections and
from common participation in a variety of local institutions, from congregations to school associations. This is the social capital of family, familiar-
ity, and engagement in everyday efforts and activities. Counteracting
forces of distrust emerge from the fears and consequences of crime, the
struggle over scarce goods, including housing, and financial obligations,
conflicts with police or other outside agencies, and divisions among ethnic
groups.

There have been popular tendencies to either idealize poor communities as well organized in terms of internal solidarity or to discredit them as
places of chaos, lacking any internal trust or organization. Neither charac-
terization is true. But the elevation of low-income communities is aided by
increasing the level of community organization and social capital through
which talent and financial resources are pooled, trust is extended, and new
opportunities are discovered. Anyone who has worked or lived in a low-
income community knows the importance of social organization as it relates to increased levels of private and public investment. Poor communities
need authentic social representation to have a voice.

The Oliver community in East Baltimore is an unlikely place to seek
sophisticated social or economic networks. It is among the nation's most
distressed communities in terms of poverty rates, the number of abandoned

housing units, and the proliferation of drugs. If you watched HBO's *The Wire*, then you know East Baltimore. It is the site of the abandoned row homes where dead bodies were deposited. But in real life it is a neighborhood with a high level of community organization that is on the verge of reinventing itself.

Fifteen years ago, in a neighborhood accustomed to shootings and the death of young people, one crime shocked everyone and made national news. A resident, Angela Dawson, who had been trying to get drug dealers off her street corner, had her home firebombed. Angela and her five children were burned to death in their sleep. Her husband died from the fire a few days later. The firebombing on Preston Street heightened the tension between neighborhood residents and city officials over crime and the inability of the city to protect people who reported crimes. Angela Dawson was one of those people who would not take no for an answer. There were threats and even a failed bombing attempt prior to the seven murders. But she refused to leave.[43]

The day after the news broke, hundreds of people came to the Dawson house and held a vigil. Many murder victim vigils are held in America's cities. But the vigil on Preston Street was just the beginning of what became an extensive effort to rebuild the community. Many churches in the community were members of Baltimore BUILD, a citywide coalition of congregations, civic groups, and unions affiliated with the Industrial Areas Foundation (IAF) network of community organizing groups.

The IAF and other organizing networks throughout the nation have continued to build the relationships and associations within low-income urban and rural communities to gain more power for those places and people. They get very limited coverage, but in communities as diverse as East Brooklyn and San Antonio's West Side, they have ignited grassroots change.[44]

After the bombing on Preston Street, BUILD recommitted to deeper organizing within the community to turn the situation around. At the center of the IAF methodology is relationship building and training: schooling ordinary people in the practice of citizenship, negotiating with public officials, and private institutions; reclaiming the need for reciprocity among various public and civic actor; and practicing what we call in this book horizontal power or, in IAF language, *power with, versus power over* someone.[45]

The East Baltimore organizing efforts eventually helped produce a new school, better after-school programs, and an expansion of community policing. But there were also capital and development finance connections that grew out of the organizing. BUILD worked with a community investment group, Reinvestment Fund, to develop a plan for the neighborhood that would redevelop abandoned housing units, which at the time made up approximately 45 percent of total units.

In the summer of 2003, eight months after the bombing, leaders from BUILD and Reinvestment Fund, along with 100 local volunteers from the community, surveyed every property and spoke to almost every available resident. By the time the one-year anniversary of the firebombing came around, they were able to present a community-led redevelopment plan at a church meeting packed with residents and officials, including Congressman Elijah Cummings and then senator Barbara Mikulski.

In typical IAF fashion they asked everyone—including their congregations—to be part of the solution. At the center of the housing plan was the need to raise high-risk capital to acquire properties and begin rebuilding. The churches put up the first million dollars and then went to other sources—corporate and civic—where they had relationships. Their religious community networks expanded far outside the East Baltimore churches to Catholic, mainline Protestant, and Jewish congregations. It started with their local relationships and then moved outward; in other words, their organizing made use of both bonding and bridging social capital. The Reinvestment Fund put up money from its own loan fund, and several Baltimore area foundations and corporate leaders did the same. A development fund was created and the housing development corporation—a partnership of BUILD and the Reinvestment Fund—got under way.

A signal had been sent that someone believed the community had a future and would continue investing over the long term. The fledgling housing development corporation was able to take very difficult early-stage risks, including acquisition and predevelopment costs. Because of its risk tolerance, the corporation was able to leverage other capital by subordinating its security position when required. It could be patient, acquiring and holding property as it built demand. The capital represented the community's own equity stake in the place, a signal that this represented a grassroots commitment.

The results have been hard-fought but impressive: a significant reduction in vacancies, hundreds of new housing units, revitalized civic groups, a reduction in crime compared to other Baltimore communities, and rising real estate values. There have also been missteps: poor property management as the developments became rentals, a result of the mortgage industry collapse in 2008; fears that property values were rising too quickly in the areas closest to other redevelopment near Johns Hopkins Medical Center; ongoing difficulties in policing and community relationships; and issues of drug dealing and violence. Nothing will come easily to a community like Oliver. But they proved that the social networks of the poorest community could be leveraged to generate connections across geographies and social class.

This is New Localism in a very profound sense, built from the neighborhood outward.

COMMUNITIES WITH LIMITED GROWTH ASSETS

Some of the poorest places in America are rural counties: in the Mississippi Delta, in Appalachia, on Indian reservations, and in many other sections of the nation. Most communities—even poor rural counties—have two attributes from which they can build: the inherent quality of the place and the future potential of educational achievement. Quality places attract others (as residents, tourists, consumers, investors) and an educated workforce attracts employers through either internet or brick-and-mortar employment.

The most important issue is always workforce quality. In a computing environment, it is as possible for people in South Dakota to work as off-site administrators or help desk personnel for distant companies as it is for people in Dublin or Hyderabad. The question is how to organize rural development institutions and schools to connect to those opportunities and build recognizable strength in a service or product.

But what about places that lack the taxing capacity for basic public goods and have no discernible growth assets that are market-based? For many lower-income localities, current fiscal stress is compounded by their inability to raise enough money for public goods owing to their limited taxing capacity. While states are major funders of local services, including education, the majority of basic public services are paid for through local taxes. State redistribution is not always adequate. It is one thing to fix a structural budget problem in Houston or Phoenix and another thing in Gary, Indiana, or a poor rural community. In some instances a more radical approach may be required that involves governance consolidation.

The cycle of inadequate budget revenue and trying to get more money from local taxes results in a downward spiral of decline and fiscal absurdity, to the point that some of the poorest cities in America pay very high property tax rates, which eats value from already low home prices and hence drives down both public and private wealth. Thus hard-hit Detroit has one of the highest property tax rates among large American cities and thriving Boston has one of the lowest.[46]

The water crisis in Flint, Michigan, had many causes, from a bad decision to change the water supply, to poor adherence to standards for the new supply, to mismanagement and possible criminal misconduct among some government officials. It was a national wake-up call regarding declining infrastructure in older towns and cities with limited fiscal capacity.[47] But one of the core issues in Flint is its lack of public system sustainability. Flint does not just have tainted water; it also has one of the highest water costs in the nation. The innovation that is needed is not just better government but a structural answer to fiscal sustainability over the long term.

Many states have emergency intervention systems for fiscally distressed localities, most of them a legacy of the Great Depression. Some states offer technical assistance for localities in distress or make special grants or loans. In the worst cases there are state takeovers, as occurred in Detroit during the 2013 bankruptcy. Few municipal takeovers have had the intended effect because they come with too little capital, too little planning, and often not enough power or legitimacy. The Detroit takeover, for all its controversy, was better than most efforts of its kind. Most takeovers are emergency actions with very limited preparation or power.

Washington, D.C., was likely the best example of turnaround success, in part because of the unusual circumstances of being a federal city, but also because of the management quality, financial capacity, and legitimacy of the turnaround effort. And, of course, Washington, D.C., has an obvious business growth niche based on federal government and related professional services.

More often than not, very poor localities do not get fully taken over. Instead, they have agencies within their government seized by federal or state agencies, as when HUD brings a housing authority into receivership, the state police take over local policing, or a state runs the school district. Some of these efforts have had short-term success but generally do little to change the overall trajectory of a city.

Departmental takeovers and bond protection do not generally get at the core problem, the lack of structural capacity for many small-towns, older industrial cities, and rural communities to pay long-term recovery costs or ongoing operating costs. Low-income municipalities or rural communities without adequate taxing capacity need a twenty-first-century solution that is not just more debt. Otherwise Camden, New Jersey, East St. Louis, Illinois, and Flint, Michigan, will continue to cycle in and out of fiscal insolvency.

When able to make the math work, sometimes states and municipalities make bets on major economic development projects that are heavily subsidized through state grants, loans, and tax credits. Some states and cities turn to gambling as a potential quick fix. The results are rarely good, particularly in a world where everyone has launched gambling enterprises and the internet is the new super-casino. Using an extractive industry like gambling to build wealth generates as many new costs as it does new revenue. Moreover, it creates a single-industry boom-and-bust cycle. The saga of Atlantic City is a cautionary tale: state and private investments went into gambling, and decades later, it is a city in financial ruin.[48]

We need fresh thinking about how to manage places where infrastructure and operating costs far exceed their ability to pay. For years there have been attempts to consolidate local governments into some form of regional system. We applaud those efforts but see very little sign that many will succeed outside the regionalization of particular functions such as transportation, infrastructure, environment, and the like. But for the poorest communities, broader consolidation becomes vital.

We propose a voluntary intergovernmental turnaround strategy whereby states, counties, and municipalities collaborate in the management of services in exchange for the loss of home rule. Consolidation works only if it is in everyone's interest. In this case, it has to be in the interest of both buyers and sellers. The distressed locality must be willing to voluntarily dissolve its home rule status and be absorbed into a larger governmental unit, and that larger county or municipal entity must be willing to absorb the added political geography. This does not work for Native American reservations, where there are sovereignty issues, though even in those cases there are options for consolidation of certain governance functions.

What is the advantage of taking over the most distressed places? That is the question for a buyer to answer. Buyers have to see strategic value where others don't and the value of using the incentives to make the transaction happen over a period of time.

In most cases, however, sellers (distressed localities) will not want to give up political control even though so much of their economic value has been expended and the quality of life for their residents is poor. And buyers (more financially able entities) will have a difficult time convincing their residents of the wisdom of acquiring a new political geography that is largely poor.

But the choices should be weighed among sellers and buyers. Some form of intermediary may be needed to help organize the merger, the way consulting firms and investment banks do for company mergers. Without experimenting with new solutions, we are left with a cycle of fiscal dysfunction, population loss, and deepening poverty.

The importance of insisting on higher levels of economic inclusion as part of any growth, governance, or finance model is that it forces us to give attention to solving the seemingly most intractable problems, whether in low-income urban communities, small towns, or rural areas. The solutions from the perspective of New Localism involve a range of tools: connections, innovations, extension systems, and community organization. These have to be applied to existing systems and across existing systems. They have to allow for a pragmatic approach to what works and the emergence of community voice and participation.

EIGHT

Inventing Metro Finance

By and large, a disruptive technology is initially embraced by the least profitable customers in a market.

—Clayton M. Christensen, *The Innovator's Dilemma*

———————————————————————

Financing the future requires unlocking new sources of capital. This is particularly important in light of the lack of public budget flexibility and the constraints of private capital. Over the past four decades, public purpose sources of capital have played increasingly more important roles as bridges between more conventional finance and development. We refer to these efforts collectively as metro finance. These innovations are modest when measured against the challenges of growth, yet they are central to the long-term efforts of New Localism and must scale up significantly over the next few decades. We review the role and potential of these various financing trends, including public sector development authorities, community investment intermediaries, impact investors, philanthropy, and universities.

———————————————————————

New Localism needs capital to finance inclusion, infrastructure, and innovation. Some of that capital will require public funding; much of it will require financial investments. But there are barriers—linked to both public budgetary constraints and private investment incentives—to making those investments. To overcome some of those constraints, new public purpose sources of capital have emerged to catalyze private investment and extend public capacity. Like other aspects of New Localism, these are multisectoral collaborations often managed through hybrid institutions, with one foot in private enterprise and one foot in civil society. We refer to these innovations and practices in this chapter as *metro finance*.

CONVENTIONAL BARRIERS TO INVESTMENT

Barriers to increased public investment derive from a lack of public sector flexibility resulting from the many legacy costs carried on the balance sheets of states and municipalities, including unfunded pension and health care liabilities, or, in the case of the federal government, from the escalation of mandatory spending on entitlements. Where there are barriers to accessing private finance they generally arise from a focus on short-term returns and the increasing disconnect of capital from the success of any one region or community.

Overcoming legacy costs requires political and public will to reform systems captive to past promises and obligations. Overcoming private finance barriers requires innovation by institutions with a deeper connection to places, private market credibility, and the capacity to lower the risks and transaction costs for many private investors.

Legacy Costs

The extent to which legacy costs make it difficult to fund local and state budgets is not the same in all places; some governments are in a much stronger position than others. Many have instituted smart reforms that anticipated the possibility of a crisis. But too many others are struggling, losing ground and in danger of facing fiscal distress.

Some of America's largest cities are overwhelmed by unfunded promises, including Chicago, Houston, Philadelphia, and Los Angeles.[1] Several have already gone through bankruptcy in part because of pension liabilities (such as Detroit), and several are edging closer to bankruptcy (Hartford).[2] Many cities with high levels of unfunded liabilities are located in states with similar problems (the city of Chicago and the state of Illinois), making fiscal rescue more difficult since there is no state backstop and federal guarantees do not exist for state and local public pensions.

Failure to reform situations of unfunded liabilities can damage fiscal capacity in several ways: by lowering bond ratings and increasing the cost of borrowing, by requiring increasingly larger annual contributions from general operating budgets to catch up to unfunded liabilities, and by detracting from the capacity to make elevated investments in future-oriented initiatives that might result in increased public wealth.

Unfunded pension and health care liabilities became a central point of fiscal stress over the past fifteen years of uneven growth as the number of people aging into pensions increased in proportion to the number working to support pensioners, leading to an unsustainable system, while poor fiscal management, including an unwillingness to update actuarial projections and face the consequences of inflated financial return expectations, exacerbated the problem.[3]

The stock market growth in the 1990s enabled cities and states to make generous pension promises to public workers, sometimes in lieu of other benefits. While employees met their required contribution levels, politicians often could not sustain public pension accounts owing to other budget pressures.

As Amy Monahan, an expert in tax and employee benefits law, notes, there is a political economy to pension decisionmaking that favors underfunding on everyone's part: on the part of politicians, taxpayers, and even employees, who might favor other benefits—higher wages, no-layoff promises, better overtime allotment—over the full funding of pensions.[4] Both employees and employers assume higher rates of return will eventually cure underfunding. But that is a dubious assumption that is not grounded in responsible investment experience or actuarial practice.

As markets turned downward, particularly during the global recession of 2008–09, and pension funds (often) took on significantly higher risks to achieve promised returns, portfolios suffered. The city of Houston saw its unfunded portion of public pensions go from zero to $4 billion over fifteen years.[5] To his credit, Mayor Sylvester Turner has led an ambitious effort to avoid fiscal meltdown by restructuring pension plans and government contributions. During the same period the Commonwealth of Pennsylvania went from a pension surplus to unfunded obligations of nearly $70 billion. Recent reforms in that state require new public employees to enter into defined contribution or hybrid plans, a welcome reform.[6]

Part of the unfunded pension problem is structural. Public pensions generally use defined benefit plans rather than defined contribution plans. A defined benefit plan creates a promised stream of pension payouts that markets cannot necessarily ensure, especially when the return assumptions are overly optimistic. But shifting to defined contribution plans can also have drawbacks in terms of both short-term effects (less new money flowing into the pension fund) and longer-term retirement security as the risk shifts to individuals.

Most reforms undertaken by U.S. cities and states to keep pension funds solvent include some combination of structural changes for future workers (defined contribution plans or hybrid plans); changes in benefits, including changes in payout calculations, retirement age, and cost-of-living increases; increased contributions from cities and states; and sometimes temporary catchup investments through pension obligation bonds or public asset sales. Some impressive reforms along those lines have been carried out by the states of Rhode Island and Utah, among others, and by many cities, including San Diego and San Jose.

Reforms also may require a reevaluation of how pension funds are managed, including, for example, whether to use active but higher-fee managers or more passive index funds. While this may not be a simple either-or choice, it brings to light a major problem, that is, the capacity of mayors, county executives, elected treasurers, or governors to understand the options, trade-offs, and risks of various financial investments and strategies. In too many instances public managers, including some on pension boards, do not understand the suitability of their investments.

Fiscal reforms require transparency about the nature of the crisis and the impact if nothing changes. It requires sustained leadership by politicians, union leaders, taxpayers, and civic leaders willing to subject themselves to reputational risk on behalf of the future. It requires shared sacrifice in the way benefits and costs are distributed as part of a solution, and it requires a working partnership between states and localities to help with everything from emergency intervention to changes in rulemaking.

The longer fixes are delayed, the less opportunity there is for public budgets to do the heavy lifting to fund additional future-facing investments. The exemplary case for delay is Illinois, which has gone nearly three years without a state budget, had its bond ratings lowered to near junk bond status, and is testing the waters of bankruptcy, which has no legal precedence for states. Moreover the Illinois State Supreme Court has made it difficult to build a workable compromise by placing legacy expenses ahead of the security position of bondholders.[7]

PRIVATE INVESTMENT INCENTIVES

In the private sector, the barriers to investment have a different source. Capital abounds, but it is not always suitable for certain projects or situations. Over the past forty years, finance has become less place-connected and more directed at short-term profit maximization. Quicker profits have increasingly taken precedence over longer-term investing, and trading in arcane financial instruments has usurped the more tangible economy of production and services. Finance, which has always been viewed as a means to support the real economy, has increasingly become a self-reinforcing system, decoupled from the real economy. As evidence of that trend, a larger percentage of corporate profits is coming from the finance sector than in the past.[8]

For most Americans, the change in finance has hit home in the form of increased levels of household debt and the diminished role of local banks.

The excessive use of debt in America and its acceptance as a fact of everyday life is one of the great cultural shifts of the twentieth century.[9] Along with ordinary consumer goods, Americans increasingly use debt to finance what individuals in other nations may view as public entitlements: education, medical care not covered by insurance, and even retirement (through reverse mortgages).[10] Household debt measured either in terms of its relationship to GDP or to discretionary income drove steadily upward until the 2008 recession, fell back as a period of deleveraging began, and has now returned to its upward climb.[11]

A system of depositors placing savings into local banks that then make business, consumer, and real estate loans in a relatively circumscribed service area is becoming a thing of the past. In its place are a small number of national money center banks (five of which control more than 40 percent of all bank assets), a more numerous group of large regional banks, new technology lending platforms, and nonbank financing companies that specialize in real estate and small business credit.[12]

The loss of independent banks is most acute among community banks, generally viewed today as banks with assets under $10 billion, and especially among the smallest banks in community banking.[13] The social consequences of that loss are significant for some communities, particularly small towns and rural communities. Small banks generally punch far above their weight in terms of small business, agriculture, and real estate lending. They use local market knowledge, including the soft knowledge of relationships, to build portfolios. Smaller local banks have not disappeared, but their numbers are in decline, as are the incentives for new startup banks. Capital is more often aggregated today to organize a private fund than a small bank. The old-fashioned notion of a bank functioning as a kind of community utility has all but disappeared.

The changing nature of finance is also reflected in the rise of new financial instruments that capture household savings, including mutual funds and exchange-traded funds, and connect those savings to Wall Street returns and risks. Households from practically every income group have a stake in the stock and bond markets. The elevation of private equity as a central feature of finance also represents a significant change in global finance, particularly as it relates to the investment focus of institutional and high-net-worth investors. The total global supply of private equity is around $2.5 trillion; but with the leverage used by private equity firms for buyout activities, total capital capacity is much higher. And as with commercial banking, a few very large firms dominate the landscape.[14]

As local leaders grapple with making significant investments in the future, they must work with a financial system that is globally connected in remarkable ways but also disconnected from many essentials needed for local growth. Some of these disconnects are linked to the changing nature of banking, some to the availability of higher-return alternatives, which drives the flow of capital, and some to the overall transition of lending into high-volume securities.

Where the connections exist, modern finance is efficient and plentiful. Capital markets and major banking and investment institutions play a significant role in financing cities through the municipal bond market, in support of those firms able to access publicly traded debt and equity, or through the provision of credit facilities to firms that have a healthy balance sheet. The efficiency of those markets and transactions is undeniable, as are the lower costs and transaction efficiency for most home mortgages and consumer credit transactions. Finance works particularly well in support of consumer goods, from homes to cars to retail sales.

Moreover, the regulatory pressures on banks based on the Community Reinvestment Act (CRA) to meet credit needs in lower- and moderate-income communities should not be overlooked. It has resulted in many billions of dollars in investments. The CRA has led to especially significant capital commitments among large banks, such as Bank of America,

Citi, JP Morgan, and Wells, which are national investors in low-income places as a result of CRA requirements. They became experts—along with many other financial institutions—in deploying debt and tax credit equity to affordable housing projects and to community facilities and small business lending initiatives. As those banks grew, largely by buying other banks, legacy CRA agreements became part of their growth obligations.

But there are major capital gaps not filled by Wall Street or banks because of the size, risk, or boutique nature of the investment or loan or because the sector or area has to be primed through information, new product development, or with capital, which can incur higher risks without necessarily assuming compensating high returns, at least in the short term. This is particularly true in many aspects of small business growth, particularly for early-stage equity investments. America has built a more robust public enhancement and liquidity system to support housing finance than for business investment.

Credit issues also exist in communities where real estate values do not appraise to achieve the right loan to value ratios and for individuals or firms whose credit scores or lack of bank relationships place them in contact with subprime lending sources.

The financing and funding needed to restructure the trajectory of a local economy and create new financial products, from the costs of planning and early-stage investments to the connection back to conventional finance, often requires a very different kind of investment framework than most conventional investors can undertake. This is where metro finance institutions often lend their balance sheets, risk tolerance, and systems-building expertise.

THE BUILDING BLOCKS OF METRO FINANCE

Metro finance does not refer to a specific financial intermediary or product but to a range of experimentation at the intersection of finance, civil society, and the public sector. As civic leaders come up against the boundaries of conventional finance for certain development projects and the lack of fiscal flexibility in local public budgets, they have to identify compensating strategies.

Some of those strategies have to do with the use of federal (sometimes state) tax credits, which enhance the returns for private investors. An industry of tax syndicators has emerged to intermediate between projects and investors using low income housing tax credits, historic tax credits, new markets tax credits, various energy-related credits, and trading carbon offsets. Some of those strategies have to do with capturing future economic value through tax increment financing (TIF).

But increasingly metro finance is less about credits, value appreciation, and offsets and more about the creation of new institutional investors and capital sources that have a stronger connection to place and public purpose. These new institutions and investors have slowly changed the landscape of how we think about development finance.

The role of metro finance is ultimately to attract, deploy, or leverage conventional capital to sectors and places it may be less incented to enter without other sources of capital leading or without structures that create some bridge—through liquidity, direct capital protection, or a reduction in transaction costs—between the capital of conventional investors and the requirements of local development.

The general goal of metro finance is to create products, intermediaries, and leverage that entice conventional capital from the sidelines and extend the capacity and effectiveness of public budgets. The five most important building blocks for metro finance today are (1) philanthropy, (2) civil society capital intermediaries, (3) impact investors, (4) public sector–related investment intermediaries, and (5) major research universities.

These five actors, though others exist, are the best positioned to play this metro finance building block role. Each has the ability to incur financial risk, each has interests over and above the highest return on its investment, and each has extensive private and public sector credibility. These three characteristics—a healthy capital base, a public purpose, and credibility with markets and public sector participants—are fundamental attributes. Following is a brief description of some of the characteristics and roles of the five building blocks.

Philanthropy

The Indianapolis and Pittsburgh stories demonstrate the social change potential of philanthropy. The power of philanthropy derives fundamentally from its financial flexibility and capacity to take risks. Many large private foundations are filling roles left vacant by a lack of public resources or by a private sector no longer focused on a local civic role. As philanthropy does not need a return in its grant-making functions, donors have the flexibility to experiment and incur costs that private capital cannot. This allows private philanthropy to function as a significant point of leverage. Of the leadership institutions common to New Localism, foundations are among the most critical.

All effective philanthropies make use of data and evidence to inform their work. And they have the ability to conceptualize leverage within a strategic framework. But philanthropies that have been particularly important to New Localism have other attributes as well: a willingness to make big bets, the ability to manage reputational risk, a problem-oriented perspective, an interest in using more of their balance sheet to align with their social mission, and a long-term view of social and economic change.

A willingness to make big bets is critical. Some well-known examples here are the Gates Foundation in its work with high schools, the Edna McConnell Clark Foundation with youth-serving organizations, Bloomberg Philanthropy grants to cities that make better use of data, and the Robert Wood Johnson Foundation's work in promoting healthy eating and countering obesity.

Wading into difficult policy issues that can trigger reputational risk sometimes follows from making big bets. The size and publicity of big bets expose philanthropy to a greater degree of scrutiny than does spreading small grants around to hundreds of grantees in different fields. But civic risk is a matter not only of size and notoriety but also of the nature of the problem. The Kresge Foundation's work in Detroit (along with the Ford and the Knight Foundations and several smaller philanthropies) during the fiscal bailout is a good example. There are other examples, including foundations that find themselves embroiled in the contentious debates over urban schools and school choice.

The most effective philanthropy partners in New Localism have to be solution-oriented more than focused on a specific type of grantee or technique. They start by defining problems they want to solve and then design strategies to achieve solutions. By attending to a specific problem and its solution, philanthropies build investment or grant-making hypotheses and identify implementation strategies with partners. Like any investment hypothesis they may turn out to be wrong, but they give rise to organizing principles and implementation processes that can be tested, measured, and redirected.

A problem-solving focus generally means a variety of problem solvers can be found among nonprofit groups, startup companies, academics, and governments. When the Kauffman Foundation in Kansas City turned its attention to reducing the local public school achievement gap it devised a broad array of strategies, from research to grant making to scholarships to new innovations, and a new school that it incubated.

Foundations involved in public purpose finance use more of their balance sheet to support their social mission than the private foundation regulatory requirement of 5 percent of last year's asset level devoted to grants for this year. Pioneering work by the Ford Foundation and the MacArthur Foundation through program-related investments, generally high-risk, low-cost loans to social enterprises, was significant in this regard. Today there are larger mission-related investment commitments—direct from the corpus of foundation assets, not just the returns—being made throughout the philanthropic universe.

This fits well with the solution-centered approach mentioned above. Some approaches need a grant, some need early-stage seed capital, and some need policy advocacy. To the extent to which a full portfolio is viewed as being in service of solutions, it is easier to fund or finance multiple strategies. A number of new social change efforts by donors are organized as limited liability companies and not private endowments, as a way to use a wider variety of tools, from investments to grants to lobbying to operational support.

As philanthropy balance sheets become converted into social change capital, the potential for more multisectoral solutions and partners grows dramatically. Increasingly the family offices of high-net-worth individuals are investing in areas as diverse as climate change and educational technology.

The best philanthropic partners also have a long-term perspective. This is inherent in a financial investment perspective as investments often have a longer-term return horizon. A long-term commitment has sometimes been missing from philanthropy, which may move from issue to issue based on changes in staff, the latest strategic plan, or the most recent consulting firm advice. While philanthropies still have plenty of short-term noise in their portfolios, the best are keepers of a long-term agenda, either in a place or connected to an issue, through funding, social networks, data, and investments.

Civil Society Capital Intermediaries

The rise of new capital intermediaries in civil society is associated with microfinance in the developing world and community development finance in the United States. Microfinance emerged in the developing world as an alternative to the poor record of international aid, to ameliorate the lack of banking services for the poor, and as an investment in the informal economies in Asia, Africa, and Latin America. In the most interesting examples in Bangladesh and elsewhere, microfinance uses social networks as peer-oriented collateral; new loans are contingent on all members of the network being paid up. Despite mixed reviews of microfinance's ability to alleviate poverty in the long term, such loans have elevated the importance of capital-led antipoverty strategies.[15]

In the United States, community development finance grew out of the "war on poverty" programs in the 1960s and the early 1970s with their focus on inner-city enterprise. It took off as the financial system began to change and the federal relationship to cities began to erode in the 1980s. In contrast to microfinance in the developing world, community development finance in the United States is more intent on restoring the real estate value of low-income places through housing and commercial real estate finance than through low-income household enterprise, an approach that in part reflects a different social system and the availability of public subsidies to support development activities.

Among the earliest of these U.S. efforts were national intermediaries such as the Local Initiatives Support Corporation, Enterprise, Neighborhood Housing, and Living Cities. By the 1980s a new breed of local community-based financial intermediaries known as community development financial institutions (CDFIs) emerged. They included regulated banks and credit unions with a low-income development emphasis as well as nonprofit loan funds and a handful of private equity investment funds with a targeted jobs focus. Over the past three decades the number of CDFIs has grown from a few dozen to about 1,000, with total assets of around $110 billion.[16]

Investors and depositors into CDFIs include individuals and institutions motivated by social investment, including philanthropy and religious institutions. The major institutional investors are banks, which invest in CDFIs in large part to meet their Community Reinvestment Act obligations. As banks become larger and less place-based, some CDFIs became a retail outlet for bank requirements to invest in their communities. As CDFIs become more sophisticated they have been able to reach new investors, including insurance companies and pension funds. Some CDFIs are now rated by Standard and Poor's, have access to the bond market, and are members of the Federal Home Loan Bank System.[17]

The big breakthrough for CDFIs occurred in the 1990s when the CDFI Fund was created at the U.S. Treasury Department to provide grants and loans to CDFIs and extend public legitimacy and visibility. This built their balance sheets and allowed them to raise debt at significantly higher levels than before. A decade later, additional incentives and visibility emerged as federal tax policy created new markets tax credits and placed the credit allocation authority at the CDFI Fund. As with low income housing tax credits, created two decades prior, the new markets tax credit uses the tax code to incent private investors. It also creates policy alliances between low-income communities and private investors. National CDFI intermediaries have become major syndicators of private equity into low-income rental housing.

There are other nonbank capital intermediaries that also emerged during this period that do not consider themselves CDFIs in that they do not limit themselves to low-income community development. Many are very effective small business and early-stage technology investors that prioritize specific lending or investment products. Small Business Association (SBA) 504 Loan Program intermediaries are other examples of effective non-CDFI capital sources. Growth Capital in Cleveland, a large SBA lender in Ohio, is a good example.

The impact of the community investment intermediaries can be measured through their direct capital investments in specific places or in certain sectors, such as supermarkets, early childhood centers, or affordable housing. The best function as bridges to the public sector and conventional capital, often building trisectoral capital investment systems that make the flow of capital and subsidy more efficient and predictable.

Impact Investors
The tendency of finance to focus on shareholder value to the exclusion of all else has a counternarrative in what is today called impact investing, broadly defined by the Global Impact Investment Network as "investments into companies, organizations, or funds with the intention to generate social and environmental impact along with a financial return."[18] It can be argued that all investments have some social or environmental impact, but the key word here is *intention*. Impact investors specify the impact they are seeking and try to quantify it within the context of their financial return decisions.

Some impact investors place more emphasis on financial return and others prioritize social return. Some impact investors think it is not necessary to give up any financial return as an impact investor, while others view concessionary pricing as an important part of certain impact sectors.

The term impact investing is new, but the practices have been around for many years through cooperative credit schemes and charitable loan associations. The first banks created in America in 1816—the Provident Institution for Savings in Boston, and the Philadelphia Savings Society— had explicit missions to serve the poor, helping them save and acquire property. Their minutes and articles of incorporation make it clear that they were social institutions as well as financial intermediaries.[19]

Indeed, for many years local banking was not just a downtown or elite phenomenon. Mutual banks, building associations, and credit unions, whose origins were in diverse civic, religious, and ethnic networks, financed the housing stock and small businesses of many late nineteenth- and early twentieth-century urban neighborhoods. In cites in the Northeast and Midwest, small savings societies appeared in every community, using street and neighborhood names for the bank's name. This group includes African

American banks, which emerged from mutual aid networks in African American churches, the only institution reliably owned by that community for a century following emancipation.[20]

Today impact investing has grown into a $60 billion a year global enterprise and is characterized by an increased demand for socially oriented capital and an increasing number and diversity of impact investors. A broader definition of social investment that includes socially screened mutual funds or investments that favor companies with strong ratings in environmental, social, and governance (ESG) standards would show the amount of socially focused capital is somewhere around $3.5 trillion.

Major wealth management firms such as Goldman Sachs and Morgan Stanley employ people expert in impact investments because their clients— philanthropies, university endowments, family offices, and increasingly pension funds—want it. While many of the large investment firms specialize in managing portfolios of publicly traded equities and debt that have positive ESG ratings, those firms are also developing expertise in more boutique private efforts. Many European banks that have been attuned to environmental and consumer issues as developed through the European Union have built very strong portfolios and practices with regard to environmental sustainability.

The integration of social and economic returns is part of today's worldview. There are many reasons for the rise of impact capitalism: consumer insistence on higher levels of corporate responsibility, greater attention to climate change and other environmental issues, concerns with rising levels of social inequality, the popularity of microfinance in the developing world, the increased interest in social enterprise as a way to solve problems, and the expanding vacuum resulting from a changing financial landscape. All of these are factors. But ultimately consumer demand will drive change, as people make informed decisions about how they save money and the social costs of various investment decisions.

The dramatic transfer of intergenerational wealth may turn out to be decisive with respect to impact capital supply and direction. With more than $40 trillion in the United States expected to be transferred from one generation to the next during the first half of the twenty-first century, impact investing may be coming into its own. Whether that happens or not depends largely on the ability of the impact field to issue the products, build the institutions, and make the case over a longer period of time.[21]

Public Sector–Related Investment Intermediaries

The public sector's role in metro finance is based on two principal levers: derisking private capital and using public affiliated agencies and authorities to access the bond market, finance projects, and play direct development and asset management roles. If the public sector wants to extend its capacity, it has to participate in the private market.

The role of the public sector as a derisker of private capital is especially well developed at the national level through a housing finance system that contributed to an expansive homeownership society. Federal Housing Administration and Veterans Administration insurance programs made it easier for households to get mortgages, and the establishment of government-sponsored enterprises created secondary markets and reduced the cost of private capital for consumers. Similarly, SBA loan programs provide large credit enhancements for private small business lenders, both banks and nonbank investors.

This derisking role is also common at the state, county, and municipal levels through small business, housing, and service programs. The value of the public sector in these situations is that it does not have the same pressure from investors with respect to returns and it is motivated by market leverage to make capital go further. While this is in contrast to our perspective on public asset management in a more profit-driven way, there is a role for the public sector to both increase its market position through how it manages certain real assets and open up new capital sources by derisking financial investments that could not be made in other ways. This latter function should especially be employed in situations to benefit people or sectors that have capital access constraints. High-quality public management produces public revenue that can be used for anything; derisking capital should open up market opportunities that would not exist otherwise.

The United States has thousands of public and quasi-public authorities and agencies that manage public assets and can access the bond market through their public status. Many of them also invest directly in civic and private sector projects (apart from bond financing) that span business and housing development of various kinds. While many of these programs are limited by the allocation of subsidy, others have been able to establish self-sustaining loan funds. Indeed, many have become among the most active small business lending organizations in the nation, making use of SBA guarantees. In housing and facilities investments, the state housing finance authorities are major investors in homeownership, mixed-use developments, and multifamily housing.

The mission, governance systems, and relationship to private sources of capital limit some of these public authorities from playing even bigger roles. Many could function more as civic capital intermediaries with deeper investor, developer, and lending relationships. Coupled with their public sector support and tax-exempt bond capacity, the potential would be significant. Some of this is happening today, but it must expand significantly. We are at the beginning of their potential reinvention.

Major Research Universities

Major research universities and medical centers are important participants in metro finance, even though they might not be ordinarily viewed in the same light as the four other building blocks. But they are among the most important place-based investors in many cities and small towns. They hold significant real estate assets, are major employers (and often provide employer housing incentives), attract students with financial aid and loans, generate demand for local housing and related business investment, manage external research dollars with commercializing opportunities, manage private endowments, and are tied to particular communities by history, customers, and real estate. Moreover, they are hybrid institutions, with nonprofit status, major investment portfolios, and a placemaking presence that affects local and national markets.

Universities are also equity investors in businesses. The history of university venture investing is complex and, like all venture investing, has a mixed history. With the exception of Stanford, many of the early funds were linked to medical centers, as at Johns Hopkins and Harvard. There are also examples of venture investment groups that began within university settings and were later spun off as private, nonaffiliated groups (such as ARCH Venture Partners, which was spun off from the University of Chicago in 1968).[22] Some universities partner with professional managers; others bring managers in-house as part of technology transfer programs. A good number of seed funds come from university alumni who view the creation of early-stage funds that benefit students and faculty as a contribution to the university.

Increasingly, major universities have taken more aggressive roles in both reshaping relations between community and campus and investing in startup businesses that emerge from students, faculty, and the related business clusters that congregate in and near university districts. Almost all major research universities have seed funds available for commercialization of research, and a good number of major venture capital funds have links to university engineering, biomedical, and other science disciplines. It is the combined effect of the three principal capital investment aspects of universities—endowment investment, real estate development, and commercialization of research—that makes these institutions central to the public purpose finance efforts of New Localism.

NORMS OF METRO FINANCE

While public purpose finance encompasses thousands of transactions and products across the nation and hence is difficult to discuss as a unified practice, a number of norms have emerged that characterize much of what they do. Five norms in particular are foundational: (1) the importance of civic connectivity, (2) getting private capital supply off the sidelines, (3) aligning interests through social outcomes, (4) making smart use of subsidy, and (5) extracting value from the value created, including that created by the public sector.

Civic Connectivity in Kansas City

Kansas City has one thing that many cities lack: a consensus on where it wants to go. If you speak with people at their Civic Council or Chamber of Commerce, local philanthropy, officials at the University of Missouri at Kansas City, or neighborhood civic leaders, they mention the Big Five, which are the macro-goals set by civic and business leaders to drive change over time. Essentially, there is agreement on what they want to accomplish in five areas: a workforce system for tomorrow, rebuilding urban neighborhoods, making the city the most entrepreneurial in America, growing the region's medical sector, and enhancing the arts community. The Big Five are regional and local, business-oriented and neighborhood-relevant.

One of the progress reports that came out of the Big Five goal-setting prioritized access to capital for Kansas City entrepreneurs. The report delineated the range of capital requirements in terms of early-growth stage investments, as well as other forms of equity and debt financing. The report authors measured the sources and gaps and compared capital investment in Kansas City with investment in other cities. KCSourceLink, a brainchild of Maria Meyers, director of the University of Missouri–Kansas City Innovation Center, produced the report.[23]

Maria Meyers is one of those connectors every city needs. An entrepreneur and civic activist, she makes everyone's list of local influencers because she knows how the place works (and how the place does not work), as well as some of what it needs to move forward.

One thing that struck Meyers as she moved around town speaking to capital sources and small businesses was the conflict of perceptions. Some capital sources told her they were frustrated there were not enough good Kansas City deals. Yet small enterprises, including technology startups, said there was not enough local Kansas City capital.

As she looked at the local deals getting done by angel investors and seed funds, she noticed that what they had in common was credentialing from particular entrepreneurial support groups. Those groups were passing on deals they believed in to sources of capital that believed in them. While this did not mean the deal would get done or that it would succeed, it elevated the possibility of early financing. The missing link in the mystery of whether there was not enough capital or not enough good deals was connectivity on the part of trusted networks. Sitting at the center of the enterprise ecosystem at a university, she was able to maintain credibility on both sides of the investment ledger.

Another thing Meyers noticed was how few early-stage investors sought visibility after making the investments. Perhaps this was a function of midwestern humility or just not wanting to be flooded with requests. Yet what

Kansas City needed, she thought, were investors to help brand the community as a place to make early-stage investments.

Finally, she noted that many gatekeepers to family wealth were not aware of the local opportunities to make investments. Family funds and offices around the country are often idiosyncratic sources of capital, highly personal and private, and this was certainly true in Kansas City. A great deal of money had been made in the city but the connections to local startups were underdeveloped. Kansas City wealth was investing, as could be expected, far more in funds that were concentrated in national business hotspots.

The work she did over the next several years involved promoting visibility, building stronger relationships among family offices and deal flow, and strengthening the linkages between business support groups and seed fund sources. She became the connector, not the aggregator, of capital. Today the amount of early-stage capital in Kansas City is expanding. And as a result of the report on capital gaps, other institutions, including several local banks, are stepping up to solve other problems the report pointed out, including the need to create new small business loan capital.

Getting Supply off the Sidelines in Chicago
Chicago has an active community investment movement that started with the early efforts of South Shore Bank, which inspired President Clinton to create the CDFI Fund, as well their many civic organizing movements connected to mortgage and housing discrimination in the 1970s and 1980s. In Chicago today there are more than a dozen active community investment organizations involved in lending, equity investing, community-building activities, and banking services.

CDFI lending in Chicago aggregates to several billion dollars over the past few decades and includes several banks, specialized housing lenders such as the Community Investment Corporation, loan funds such as the Chicago Community Loan Fund and IFF, national intermediaries such as the Local Initiatives Support Corporation, specialized micro and small business lending funds such as Accion, and credit unions such as the Self-Help Federal Credit Union. The result has been thousands of affordable housing units, millions of square feet of community facilities, and countless neighborhood businesses, child-care centers, charter schools, urban food markets, and energy efficiency projects.

An important catalyst for CDFI lending in Chicago is the MacArthur Foundation, one of the largest American philanthropies and perhaps the most innovative in the nation in terms of impact investing. The MacArthur Foundation is probably best known for its so-called genius awards, but those awards are just a small fraction of its grant making and investments, which are heavily targeted toward global environmental sustainability, poverty reduction, and juvenile justice reform.

MacArthur's managing director and head of impact investing, Debra Schwartz, is among the field's most important alchemists, always trying to figure out ways they can use their balance sheet to move money that is on the sidelines into social change–oriented programs. She can play this role because she acquired a deep background as an investment banker prior to working at the foundation and hence understands the multiple languages of finance, and because the MacArthur Foundation is willing to subordinate its capital to the security interests of conventional investors, whom they want to attract to the impact and community investment fields.

Recently, in partnership with the Chicago Community Trust and the Calvert Foundation, the MacArthur Foundation helped launch Benefit Chicago, a new $100 million fund that is aggregating donor-advised funds, prior to their grant deployment, for local projects in Chicago. The MacArthur Foundation is playing a variety of roles, including providing some credit enhancement for the Calvert Foundation, which is issuing the notes, and also providing a partial liquidity guarantee to match investor and loan maturities.[24] A flexible impact investor such as the MacArthur Foundation is able to help build systems with sophisticated partners by identifying system gaps that need to be filled.

Benefit Chicago wants to demonstrate the ability to move donor-advised grant funds into impact investing. The amount of capital that sits in donor-advised funds in large mutual fund companies that have created gift advisory services, such as Vanguard and Fidelity, is huge. The Chicago effort is one of several emerging mechanisms that seek to direct the short-term investors of donor-advised funds, and mutual funds in general, into various forms of impact investing.

The major constraints to transforming mutual fund assets into longer-term community or urban investment notes has to do with the liquidity investors require and the ability to post asset prices each day. Those issues can be overcome, but it will take the kind of experimentation and product development that are going on in Chicago.

Banks convert short-term deposits into long-term loans through the system of fractional reserves and through access to secondary market sales. But if bank money is not there for certain purposes or if the secondary markets are not available for nonconforming investments, how can other capital investors that may be predisposed to social outcomes but have short-term time horizons play a longer-term lending role? That is what Debra Schwartz and her colleagues are figuring out by experimenting with a variety of civic and private entities.

Aligning Outcomes in Salt Lake City

It would be hard to find a better example of a public purpose finance product than a social impact bond, also called pay-for-success bonds. The reason is that they reflect participation and risk by every sector of society. They are also a very small experiment, still at the margins of finance and public sector focus. They do two important things: they provide significant working capital (which governments cannot generally provide) to scale up promising programs managed by expert agencies, and they give us more information about what programs have evidence-based impact. Sometimes even small efforts from the perspective of capital deployment have significant longer-term meaning, and this may be the case with social impact bonds.

The theory of a social impact bond is simple in design but hard to achieve. It is a contract with the public sector to pay for outcomes that represent success and generally result in savings for the public sector. There are generally four parties to the transaction: a service provider, which receives a significant infusion of capital from investors to provide services; the public sector, which pays for the outcomes as they are realized; an investor group, which provides the upfront capital to the service provider but is repaid only based on the outcomes; and a third-party evaluator, which evaluates whether the outcomes were in fact realized. The goal is to create private incentives for social outcomes that lead to public sector savings and allow for longer-term replication based on what is learned.[25]

In Salt Lake City, a social impact bond was directed toward early childhood learning, seeking to test the theory that higher-quality early learning would result in cost savings later as fewer children would need special education, and hence there would be a reduced societal cost per child. The investors included Goldman Sachs and J. B. Pritzker. They used the local United Way to manage relationships with the early childhood care providers. Every sector of society was involved, including business participation through the United Way board. Investors included a public school district, the state, local nonprofits, and two major national investors. There has been preliminary success, and some bond repayments were made. More data are needed to fully evaluate the impact of the bond.[26]

Pay-for-success bonds are now being explored throughout the United States. They are best used where there is social science to back the strategy, a high-quality provider, and a field in which outcomes can be easily monitored. The first bond was launched in the United Kingdom in 2010, but since that time they have taken off in fifteen nations, with more than sixty transactions in various stages of demonstration or completion.

While the Salt Lake City bond represented a typical pay-for-success format, new experiments are emerging. A recent social impact bond issued in Washington, D.C., does a few things that other social impact bonds have not done to this point: fund environmental infrastructure (with the D.C. Water and Sewer Authority) and function as a tax-exempt bond through a hybrid payment structure. The function of the $25 million bond, which was purchased by the Goldman Sachs Urban Investment Group and the Calvert Foundation, is to construct green infrastructure that slows surges of stormwater, which can result in sewer overflows.

The bond is issued with a predictable payment stream based on expected performance, but it can also generate a premium payment based on greater environmental outcomes, as well as the ability to recapture some of the return if the performance is below expectation. This kind of hybrid bond structure may be extremely important as organizations identify new ways to finance smart infrastructure.[27] Having closed the bond successfully, Quantified Ventures, the intermediary that structured the transaction, is seeking to replicate this work in a variety of other environmental and sustainable agricultural contexts.

Smart Subsidy in Pennsylvania

Dwight Evans is now a U.S. congressman, but before that he served for years in Pennsylvania's General Assembly, rising to lead the House Appropriations Committee. In the 1980s he started out as a community organizer in his West Oak Lane, Northwest Philadelphia community. His section of Northwest Philadelphia is overwhelmingly African American and working class in the Philadelphia row house style of modest homeowners. Congressman Evans used legislation to solve constituent problems and transferred his community efforts into a demonstration platform for replication. His efforts touched on a variety of issues in the 1980s and 1990s, from crime and safety to retail revitalization to schools. In the early 2000s his constituents were frustrated by the lack of fresh and affordable food in the community. He wanted to take action.

In 2004, after years of study and advocacy, Evans helped launch an unusual partnership with the Commonwealth of Pennsylvania; a Philadelphia-based CDFI, the Reinvestment Fund; a nonprofit organization that concentrated on healthy food issues, the Food Trust; and a citywide group that assisted with minority contractor compliance, the Urban Affairs Coalition.

The purpose of the partnership was to finance high-quality grocers to locate to or expand their stores into communities without access to fresh food. Based on research, supermarket operators identified certain costs that made it difficult to enter the market without raising prices above suburban store prices.[28] The goal was to ensure that high-quality stores with the same healthy food options and the same prices could be located in those communities. Supermarket operators told Evans that there were costs in terms of land development, security, higher insurance costs, the higher cost of training workers, and sometimes higher financing costs that resulted in either inferior products, higher consumer prices, or both.

To accomplish the goal of creating high-quality stores with suburban prices and products, the state put up $30 million over three years and the Reinvestment Fund matched the grants with more than $100 million in

private debt and other financing, including new markets tax credit allocations. The debt came through loan syndication from major banks. The
Reinvestment Fund managed both the grant and debt financing; the state
monitored the program, the nonprofit Food Trust ensured that the stores
met the standards of high quality and comparable pricing, and the Urban
Affairs Coalition worked to ensure minority contractor participation.[29]

The grant money was used to subsidize costs that were a barrier to entry,
including workforce training, environmental remediation, and higher infrastructure costs. This was *smart subsidy* because it filled a gap the market
could not. Public subsidy is not useful if it crowds out a market mechanism that could do a comparable job, hides operating inefficiencies, or
has no trajectory for longer-term sustainability (when that is feasible). The
grants were underwritten to make certain they did not play those roles.
The debt financing was used as with any grocery store development for
commercial real estate and business operations.

The Pennsylvania program led to a variety of unexpected national outcomes: the replication of the program in other states, support from the
Obama administration for a national program, and the emergence of entrepreneurs such as Jeff Brown, who benefited from the program and then
went on to found a national nonprofit, Uplift Solutions, to provide assistance to others who want to bring better food options to the inner city.[30]

Extracting Value in Copenhagen
One of the important rules for any kind of metro finance investor is to be
able to have a longer-term advantage in the value of what he or she helps
create. Otherwise the business model of only doing the hard and risky stuff,
without any upside benefit to the social benefit corporation, generally
translates into long-term reliance on external subsidy.

Chapter 6 discussed the remarkable story of Copenhagen's revival over
the past three decades. The story of Copenhagen is also one of norms.
Copenhagen is cleverly extracting value from the value that the public
creates through the building of infrastructure and the promulgation of smart
land use and zoning for assets previously owned by the public. This norm
is followed in the United States but not to the same extent and not for the
same purposes as in Copenhagen and other northern European cities, such
as Hamburg and Helsinki.

U.S. cities and metropolitan areas do use innovative mechanisms to capture upfront the anticipated value appreciation of local property from improved infrastructure, thereby making available resources to finance the market-shaping improvements. Many cities already use tax increment financing to support infrastructure projects by borrowing against the future stream of additional tax revenue the project is expected to generate. For example, a TIF was used to finance infrastructure improvements for the Atlantic Station project in Atlanta, a streetcar in Portland, and urban renewal projects in Fort Worth. Many cities also use land use and zoning changes to enhance the market value of properties in downtown, midtown, and waterfront areas, thereby unleashing private investment.

The TIF model has been used by many U.S. cities to spur urban regeneration. But for city building it is inferior to the institutional mechanisms used in Copenhagen and elsewhere. TIFs use the value of projected tax revenues to support district infrastructure and economic development, thus preventing future taxes to flow to schools, parks, and other critical services. Copenhagen, by contrast, uses the value of projected land sale revenues to support district *and* citywide infrastructure and economic development, thus preserving future taxes and value appreciation for needed services.

Extracting value from the value that a metro finance transaction creates runs counter to the logic of some involved in public purpose finance. They view their role largely as catalytic to private capital. But a balance has to be reached between transferring and capturing value so that the social intermediary or public affiliate can sustain itself over time and therefore have a platform for continued impact.

METRO FINANCE NEXT

The norms we discussed above each focus on ways to identify higher levels of investment, sustainability, and replication. They are more than transactions. Each transaction—civic connector, the donor-advised fund modeling, pay-for-success bonds, the integration of subsidy, private debt, and civic capital, and Copenhagen's public asset management strategy—is transferable and creates new investment opportunities. Each has the potential to bring in additional private capital either directly through the transaction, or through multiplier investments (as in Copenhagen), or by creating models that the private sector will run with in the absence of other metro finance inputs.

Metro finance in its many forms is leading to expansive forms of social and conventional investment throughout the nation. Cities and states are creating credit enhancement programs that allow lenders to more easily finance early-stage land acquisition or pay for predevelopment costs. Foundations are enhancing structured finance pools to meet a variety of capital gaps in real estate, small business, and retail strategies. Entrepreneurs are creating socially motivated investment funds to redevelop former industrial sites and turn them into multi-use commercial and residential communities, using subordinated debt instruments from impact investors. Major investment houses such as Bain Capital and UBS are launching or sponsoring double bottom-line (financial and social returns) investment funds.

Those in metro finance have learned how to function as financial chefs over the past several decades, using every available ingredient in the civic and public kitchen to bring in private participants and extend the capacity of the public sector. In so doing they have built new capacities to direct capital in increasingly efficient ways toward public purpose solutions. The problem is that not enough of these efforts are at the scale needed to accelerate change. If New Localism is to thrive, the activities that have evolved over the past four decades need to achieve greater scale and impact. This means that their focus will have to be adopted by greater numbers of market participants and the level of institution building will have to scale up significantly.

In the next chapter we turn from what has emerged over the past four decades to what must be developed over the next few decades if New Localism is to succeed.

NINE

Financing the Future

You do the math. You solve one problem and you solve the next one, and then the next. And if you solve enough problems, you get to come home.

—Matt Damon as Mark Watney, *The Martian* (2015)

Now is a time for bold ideas. Markets have revalued city growth at the same time that national politics has led to a devolution of authority to cities and the networks of actors within them. The leaders of New Localism need to think with clarity and ambition. In this chapter we lay out a provocative agenda for supporting and scaling up the most critical investments needed in cities around the United States in the areas of innovation, infrastructure, and inclusion. The right investments in terms of scale, quality, and public value require civic and public decisionmakers with a long-term view of growth and the ability to negotiate complex transactions.

Economic competitiveness and social cohesion require intentional investments in innovation, infrastructure, and inclusion.

Innovation investments support the commercialization of research so that scientific discoveries can perpetuate the testing, deployment, and adoption of next-generation technologies. Innovation is also accelerated through support for business ecosystems and for institutions and places that enable the organic collision of people and ideas across different institutions, businesses, and practices.

Investing in infrastructure must begin with the retrofitting of crumbling twentieth-century physical infrastructure (water and sewer systems, energy grids, and freeways that are coming to the end of their useful life) and the creation of new transit and communication systems aligned with the twenty-first-century economy and lifestyles.

Including a broader segment of society in economic growth requires better opportunities for children through investments in quality early education, more effective schools, and cutting-edge post–high school skills training—that is, a new social contract with young people. The reinvention of public purpose finance has a role to play by bringing more people into the financial services mainstream.

As described throughout this book, many on-the-ground investments are turning around communities and cities. Three drivers are necessary for these changes: one predominantly civic, a second predominantly private, and a third predominantly public. In turn, each sector catalyzes, shapes, and generates capacity for the others.

Civic capital transformations rooted in metro finance must increase in scale and, in some instances, refocus on new opportunities and needs. The importance of those transactions and intermediaries will not recede as communities gain more market traction. Civic and public capital is crucial as the first mover and as the guardian of public interest. Metro finance is leading to self-sustaining institutions able to manage market and public purpose requirements in increasingly sophisticated ways. Many of the major nonbank capital intermediaries will reach capitalization levels that make them important market participants over the next decade. As such, their ability to increase the level of economic inclusion through financial services is vital.

Revaluing cities with market-based capital offers greater opportunity to channel global capital into the rebuilding of larger parts of American cities and towns, stretching from the downtown, midtowns, and innovation districts into older residential neighborhoods and industrial districts. However, civic and public leaders must ensure that market investments have long-term value, are inclusive, and are environmentally sustainable.

The public sector has to step up significantly to meet the demands of the future. Better management of public assets will generate higher levels of public wealth. Disparate learning systems, from early childhood care to K–12 to post–high school career placement, should be forged into a meta-system accountable for results. Some public institutions developed in a prior era of growth have to be restructured.

To scale investments in innovation, the following are needed:

- *Innovation districts 2.0:* Building on recent real estate and business development trends, universities and others should market innovation districts as a unified investment sector, enabling more private capital to flow to the heart of city and metropolitan economies.

- *Regional investment funds:* Institutional endowments, impact investors, and public entities should capitalize regional investment funds at a significant level to promote business growth using a variety of equity and debt instruments and to function as sources of liquidity and investment for smaller metro finance business investors.

To scale investments in infrastructure, the following are needed:

- *Infrastructure investments:* Local government should detail transformative infrastructure projects and market them to public and private sources of capital. Investment intermediaries can help governments finance public projects in cost-effective ways. Local jurisdictions should also consider bundling projects with their peers to have greater leverage in the capital markets.

- *Public asset corporations:* New public asset corporations must be organized to capture more public wealth and reinvest it into local infrastructure. All public authorities must be better aligned in the pursuit of long-term growth strategies.

To scale investments in inclusion, the following are needed:

- *Investments in children:* A national campaign led by cities and counties must reorganize educational investments based on cradle-to-career life-cycle milestones and cross-system agreements. Only through clarity of strategy and commitment to effectiveness can additional public and private investments be raised to achieve campaign goals.

- *Local lenders of first resort:* Significant growth is required for public purpose banks and nondepository capital intermediaries, with the goals of bringing people into the financial services mainstream and increasing the supply of affordable housing.

INNOVATION DISTRICTS 2.0

Urban innovation districts have emerged as a new spatial platform for the invention, deployment, and prototyping of new technologies, products, and processes. These clustered districts represent small geographies, often not more than one square mile in size, in which are colocated advanced research institutions, mature companies, small entrepreneurs, and specialized intermediaries that focus on nurturing businesses, supplying skilled workers, and creating magnetic places. This concept stems from specialized centers of excellence such as the Robotics Institute in Pittsburgh or BioCrossroads in Indianapolis.

Unlike the exurban and suburban research parks of the 1960s and 1970s, these innovation districts are multi-use, open, and connected to the broader city and metropolis by transit and other infrastructure. They offer vibrant and vital gathering spaces that knit people, products, and ideas together. They also represent the convergence and reinvention of three spatial archetypes in American culture: the downtown, the suburban office park, and the college campus.

Innovation districts can be found throughout the nation: in Indianapolis, Pittsburgh, Austin, Atlanta, Birmingham, Buffalo, Cambridge, Philadelphia, Phoenix, Providence, St. Louis, and Winston-Salem. In all of these places, research universities, medical complexes, and clusters of technology and creative firms are sparking business expansion, as well as residential and commercial growth.

Innovation districts are supported through a variety of finance mechanisms. In Oklahoma City and St. Louis, tax increment financing was used to provide the necessary capital for district infrastructure investments. In Atlanta and Pittsburgh, the balance sheets of major universities, such as Georgia Tech and Carnegie Mellon, were used to acquire land and expand research and other facilities. In Philadelphia, a major real estate investment trust (REIT) and Drexel University joined forces to develop Schuylkill Yards.[1]

Market-rate developers of commercial real estate and major investors increasingly view these areas as the business parks of the future. Innovation districts were a scattered phenomenon without generalizable content and activity just a few years ago. Now urban innovation districts can be marketed as a single investment sector that enables the flow of institutional capital interested in long-term value appreciation and returns. This is an asset that REITs, pension funds, and others are following with interest.

A good example is King's Cross in London. A sixty-seven-acre former industrial site, King's Cross was fundamentally revalued by the decision in 1996 to locate the Channel Tunnel Rail Link at St. Pancras station in central London. When the owners of King's Cross—London and Continental Railways Ltd. (a subsidiary of the U.K. government) and DHL—decided to develop the land, they selected Argent and ultimately formed the King's Cross Central Limited Partnership.[2] The approved plans call for twenty-five new buildings, twenty new streets, ten major public spaces, and the restoration of twenty historical buildings and up to 2,000 homes. In September 2011 the University of the Arts–London moved to Granary Square, the center of the King's Cross area. Since then, restaurants and retail establishments have opened and, most notable, Google is building a vast headquarters capable of housing 7,000 staff.

Google's announcement reflects the convergence of possibilities represented by these new innovation hubs. Google's chief executive, Sundar Pichai, described the significance of it: "Increasingly, for the kinds of complex things we do, we need to bring people who are across many disciplines—with many different backgrounds—together to solve problems. That's how you can build newer things."[3]

In January 2015, the U.K. government and DHL announced the sale of their investment in the King's Cross redevelopment to Australian Super, Australia's largest pension fund. The fund manages more than $91 billion (in Australian dollars) of member assets on behalf of more than 2 million members from across 210,000 businesses.[4]

Pensions such as Australian Super recognize the synergistic effect of disparate investments that strengthen and reinforce each other's value. This is a major departure from the status quo, in which large commercial banks and government agencies compartmentalize all aspects of financing (equity investments, lending, grants) even though the targets of these investments (such as housing, infrastructure, or small business) may be physically located in small geographies and interact in a way that enhances value for each of the disparate elements.

In the same way that investors and developers seek certain types of properties or specialize in certain developments—from business parks to golf courses, from hotels to suburban housing tracts—the innovation district is a quantifiable real estate asset that commercial developers such as REITs or other investors will specialize in over time.

As the districts become their own investment class in which investors and developers calculate risk, return, and time horizon, the organizers of the districts—universities, medical centers, philanthropies, technology companies, and the public sector—have to market and manage the districts to ensure long-term advantage. A design strategy that will make the districts part of a walkable city with quality public spaces and multi-use opportunities has to be articulated. This is an opportunity to reinvent major parts of a city; such opportunities do not come about frequently. The market capital is there, but it must be leveraged with the right civics and purpose.

REGIONAL INVESTMENT FUNDS

While there has been a diffusion of venture financing from traditional hotspots on the coasts and a few university towns, many cities are still in need of more early-stage and even growth-stage equity, as well as some types of early-stage debt. Most cities have existing public economic development investors, university-linked incubators, angel investors, and a small number of venture funds. They also have a variety of metro finance sources for debt financing in support of small business development. However, they are often inadequate to meet demand. To solve the lack of early- and growth-stage capital, we favor the development of regional investment funds that are privately managed, with investment support from local institutions with an economic and civic commitment to place.

The past decade witnessed greater diffusion of the support infrastructure for the startup community and small enterprises than has been reflected in the aggregation of capital for those same purposes. Said differently, demand is being generated today that needs more capital to realize the best opportunities. That proposition has to be proven through a market analysis of whether existing demand would really pass muster with investors, whether there is local capital on the sidelines that can be organized for these purposes, and what business sectors make the most sense to back with the right investment and advisory capacities.

There is an institutional base of support for regional investment funds, if aggregated by the right private managerial expertise and business strategy. Investors include family offices, university endowments, impact investors, and philanthropy. Public recognition of vibrant startup companies and economic development agencies that are already doing early-stage investing helps build momentum.

Regional investment funds could have a window for both early-stage equity and small business debt. On the equity side, they could focus on deal flow coming from universities, medical centers, and the local technology startup community. They could participate with existing economic development investors who already have a strong deal flow and investment process but need to have their capital capacity extended. Equity investments could be made at the early stage through convertible debt, as well as through more growth-stage investments. The exact portfolio and products would be shaped to the requirements of the region, including the innovation districts and the broader economic system.

The availability of debt originations by the regional investment fund may be less needed in some markets, but not in all places. The capacity to use debt by the regional investment funds would diversify risk. Moreover, debt could also be used to recapitalize existing smaller civic capital funds or to buy their portfolios and give them more liquidity.

The structure of a regional investment fund could take a variety of forms, including the traditional partnership used by venture capital or a corporation that sells equity and debt positions with various rights and security. It would be profit- and place-focused and would have as its central mission the growth of regional business activity.

Like any major fund, the regional investment fund would seek coinvestment relationships with investors that have aligned interests in building strong companies and providing competitive returns to their own investors. It would also encourage additional investors to form funds or make parallel investments. While the size of the fund should reflect the ability to deploy capital in the designated business space, the fund should be large enough to warrant strong deal flow, send the right market signals, and increase the capacity of smaller but effective metro finance partners.

INFRASTRUCTURE INVESTMENTS

It is a truism of American public policy that the nation suffers an infrastructure-financing gap to pay for managing the old and developing the new. Yet America requires an infrastructure compatible with the next wave of urban living and business innovation. Although infrastructure became a popular platform theme for both parties during the 2016 presidential campaign, most public infrastructure finance comes from state and local sources and not the federal government. Increasingly, infrastructure investments also come from private sources that use fees, rents, or tolls from bridges, highways, airports, or utilities to repay the investments over a period of time.

Rebuilding America's infrastructure is a herculean task that will need public and private investors and strong local managers. Global funds want to get out the bulldozers. In fact, the next wave of private investments in U.S. infrastructure may well come from global pension funds like those in Canada, such as the Ontario Teacher's Pension Plan, the Ontario Municipal Employees Retirement Fund, and the Canada Pension Plan Investment Board.

Among global pension funds, those in Canada and Australia have dominated infrastructure investing. The Canadian model of infrastructure investing has been through direct investments more than through external fund managers. Thus far these funds have had success and, in the process, built deep knowledge of managing infrastructure projects over the long term. It is possible that Canadian pension funds, which invest in infrastructure projects around the world, will invest directly in the United States or partner with American pension funds to coinvest.

Some large American pension funds, among them the AFL-CIO fund and CalPERS, make impact investments in housing finance and environmental funds. In general, however, the American landscape of pension funds suffers from the same fragmentation as our public authorities. Even with the lion's share of pension fund assets, U.S. funds are mostly inefficiently managed and unable to aggregate the capital for transformative investments. Illinois, among the worst states in the nation in terms of unfunded pension liabilities, has 457 governmental pension funds.[5]

Pension funds, sovereign wealth funds, and specialized infrastructure funds are critical for rebuilding America. Cities and urban counties are going to have to negotiate complex financing and management arrangements with these funds. Many places are not prepared for those negotiations and will need the assistance of intermediaries and advisers.

Incurring market interest will involve prioritizing public infrastructure needs according to public safety and use priorities, followed by projects that can be transformative in terms of everything from transportation to the reclamation of ports and waterways. Especially with global capital, the potential for transformation is greater than simple repairs.

The public sector has to wade through the various public-private partnership models that exist and understand where they are or are not applicable to their situation. These models cannot be applied without significant due diligence and the right internal capacity. Yet they are essential because there is not enough public money to fund infrastructure needs through public grants or the public bond market.

Where will the sophistication come from, and how will smaller public entities in particular negotiate the capital markets? Sometimes the best approach is for localities to band together. Several early examples of cities acting as collectives are worth noting.

In 1986, a group of cities in Sweden joined together to create Kommuninvest. The goal of this new institution was to create financial instruments that served the disparate needs of individual cities. Ninety percent of Sweden's municipalities and regional councils are now members and are able to access low-cost capital for a wide variety of infrastructure projects. As the *Financial Times* reported, "The philosophy behind Kommuninvest is simple—big is better, because size provides the necessary muscle to compete in the capital markets. Sweden's local authorities can raise money more cheaply by joining forces under the Kommuninvest umbrella than on their own."[6]

Over the years, Kommuninvest has innovated a variety of products. Multiple municipalities are able to issue joint bonds, enabling them to raise substantially more capital than they could individually. In recent years the company has pioneered green financial instruments. Kommuninvest also invests heavily in knowledge transfer and represents municipalities and regional councils on issues of financing and debt management.

In the United States, cities and counties are beginning to organize based on shared assets, which can be bundled together, allowing investors to invest in a portfolio of projects to lower risk and provide safer returns. As the National Association of Counties has observed, counties are beginning to move to a bundled approach to retrofit structurally deficient bridges rather than proceed one project at a time. Northampton County, Pennsylvania, for example, recently entered into a public-private partnership with a private construction firm to retrofit thirty-three bridges. The approach will potentially save the county between 20 and 30 percent per bridge.[7] This pooled approach is critical since counties invest more than $100 billion annually in roads, bridges, transit, water systems, and other public infrastructure. Incredibly, counties build and maintain 45 percent of public roads and 40 percent of bridges.

One initiative under way involves consortia of cities that share natural assets because of their location along waterways. In the past, organizations such as the Great Lakes and St. Lawrence Cities Initiative and the Mississippi River Cities and Towns Initiative were created to represent the mutual interests of waterway cities before the federal government. These organizations, and others, such as the Chesapeake Bay Foundation and the San Joaquin River Partnership, were particularly adept at gaining earmarks for related projects.

With earmarks eliminated and Washington scaling back, consortia have evolved to meet current demands. The Mississippi River Cities and Towns Initiative, for example, has approached large institutional investors who are looking for projects that are sustainable, resilient, and complement the ecological assets of the Mississippi River. Research has shown that these kinds of projects tend to be cheaper, have more benefits, last longer, are less risky, and have a larger return on investment over a longer period.

Another example of organizational evolution can be found in the rise of intermediaries to bridge the gap between innovative city projects and institutional capital. Many urban transactions—the recapitalization of public housing; the retrofit of metropolitan transit systems; the redevelopment of rail stations, rail yards, waterfronts, and other major underutilized parts of the metropolitan core; the shift to low carbon energy use—require capital that is multilayered and multisectoral. Intermediaries are essential to help cities understand the possibilities and complexities of sophisticated finance deals so that transformative projects can be delivered efficiently and effectively.

A new multicustomer intermediary capable of using real projects on the ground to inform federal infrastructure policies as they are being crafted is important. While philanthropy and the public sector, along with some private investors, helped to build intermediaries to rebuild neighborhoods, intermediation that links capital markets and the broadest public purpose for infrastructure is necessary.

Infrastructure is a complex business, comprised of multiple investment sectors as diverse as a water treatment plant, a river or lake reclamation, an airport or port expansion, a road, rail, or transit hub retrofit, a rail station redevelopment. Digital technologies serve them all. Yet each is different in terms of project design, revenue streams, and market impacts, and in how they are governed, regulated, owned, and operated. As such, federal plans for infrastructure often are not responsive enough to local needs and concerns.

What if we reversed the process to flow from the local level to the federal?

What if several governors, mayors, and county executives, from across both parties, nominated a group of emblematic projects? A trusted intermediary—perhaps a newly formed entity co-owned by the existing constituency groups representing state and local elected officials—could use a uniform template that made the business case for each project and then sorted out options for federal financing. In this way, Congress could ultimately enact legislation and provide tools fit to purpose and designed to succeed.

Infrastructure should not, of course, be the only domestic policy subject to reverse engineering. States, cities, and counties should be consulted, at a minimum, on health care, housing, and education reforms.

Other federal republics have structured ways for local knowledge to inform and guide national policy. In Germany, city-states such as Hamburg and Berlin have representation in the national legislature and the right to initiate legislation. In Denmark, cities actually engage in negotiations with the national government on annual budgets.

U.S. local needs cannot be left to a federal government that is increasingly removed from the reality of how the world actually works.

THE PUBLIC ASSET CORPORATION

As the Copenhagen model shows, the ownership and management of public assets—land, buildings, ports, airports—is one of the most critical tools that cities have in the modern era to generate capital for a wide range of transformative projects, as well as to fund their basic operating budgets.

Over the past 100 years, the governance of public assets has become inordinately fragmented and complex. Many U.S. communities have multiple, often independent public institutions that own and manage public assets. The list of these institutions—airport authorities, port authorities, water and sewer authorities, convention center authorities, stadium authorities, redevelopment authorities, parking authorities, public housing authorities, land banks, public school boards—is long and differs across states and regions. They are often established by legal, governance, and operating mandates that limit collaboration and profitable management incentives.

The origins of semi-autonomous public institutions are well documented. In some cases they were designed to prevent the corruption of urban political machines and take power away from certain racial and ethnic groups; in other cases they were incorporated to obtain federal resources; in still other cases, they were designed to garner the efficiency effects of institutions that had specialized expertise based in distinct segments of the urban ecosystem. In recent decades, special-purpose entities have grown to circumvent onerous state restrictions on taxation and borrowing.

Here is the challenge. When multiple public authorities are powerful, the power of the broader public may actually be diminished. Specialized institutions often act in their own self-interest rather than the interest of the collective.

A robust academic literature has developed with regard to the fragmentation of general-purpose local governments within counties and metropolitan areas. A sharp focus on special-purpose government is equally critical and urgent during a period when fiscal responsibilities are devolving.

The bottom line: over the past century, the emergence of separate public institutions has chipped away at the concentration of political power in cities. This could be a time for consolidating some of those separate entities to aggregate and rationalize public assets and to offer the potential for generating new sources of revenue, as was done in Copenhagen. Yet reforming, rationalizing, and restructuring public institutions will not be easy. In many cases, special purpose authorities are creatures of state law and relate to separate state agencies and legislative committees. States rarely eliminate what they create.

In the near term, cities will be best served by complete transparency on the ownership of public assets by disparate institutions. This will enable the leadership of these institutions—which either include or are appointed by county executives, mayors, governors, or other elected officials—to start aligning the functions and strategic value of the assets informally.

Transparency and alignment are merely the first step. As prior chapters have discussed, the theory and practice of public asset management must change. The Copenhagen model works because the public sector partici- pates for the long term, reaping benefits as value naturally appreciates. The Copenhagen model also works because the public, private, and civic owners of assets understand current land patterns and imagine new ones.

Many U.S. cities are pocked by prior legacy uses—tow pounds, rail yards, warehousing, and department stores—that either are no longer needed or could be relocated given economic restructuring and population shifts. The potential for smart public-private land swaps and joint partnerships are limitless as the cores of metropolitan areas are revalued and remade.

At the heart of the issue is the need to create one or more public asset corporations within cities and counties that do function like Copenha- gen's CPH City & Port Development: managing public assets without political interference, delivering better returns on those assets, and, when capital is available, investing that capital back in local infrastructure. This will be the hardest thing for the U.S. public sector to do, but it has become increasingly necessary. Once it is done and there are tangible public benefits, customer and voter demand for greater levels of transfor- mation will more likely ensue.

INVESTMENTS IN CHILDREN

The institutional infrastructure that invests in children is both vast and fragmented, too often working without a common set of metrics beyond statewide testing requirements, licensing procedures, or a few independent

ranking studies. In fact, few cities or counties know the full extent of
what they spend, and how effective the investments are, in a range of areas
related to children. Most communities cannot produce a meaningful report card.

There are hundreds of different early childhood centers, some with
public subsidies and others that are fully private. There is a K–12 system
that in many cities is increasingly decentralized by a variety of school
management arrangements. There are private schools, mazes of after-
school and summer educational programs, school-to-career programs, and
a social service infrastructure that deals with foster children, homeless
families, and a variety of behavioral health issues. Many of those social
service budgets manage programs through community-based nonprofit or
for-profit firms. There are community colleges and technical schools. And,
to further complicate the picture, the juvenile justice system imprisons or
institutionalizes many teenagers and young adults, who will ultimately be
released with limited opportunities.

Very few cities have a clear grasp of the performance of these disparate
systems, beyond their basic legal compliance. While the local public sector
may manage most of these systems, capital flows from different budgets.
Since many of those budgets have distinct mandates, multisystem planning
is a challenge.

To deal with this fragmentation, many mayors and county executives
have created children's commissions or children's cabinets to better organize data and budgets, integrate strategies, manage gaps and redundan-
cies, and issue public report cards regarding the state of children's health
and well-being. The value and depth of the children's budgets and commission vary greatly from the cosmetic to the deeply substantive.

We favor this intentional approach to understanding where the gaps are,
and, most important, we favor building a system of milestones based on
strong results. The goals should prioritize long-term achievement. We know
what works. Whether the goals are based on the Brookings Social Genome Model (our preference) or on some other strategy, the path forward
must be data-based and accountable.

Ultimately, we need a city-driven national campaign for economic inclusion to raise the resources and investments on behalf of children. Imag-

ine cities and counties committing to a national Children's Accord! Like the Paris Climate Agreement, it would commit cities and counties to clear goals (grounded in real evidence) and would hold places accountable through uniform metrics. As with the climate response, a substantial emphasis would be placed on capturing and codifying proven innovations, so that a smart solution invented in one city or county could be adopted and adapted to other places quickly and effectively. And as with the climate response, a commitment to uniform data and measurement would ultimately enable insights that could be routinized from place to place, enumerating projected returns on investment for example.

Public referenda represent the best, most democratic vehicle for raising needed funds. In recent years, voters in communities as disparate as Broward County, Florida, Dayton, Ohio, King County, Seattle, and San Antonio, Texas, have agreed to pay additional taxes that can generate hundreds of millions of dollars in local revenues to provide children with high-quality early education and other proven strategies. But such referenda are best supported with a clear accounting of the resources currently available and how those resources will be managed toward greater levels of effectiveness and accountability.

The role of mayors, county executives, and other local elected officials in leading referenda contests is of particular note. Mayors and county leaders bring multiple skills that are particularly useful in the successful waging of campaigns. They have expertise in message development and communication. They are skilled at building coalitions across disparate constituencies. And they know how to get out the vote.

Dayton's mayor Nan Whaley put all these skills to work in 2016 when voters approved Issue 9, mandating a quarter of a percent income tax increase, to fund greater access to preschool for the city's four-year-olds. In Dayton, "access to high quality pre-school had been a local conversation for almost a decade," said Ariel Walker, senior policy aide to the mayor. "It became clear that without a local funding champion, the program would continue to be a dream."

Mayor Whaley became that outspoken champion. Armed with strong data indicating the need for and benefits of greater access to preschool programs and a successful pilot program, she was able to garner the support of more conservative organizations, such as the chamber of commerce and traditionally liberal groups, among them labor unions and the NAACP. The measure is expected to raise about $11 million annually for preschool programs, and also will provide funding to law enforcement, emergency response services, road maintenance, and city parks.

States can be helpful here as well. Florida has a unique arrangement that allows counties to create independent bodies with taxing powers to administer a wide range of services for children and youth. These children's services councils have been approved by voters in eight counties. They are generally funded by property taxes of up to 50 cents per $1,000 of assessed property value.[8] Two of the largest counties, Broward and Palm Beach, generate close to $100 million per year through the levy.[9] Funding goes to a full spectrum of cradle-to-career activities. In 2014 the Children's Services Councils were challenged in the state legislature, and counties were forced to hold a vote on whether the councils should be reapproved. Every county that has held a vote has reauthorized its council, with approval rates ranging from 78 percent to 86 percent.

In 1992 the state of Missouri passed legislation that allows counties to create tax levies to expand mental health services for young people. Eight counties have elected to create these levies through a sales tax, and over $100 million has been funneled to mental health services for children.[10] In 2012, 57 percent of voters in Boone County approved its "Putting Kids First" initiative, which increased sales taxes by a quarter of a percent and established the Boone County Children's Services Fund. In 2015 the Children's Services Fund supplied $6.5 million for services including mental health screenings for every child in the Boone County public school system, thousands of hours of counseling and therapy for troubled youth, and training for over 1,000 mental health professionals.[11]

LOCAL LENDERS OF FIRST RESORT

The public's trust in the financial services system cratered during the run-up to the recession and in the period since. The resentment over the sub-prime mortgage fiasco and the bank bailout led to the establishment of new rules regarding risk and a new consumer financial bureau. But the major legislative overhauls did not result in any large scale re-thinking of the public purpose of banking itself or whether the old system of local depositories had to be re-invented. Moreover, as is true with many financial downturns, the global recession of 2008–09 enabled higher levels of consolidation in the banking industry.

For all of the hearings on Capitol Hill, not enough changed. On the positive side, higher capital standards and better stress tests were put into place and systemic risk oversight was given a home at the Federal Reserve Bank. And the Consumer Financial Protection Bureau, which came about as a result of the Dodd-Frank Wall Street Reform and Consumer Protection Act of 2010, has successfully negotiated a better deal for many consumers. On the negative side, some of the new regulations made it more difficult for community banks to compete because they could not incur regulatory costs. And as always, regulation after a crisis places too much weight on avoiding the problems of the past and not enough on organizing solutions for the future.

The cynicism about finance and its disconnect from Main Street did not go away. If anything, bitterness continued to simmer during the 2016 campaign season. Consumer resentment has led to several things.

First, there has been a significant increase in the role of American credit unions, with combined assets of over $1 trillion and more than 100 million customers. But as with banks, the actual number of credit unions is in decline, even while participation overall has increased. It is noteworthy that among the largest community development financial institutions in the United States is a credit union (Self-Help) with branches in California, Illinois, Virginia, Florida, and North Carolina and another one (Hope) with branches throughout the Mississippi Delta and Gulf Coast.

Second, consumer anger has likely contributed to the wider acceptance of nonbank financial transactions. While fintech companies are largely unproven in terms of their algorithms and retail tactics, some have used anti-banking sentiment to rally consumer favor. Some of their advertisements have an almost populist flavor regarding the banking industry. At the same time, their sales tactics and financing costs can create significant problems for small business borrowers unaware of the real cost of the loans, despite being pleased by the speed and ease of the transaction.

And third, there has been increased interest around the country in advocating for financial institutions that have more public purpose. This calls to mind another period of populism when the only real public bank in America, the Bank of North Dakota, was formed. The establishment of the Bank of North Dakota came about in 1919 as a way for farmers to get better leverage against high-priced lenders from out of state. The bank has been consistently profitable, including during the recession of 2008, and still manages the assets of the state and makes participation loans to businesses, farmers, students, and homeowners, as well as infrastructure loans.

Managing public banks can be difficult, and there are many examples of public bank failures throughout the world. The same political cronyism that sometimes emerges with public authorities can occur with a publicly owned bank: excessive self-dealing, poor underwriting, and politically motivated staffing. The issue is always how to professionalize governance and staffing and keep politics out of lending and asset management. But there are also many examples of public banking working well, including in Germany, where there are eleven regional banks and scores of municipal banks. The total public banking assets in Germany amount to well over $1 trillion.

The United States today is unlikely to create publicly owned banks. But there is a growing space for CDFIs and public benefit banking corporations. The former include banks with a community development mission and the later represent the B Corp movement, which designates companies as benefit corporations if they can demonstrate a broader beneficiary practice, over and above shareholder value. B Corps are an actual legal designation in many states and nations.

A variety of banks in the United States are either community development or B Corp companies, including Sunrise Bank in Minnesota, Amalgamated Bank in New York, Beneficial State Bank in Oakland, California, and Virginia Community Capital, to name a few. Many are doing remarkable things by opening up financial services to those who may have been excluded in the past. The public sector could certainly elevate many of these banks by doing business with them, including using them as depositories to the extent financially feasible.

The most sophisticated of the nondepository capital intermediaries among CDFIs, SBA lenders, and public economic development authorities are at an inflection point in their growth. The strongest have assets of several hundred million or more. Many have invested more than $2 billion over the past few decades, they have strong balance sheets in terms of capital ratios and hence are likely underleveraged, and an increasing number have active bond market, Federal Home Loan Bank memberships, or SBA lending authority. Many have become expert at the management of bank loan consortia and the organization of public and private systems that integrate public subsidy and private debt around particular project types, such as child-care centers and affordable housing developments.

The nondepository capital intermediaries will be able to scale up if they can do the three things that have constrained their growth in the past: improve earnings as a way to eliminate dependence on subsidy while still meeting the mission standards of the organization, build stronger technology systems as a way to reduce transactions costs, and improve the quality of treasury functions as they become more interest rate sensitive on both sides of their balance sheet. All three of these can be accomplished as they increase assets under management and loan production.

It will be easier to scale up if the support system for those public purpose entities—philanthropies, the public sector, and impact investors—invests heavily in their transition from niche investors to midsized financial intermediaries.

One key to this transformation, just as with the regional investment funds, is connecting the impact investment field with community investment. It would seem that they would be naturally aligned, but impact capitalism has concentrated on equity investing in environmental issues far more than on debt financing and the placemaking products of small businesses and real estate. The community investment institutions and public authorities with active loan portfolios are in a position to connect these worlds but will need to market themselves in new ways to do so.

It is likely that within a decade there will be a significant number of nondepository community investment institutions with a billion or more in assets under management that are able to focus on larger transactions, particularly in real estate development.

The two most mission-critical issues for public purpose banking and finance are increasing the supply of affordable housing—for homeowners and renters—and bringing more people who are outside the conventional financial system into a stable credit relationship. Even in those cities not experiencing widespread gentrification there is a widespread decline in affordable rental housing. The right kind of finance can aid in the recovery of units. Small dollar lending and managing small savings accounts by credit unions and small banks are among the hardest things to do profitably. They are also among the most important things to do socially. Innovations by banks, retailers, CDFIs, and many others to create manageable credit systems for lower-income households are vital to pursue. There are small-scale experiments in this area but not enough breakthroughs.

Rental housing and consumer finance are two areas in which poor households rapidly deplete income. Relief can only come from new housing finance priorities at the federal level, but a great deal will have to be pursued locally, including by capital intermediaries that have emerged to serve those roles.

Our view of what must happen in the future requires concerted action by civic, public, and private sectors. It is neither a left-wing menu of public solutions nor a right-wing menu of privatization. Nothing that works is that simple. Instead it requires that we construct new institutions and challenge existing ones. It requires that we use the power of markets but insist on long-term value creation for places; that we rethink the basic DNA of pubic asset management in service of public wealth; and that we direct efforts to invest in children and youth in much smarter, better funded, and more accountable ways.

As we turn to the conclusion, the vital issues of leadership and institution building are the natural focal points for tying together the many arguments in this book.

TEN

Toward a Nation of Problem Solvers
A CALL TO ACTION

**When you are facing a truly hard problem,
you should look outward.**
—Reid Hoffman, Founder, LinkedIn

This is a book about reimagining power. New Localism at its core is about the multiple sources and untapped potential of local power that can make cities and regions unrivaled engines of economic growth, inclusion, and renewal.

New Localism is not abstract theory but hard practice. Every story in this book exemplifies how cities are discovering new sources of power to solve problems and drive change.

Conventional wisdom holds that cities are powerless, mere creatures of the state, subordinate political units of nations. In this view, cities have no natural powers, only governmental powers devolved by higher levels of government.

But conventional wisdom is wrong. It mistakenly treats cities as just another layer of government rather than as what they truly are: powerful networks of institutions and ecosystems of actors that coproduce the economy and cosolve problems.

Activating these networks, however, requires leadership, the means by which power is translated into impact.

Leadership, so absent in our national and state capitals, is abundant in our cities and communities. Every success story in this book involved individuals and collections of people who stood up, took responsibility, recognized power in all its forms, and deployed it with vigor and affect.

The leaders of New Localism are discovering and activating the hidden powers of cities. Cities start with market power, the cumulative effect of real economic, physical, and social assets. Successful cities then actively experiment with deploying this power in a way that unlocks more public capital (fiscal power), as well as private and philanthropic capital (financial power). The aggregation of fiscal and financial power in turn is used to finance the future through transformative investments in innovation, infrastructure, and inclusion. The amassing of market, civic, fiscal, and financial power can ultimately lead, if intentionally harnessed and organized, to political power and the ability both to bend the actions of nations and states to the will of cities and to help solve global challenges such as mitigating the effects of climate change from the ground up.

City leaders are inventing an urban alchemy whereby one kind of power can be responsibly converted into another. Market power is a currency that has real, tangible value. In many cities, this value has not been realized because of a lack of transparency, the persistence of legacy rules, and a paucity of instruments, intermediaries, and institutions. When the right mechanisms are in place, value is assigned and capital flows.

Civic power is also a currency to be expended. Cities represent a hyperconcentration of problem solvers who are able to fuel a virtuous cycle of creation and innovation, transformation and transfiguration. At its best, the power of cities flows not from the dictates or decisions of central governments but from the actions and decisions of local grass tops (the heads of municipal governments, companies, universities, and philanthropies) and local grass roots (community groups, residents, and countless small and large organizations) working in concert. When unveiled and coalesced, the power of these disparate actors expands and multiplies in ways that are often unpredictable, even magical. A smart intervention (a quality park, an entrepreneurial business incubator) often creates the platform for broader economic and social transformation.

A narrow vision of cities as governments and city power as governmental power, in other words, is self limiting. It treats power as a zero-sum game, to be divided among multiple layers and levels of government. A broader vision of city power as organic market and civic power is self-generating. Like interest, it compounds and grows with use, because it opens up new possibilities and brings to the table more resources, more expertise, and more innovation.

City leaders are accumulating new forms of power by nontraditional means. They are rarely traveling to Washington, D.C., or their state capital as supplicants, begging for scraps of public resources or delegated powers. If they do make the sojourn, it is primarily to try to prevent higher levels of government from doing harm or to minimize the damage of bad policy. Federal and state governments, for the most part, are no longer in the problem-solving business; they have dealt themselves out of the equation through a combination of dysfunction, incompetence, and hyperpartisanship.

We are moving fast from a policymaking world to a problem-solving reality.

Cities such as Pittsburgh, Indianapolis, and Copenhagen are in the vanguard of New Localism. Leaders in these cities are inventing, applying, and perfecting new norms of growth, governance and finance that can readily be adapted, tailored, and replicated by cities throughout the world. Most important, leaders in these cities have accepted the central idea that "everything has changed," and have themselves changed accordingly.

Each city has built a growth model that is authentic and deeply rooted in its distinctive history and culture. Pittsburgh has willed itself to once again to be at the forefront of making things that are complex, intricate, and multidimensional. Indianapolis has burnished its starting collection of life sciences companies, universities, and hospitals into a tightly honed ecosystem that acts on the global stage. Copenhagen is restoring the core of its city at scale and is using sustainable growth that emphasizes both livability and transportation choice as a platform for economic competitiveness and talent attraction.

Each city has built a network of institutions and leaders that have the capacity to design and deliver solutions and initiatives in seriatim. In Pittsburgh, an informal coalition of philanthropies and universities has made large, strategic bets on technologies that set the platform for continuous innovation. In Indianapolis, a more formal structure of CEOs is enabling a city to make surgical and informed investments that exploit distinctive market opportunities. And in Copenhagen, a series of publicly owned, privately managed corporations has enabled the city both to catalyze growth and to productively engage the expertise of a much broader network of pension funds, real estate developers, and climate and social activists and entrepreneurs.

Each city has unlocked public, private, and philanthropic capital in novel ways to reshape economies and remake places. The philanthropies in Pittsburgh have essentially supplanted the state government as the go-to source of risk capital for investments in critical intermediaries such as business incubators and technology clusters. The pension funds in Indiana have become a vehicle for venture funding. And Copenhagen's public asset corporation is creating value in areas of the city where there was none, then using that value as public wealth to finance a modern city transit system.

The designation of Pittsburgh as a "growth" story or Indianapolis as a "governance" story or Copenhagen as a "finance" story is thus artificial. Any successful urban transformation has all three essential elements: growth, governance, and finance.

Here is the challenge.

For every Pittsburgh, there are dozens of cities still involved in traditional economy shaping efforts that subsidize simple consumption (such as major league sports stadia) rather than smart innovation.

For every Indianapolis, there are hundreds of cities that are collaborating on a shoestring in ways that are unstructured, poorly focused, and organized for failure.

For every Copenhagen, there are thousands of cities that are creating value for the private sector and then failing to maximize it for the public good.

For New Localism to thrive, we need to get serious about building a new class of city and metropolitan leaders and a new modus operandi in communities that enables leaders to flourish. We have no choice. The more angry and shallow and leaderless our national politics and culture become, the deeper and more intentional and affirmative and leader-rich our cities must be.

So what will it take for cities to adapt and tailor the transformative innovations invented in Pittsburgh, Indianapolis, and Copenhagen (and other cities)?

Information dissemination is no longer the constraint, as it was in the pre-internet era. Twenty-five years ago, the spread of "best practices," even between cities a short distance away, was painfully slow.

That is no longer the case. Each of our success stories is open sourced: it can be analyzed to its constituent parts, demystified, and widely circulated through new technologies. Their enabling features can be identified and distilled; we have done so in this book.

Local innovations, in essence, travel fast. What can be done can be captured and codified. What can be captured and codified can be replicated. What can be replicated can become a new local norm. There is, in short, method (and speed) to the madness.

And capital is not a constraint. The costs of formal or informal collaboration, the platform for transformative change in the three featured cities, are de minimis. Virtually any city and county of any measurable size in the United States has the resources to fund collective action.

The key missing ingredient is leadership. The range of excuses not to pursue these models is well rehearsed and quite common: "We don't have a Carnegie Mellon. . . . We don't have a Lilly Endowment. . . . We don't have the backing of national government. . . . Our local government is broke."

All those things may all be true. But we don't need to travel farther than Erie, Pennsylvania, to see that grand things are possible and that cities can leverage their distinctive advantages.

Erie, like many older industrial cities, has been through tough times. From its peak of 140,000 in the 1960s the city's population has fallen to 100,000 (the county population now hovers around 276,000). As in many rust belt cities, deindustrialization in the 1980s and 1990s hit the community hard: it lost 40 percent of its manufacturing jobs.[1] And these industrial losses are not in the distant past. In November 2015, GE Transportation announced that it would lay off one-third of its 4,500 workers at a locomotive manufacturing plant.

Yet the city still retains enormous assets, many of them concentrated in or near the historic downtown. The headquarters of Erie Insurance Group, the twentieth largest insurer in the United States and the city's only Fortune 500 company, is located in the heart of the downtown and is substantially expanding its headquarters with a new $135 million facility and 1,000 new jobs.[2] The campus of Mercyhurst University, which is strong in data sciences and cybersecurity, is literally a bike ride away.

Change took leadership, from these institutions and from Velocity Network, a local company that helps small businesses solve their IT issues, just relocated to the downtown, and McManis and Monsalve Associates, a small business development consultancy, which came together in 2016 to create a downtown innovation district. Mercyhurst received a $4 million grant from a consortium of funders: the Erie Community Foundation, the Erie County Gaming Revenue Authority, and the Susan Hirt Hagen Fund for Transformational Philanthropy. This gift is already yielding additional investment, including $1.25 million in funding from a graduate of Mercyhurst to develop and expand academic programs that align well with Erie's competitive advantages: risk control and insurance underwriting and cybersecurity and data analytics.[3]

As David Dausey, Mercyhurst's provost and vice president for academic affairs, said, "The field of risk management is changing rapidly. The insurance industry is moving more and more towards a big-data approach. The industry will need more people to interpret, analyze and make sense of that data."[4]

The vision: create a strong pipeline of available talent to fill employment demand for risk managers and cybersecurity experts and provide continuing education and training opportunities for existing employees in the insurance field. In other words, do what Erie does best, better.

Erie is following the path of customization and alignment. As Ted Smith, the former chief innovation officer of Louisville has opined, "Say you're a midsize city, you really have to decide what you're going to be best at and you can't be all things to all people like some of the larger metro markets. We have a handful of industry clusters that we are known for, that we continue to invest in as the area of greatest strength for us, competitively in the country and perhaps internationally at times."[5]

The momentum in Erie's downtown has resulted in over $500 million in recently announced investments by major anchors. In addition to the efforts of the innovation district partners, the Lake Erie College of Osteopathic Medicine has grown in just a few decades to become the largest medical college in the country, with over 1,000 graduates in 2017, and the Saint Vincent Hospital network has announced a $115 million expansion in the downtown area.[6]

James and Deb Fallows of the *Atlantic* recently completed a series of insightful reports from Erie. Their stories show how an eclectic mix of usual and unusual suspects is powering the momentum in Erie. As in many communities, the heads of the major public, private and civic institutions are stepping up. But leadership is also being found in unexpected corners, the county gaming revenue authority being the most unusual. "Erie has matched a familiar source of money (gambling) with a widespread civic goal (economic and technical renewal) in a novel and apparently successful way," writes James Fallows.[7]

The Fallowses also found an infectious enthusiasm, particularly among young entrepreneurs and millennials. James Fallows highlights Radius—the city's first coworking space—which is helping technology providers work with local manufacturers, using its space to facilitate the creation and distribution of local art and spreading passion about downtown revitalization.

The Fallowses finally discovered a hidden pool of talent and optimism among recent and former immigrants. The city has become one of the main refugee resettlement cities in the country. As a result, a key leader in Erie today is Ferki Ferati, president of the Jefferson Education Society, who came to Erie from Kosovo in 1998.

GROWING LEADERSHIP WITHIN CITIES

Erie is not alone. Many of the other stories in this book show similar bursts of leadership, evident in Chattanooga's rebuilding of its downtown, Louisville's commitment to its lifelong learning initiative Cradle to Career, Oklahoma City's recovery in the aftermath of the 1995 bombing.

These stories illustrate that power is not what it used to be and is not confined to national or state capitals or high-flying cities on the coasts. And neither is leadership.

The United States is a vast consumer of literature on leadership. We have grown quite familiar with archetypical figures—the strong mayor, the charismatic CEO, the battle-tested police chief, the brilliant entrepreneur, the courageous investor. Those stories make for great copy and dovetail with a culture that celebrates the individual.

But conventional leadership norms do not quite fit the configuration of localities. For Erie and other communities, the path to collective problem solving relies on leaders who can navigate and leverage the networked reality of urban power. Cities are neither vertically integrated companies nor governments that have a set command-and-control structure. Rather, they are networks of public, private, and civic institutions that coproduce the economy and cogovern critical aspects of city life.

The essence of a successful local leader, therefore, is the ability to bring groups of people together to solve problems and do grand things that they cannot do as individuals. To reflect the distributed genius of the city, leaders must be adept at creating and stewarding horizontal relationships rather than issuing and executing hierarchical mandates. And they must do so in a way that enables maximum flexibility and adaptability, in light of the fast-changing nature of markets, technology, and society.

This requires qualities that in some respects are similar to, but also distinct, from the qualities found in most leadership treatises. And it requires a look forward, as demographic changes and technological advances are altering who leaders are and how they operate.

First, leaders must learn to cultivate collaboration, connection, and trust among people who rarely interact and entities that often have vastly different missions and organizational cultures. This is not a small task, in part because of the excessive fragmentation of urban constituencies. The curse of modern cities is that they are overly organized and highly compartmentalized.

The list of established constituencies in cities and counties is lengthy. City government. County government. Public authorities. Universities. Community colleges. Hospitals. Large employers. Small businesses. Real estate developers. Real estate owners. Banks. Philanthropy. Media. Unions. Architects and planners. Service providers. Cultural institutions. Community groups. Ethnic groups. Religious groups. And on and on and on.

Each of these entities has its own board, its own driving principles, and its own distinctive culture. Like the blind men and the elephant, they each experience the city in their own idiosyncratic way. Architects and planners perceive cities primarily through the lens of aesthetics (say, the quality of architecture) or the physical dimension (the presence of cycling lanes or waterfront trails). Businesses experience cities through their ecosystems, intricate webs of mature companies, startups and scale-ups, supply chains, universities, investors, workers, consumers, and local government. Technologists are eager to use cities and the data they generate to create new tools for navigating the city and maximizing the use of existing transport, energy, and other systems. It is rare that these stakeholders think about power or problem solving in a multidimensional and multisectoral way.

Urban organizations also have varying degrees of racial, ethnic, and gender diversity. Along a continuum, government and community organizations tend to be the most diverse, business groups the least. The reasons for these differences are deep-rooted: the past is always present in cities.

The gift of urban leaders, ironically, is to recognize the potential in fragmentation. The presence of many organized constituencies means that there are many stakeholders whose energy, expertise, and enthusiasm can be leveraged. The lack of diversity in many leading organizations provides an opportunity to match them with groups that are more naturally representative of the broader community. The key is to find a challenge and a solution that unifies rather than divides. Sometimes geography (neighborhoods, districts) is the unifier; at other times burning issues such as the quality of schools, the health of the environment, or the sorry state of infrastructure provides the motivation.

Local leaders, in short, display a high degree of "network intelligence," a phrase applied to management by Reid Hoffman, the founder of LinkedIn. Hoffman's clear advice to corporate CEOs is to "look beyond your office" when trying to solve hard problems. As Hoffman writes, "When your employees share what they learn from the people in their network (about technologies, competition, talent), they help you solve key business challenges faster."[8]

Applying network intelligence to cities has similar affects. The urban leadership class consists of multiple stakeholders, including established institutions, constituencies, and communities. City leaders treat these disparate groups much as a CEO treats her disparate employees, as a vehicle for smarter and more sustained problem solving and strategic decisionmaking.

In Abilene, Texas, Mayor Gary McCaleb found that prioritizing children was the unusual path toward revitalizing the core of his economically challenged city. The simple act of reading illustrated children's books at local schools led to the idea that this West Texas city should create a National Center for Children's Illustrated Literature.[9]

McCaleb characterizes his approach as "we need everybody on board." He would visit with every civic club and say that the city needed everybody's ideas. Every time the city appointed a committee, he'd say, "Let's try to get one where everybody in Abilene could look at the names and see somebody they know."

McCaleb found that different constituencies were drawn to his idea for different reasons. The Abilene Cultural Affairs Council had already been revitalizing downtown but they were continuously looking to keep residents there, especially graduates from the three universities. "We needed to find a way to turn the magnet into glue" is how he puts it. What began as an effort to increase quality of life became a way of differentiating Abilene nationally from other cities and making a distinctive children's center an "export" through tourism. Now they have the full museum and a large annual festival.

Significantly, McCaleb's definition of leadership comes back to the elusive notion of trust. "I've always subscribed to the philosophy that the best leaders are those who others are following. You need to get people in leadership who have the faith of others."

Second, leadership comes from the deployment of soft rather than hard power. American culture often celebrates the hard power of a General Patton, barking orders. And it is accurate to say that many heads of large organizations in cities, such as companies, governments, and universities, do act as decisionmakers for their institutions, setting priorities, crafting strategies, and measuring results.

But modern challenges often require solutions that cross the boundaries of traditional sectors and expertise. The less explored power of people "in charge"—CEOs, mayors, county executives, university presidents—is the ability to convene networks of leaders and design, finance, and deliver multidisciplinary efforts to resolve difficult challenges and exploit promising opportunities.

Chapter 4, for example, discussed the importance of a new growth model that can shape both the supply and the demand sides of the economy by helping workers get the skills they need to engage fully in the labor market and businesses grow quality jobs that pay well and provide decent benefits. It becomes apparent fairly fast that no single entity can design or deliver these critical outcomes. The task is shared across different levels of government, disparate sectors of society, and a vast array of public, private and civic institutions. The new growth model, in other words, is a perfect place for the exercise of soft power and the powerful role of convening, coordinating, and mediating.

As the stories in this book demonstrate, soft power requires leadership traits that are qualitatively different from the more conventional ones used to run a hierarchical organization in which command-and-control lines of authority are in place. Soft power requires the ability to cajole and even shame private, civic, university, and community leaders to come together and collaborate to compete and solve problems. This is community organizing at the highest level, and it requires mayors and others to lead disparate actors toward common visions, tangible actions, and sustained commitment.[10]

Soft power also requires the ability to synthesize disparate bits of information, particularly regarding flows of capital. Investments in cradle-to-career services (and in children and youth more generally), for example, are balkanized and often opaque. The resources that fuel local efforts may come from federal grants, state programs, local government allocations, philanthropic initiatives, local businesses, and other sources. Mayors and their peers are often the players in a federal republic who bring alignment to fragmentation and order to chaos.

Soft power, finally, requires local leaders to sit at the intersection of multiple agencies, nonprofit organizations, and specialized disciplines that literally speak different languages while seeking similar if not the same outcomes. The Pittsburgh story showed how the convergence of advanced industry sectors often sparked product and process innovation. In many respects, the same happens in the realm of urban networks, irrespective of whether services are delivered by traditional government or by aligned providers. Convergence and the ever-present reality of resource scarcity compel new priorities, new approaches, and new coalitions.

Third, leadership is often exercised by individuals who have not achieved a place at the table through the ballot box or by dint of being the largest employer or benefactor in the city. In a world driven by collaborative governance, the people who are often responsible for transformative change are connectors who bridge the gap between major stakeholders, forge consensus solutions and initiatives, and then execute with firm backing.

Several stories in the book underscore this point. David Johnson of the Central Indiana Corporate Partnership (CICP) and Paul Levy of Philadelphia's Central City District are leaders because they form the connective tissue within their organizations and between their organizations and external constituencies. They run relatively small organizations that have large impact.

In some respects, these exceptional individuals are applying the laws of physics to the chaos of the city. Archimedes once famously said, "Give me a lever long enough, and I will move the world," when he uncovered the physical principles behind the lever. The CICP and Philadelphia's Central City District are essentially acting as levers to lift the Indianapolis economy and Philadelphia downtown, respectively.

The role of connector requires hard structure and diverse talents. Indianapolis and downtown Philadelphia work as well as they do because David Johnson's and Paul Levy's job (and that of many people who work with them) is to wake up every day and pursue collaboration, coordination, and impact. In many respects, our society has deified specialized expertise and diminished individuals who have general knowledge and can seamlessly move across sectors and disciplines. New Localism places equal emphasis on these very different skill sets. We need the technical experts *and* the people who excel at working the civics. One without the other has the limits of one hand clapping.

These new kinds of leaders come from disparate professional backgrounds with varied educational credentials. David Johnson was a well-respected public finance and securities lawyer before taking the helm first at BioCrossroads and eventually at CICP. Paul Levy had a background in academia and city government before becoming the head of Center City District. Richard Shatten has an MBA and worked at McKinsey before becoming the second executive director of Cleveland Tomorrow.

But these leaders share similar characteristics.

They are political but not partisan and are comfortable navigating very disparate environments: dealing with top CEOs and elected officials in the morning, global corporations and investors in the afternoon, community groups and neighborhood leaders at night.

They are part visionary, part implementer. Their power largely derives from their ability to execute in complex urban environments where many existing challenges go unmet and many constituencies and leaders are known more for a propensity to obstruct and oppose than to act.

Their ability to get stuff done also explains their longevity. Continuity of leadership is unusual in environments where elections take place every two or four years and when the heads of key government agencies such as the public schools or the police service rotate every eighteen months.

They speak multiple "city languages." Success means being familiar with the latest trends in finance, innovation, real estate, placemaking, and skills development and requires leaders to engage in do-it-yourself lifelong learning.

The premium on curiosity helps explain why longevity does not dull creativity or innovation. In fact, many of these leaders, like a fine wine, get better with age. They know more. They try new things. They see and act on connections.

And they are simultaneously ambitious and humble. As Paul Levy has written, "BIDs are not elective bodies and their leaders do not stand for office in the traditional sense and little aggravates local elected officials more than referring to a BID manager as 'the mayor of downtown.' "[11]

Fourth, leadership depends on the power of affirmative vision. Every successful story starts with a compelling vision: Pittsburgh as the center of robotics innovation. Indianapolis as a competitive metropolis. Copenhagen as *the* sustainable, livable city.

To quote *The Metropolitan Revolution*: "Visions clarify. Visions inspire. Visions catalyze. Visions matter."[12]

An animating vision builds on the cultural preferences of different places. Leadership thus requires both the technical skills to craft a vision and the emotional intelligence to find one that fits a place at a particular time.

A vision enables a common narrative that can be repeated and customized to different audiences. Cities that succeed have leaders in different sectors "singing from the same song book," often using the same statistics and examples. This clarifies and simplifies communication for both internal and external audiences, including investors, companies, and the media.

A visit by Bruce Katz to Eindhoven in Holland several years ago illustrated the power of the common narrative. Eindhoven, the fifth largest city in Holland, was rocked by the decision of Philips Lighting to offshore manufacturing facilities in the 1990s. The city has come back on the strength of an ecosystem that cultivates and celebrates technological problem solving, particularly with regard to medical devices.

What is uncommon about their common narrative is how the mayor, business leaders, investors, entrepreneurs, and the faculty at the local technical university use the same phrases, same language, and same facts to describe their collective enterprise. There is no space between sectors.

A vision also forms the platform for storytelling. In many respects, cities have certain characteristics and attributes that stories help elucidate and bring forward. The Pittsburgh, Indianapolis, and Copenhagen stories are illustrative of cities with radically different cultures even though they share many similarities on the surface. Stories humanize places and make them more accessible and marketable.

Fifth, leadership depends on grounding affirmative visions in affirmative *evidence*. Prior chapters described the frustrating tendency in modern life to focus on the negative to the exclusion of the positive. As described in chapter 6, cities tend to know more about what the government owes than what the government owns, and the value of those public assets.

The connective thread through most of our stories and recommendations is the contrarian fixation on mapping assets rather than assessing liabilities and on designing "business plans" rather than diagnosing problems.

This raises some challenges. All of our solutions—the Social Genome Model, public asset corporations, innovation districts, pay-for-success bonds, child referenda, regional venture funds—require different kinds of data collection and analysis than what is typically available or performed in most cities today. This information is collected so that economic and social returns on investment can be objectively unveiled. Such analyses also require technological applications that can routinize such information and enable the matching of capital to investment to occur more seamlessly and with less friction.

Technology is transforming the ways in which city governments and other entities are staffed, assets are unveiled, investable propositions are identified, resources are allocated, and progress is measured.

This brings an entirely new meaning to the notion that information is power. In government, this phrase often refers to lobbyists gaining inside knowledge of whether federal or state legislation has a chance of becoming law, and if so, which provisions would end up in the final resolution. This is the traditional view of government, characterized by backroom deals, campaign contributions, and the undue influence of special interests.

"Information is power" has a different meaning at the local and metropolitan level. Governments are huge repositories of data on everything from land ownership and crime statistics to neighborhood demographics and energy use to school performance and transportation preference. The past decade has witnessed a discernible move toward open government as cities and other localities have raced to put government data files on line for all to see.[13]

We are on the cusp of applying big data analytics and other technological advances to urban growth, governance, and finance, just in time to compensate for the dysfunction of higher levels of government.

Finally, leadership depends on, as James Fallows observed in his Erie series, "being active rather than passive."[14] Most U.S. cities have been studied to death and suffer from report fatigue. Restating the origins and nature and scope of familiar problems for the twenty-fifth time has ceased to motivate or inspire. The search for the perfect "evidence-driven policy" is endless and debilitating. Cities are not mathematical formulas; evidence-informed policy is sufficient. The premium now must be on action.

The cities and leaders highlighted in this book are models because they have perfected a practice of using independent analysis to guide practical action rather than inspire more academic debate. They are cleverly using sound research as the starting point to craft smart and strategic solutions rather than as an end point. They are narrowing the gap between the academy and practice.

But action is not confined to large structural interventions, as important as those are. The cities highlighted are also speeding and democratizing the process of problem solving. On one level, the "lighter cheaper quicker" approach to placemaking—starting small to showcase quick results—practiced by the Project for Public Spaces (such as pop-up parks and food hubs) is now translating into other arenas of urban life, including the innovative economy. In Oklahoma City, for example, health and energy researchers are exploring common technologies and applications that cut across their sectors, breaking down long-standing disciplinary silos in the process.[15]

Cities are also crowd-sourcing (or citizen-sourcing) the diagnosis of challenges and, by extension, the design of solutions. Innovative city governments in particular are reaching out to local entrepreneurs, technologists, and makers to solve problems. As Steven Johnson has written, borrowing from Poincaré, "Great ideas rise in crowds."[16]

In 2015, for example, the city of Louisville was experiencing a spike in arson in abandoned buildings. This was not just a matter of vacant properties burning down; as fires spread, they put other properties and people in serious danger. Mayor Greg Fischer held a weeklong hackathon with local entrepreneurs to see if they could find a low-cost solution. CNET reported on what happened next:

> The judging panel comprised members of the fire department, the emergency dispatch team and the fire protection industry, and it settled on a project that's now called Casper for "completely autonomous solar-powered event responder."
>
> Casper's 3D printed case contains a circuit board, battery, antenna and a microphone circuit. Essentially, Casper is a device that can listen for the specific frequency a smoke alarm emits when it goes off and then can alert emergency responders.[17]

Cities like Louisville are tapping into a growing maker movement across the country. As Peter Hirshberg and Marcia Kardanoff have written, Louisville has become a maker city, "inviting citizens and industry to go hands-on with the modern tools of production: computer science, robotics, electronics, computer-aided design and advanced manufacturing."[18]

The upshot is that cities and their disparate public, private and civic institutions are becoming increasingly tech savvy, making them more aware of the technological innovations that are coming on line and those that are moving from lab to testing to prototyping to ubiquitous adoption. This intimate proximity to and engagement with market actors helps explain why cities are becoming living laboratories for the deployment of new technologies like drones or autonomous vehicles as well as new technology driven solutions.

Chapter 9 exalted "blue sky" thinking and put forth a series of ideas that could unlock capital and transform cities, the twenty-first-century urban equivalent of the Federal Housing Administration and other institutional achievements. The search for the smart idea or tool or hidden asset is a worthy one. Yet the stories we have told point to an additional conclusion: leadership in all its varied configurations is itself a form of blue sky thinking and action.

A NEW ERA OF INSTITUTIONAL INNOVATION

Daniel Patrick Moynihan, the polymorphous public intellectual and public servant, once famously quipped, "If you want to build a great city, create a great university and wait 200 years."

Moynihan's observation about the length of product cycles and impact cycles doesn't hold true under scrutiny. Each of our stories showed real, measurable progress within several years, which formed the basis for long-term outcomes.

But his insight about the power of platform institutions was spot on. Leadership excels and thrives when it has the right institutional base and support. In a period when responsibilities have been radically devolved, the nexus of power, leadership, and institutions is stronger and more necessary than ever.

Our stories are, in essence, tales about institutional evolution and creation, as well as the leadership of individuals.

Pittsburgh would not be Pittsburgh without Carnegie Mellon University, the University of Pittsburgh, and philanthropies such as the Heinz Endowments and the Hillman and RK Mellon Foundation.

Indianapolis would not be Indianapolis without the Lilly Corporation, the Lilly Foundation, a core group of universities and corporations, and, since 1999, the CICP.

Copenhagen would not be Copenhagen without first the Ørestad Development Corporation and ultimately Copenhagen City & Port Development.

These institutions form a strong foundation on which economies are restructured, places are reshaped, capital is raised, and global brands are made and marketed.

In some cases, existing institutions have been repurposed for a new, networked era. The advanced research universities in Pittsburgh have altered their perspective from being world-class academic institutions that happened to be located in Pittsburgh to being globally significant economic players with an enormous stake in the economic success and vibrancy of the city and metropolis.

In other cases, existing institutions have been merged, combined, and recombined to enhance market power, reflect critical lessons, and take on new responsibilities. The Copenhagen City & Port Development is a powerful example because it shows the rapid cycle of institutional creation, experimentation, improvement, and expansion, all within the relatively short period of fifteen years.

In still other cases, new institutions and intermediaries have been established to fill gaps in economy shaping, placemaking, and skills preparing. The formation and creative evolution of the CICP in Indianapolis, the anchor-led Cortex district in St. Louis, and 3CDC in Cincinnati shows how leaders in three distinct cities realized the limitations of current institutions and took on the risks inherent in building something new and novel.

In this era of New Localism, smart institutions play multiple roles.

First, they develop the capacities and competencies to carry out complex initiatives and transactions. The tasks of New Localism—leveraging distinctive advanced industrial advantages, spurring large-scale urban regeneration and infrastructure building, arming a workforce with the technological skills necessary for the modern economy—are neither small nor routinized. They require specialized expertise either to be built in-house or to be on regular call. This is the major leagues of city building, carried out in tandem with institutional investors, global corporations, and informed intermediaries.

Second, they enable talented individuals to lead while simultaneously depersonalizing success. The success of the CICP or Philadelphia's Center City District is inextricably linked to the exceptional qualities of leaders like David Johnson and Paul Levy. But these individuals have also built teams of talented staff and networks of local, regional, national, and global partners. There is a depth and breadth to smart institutions, and a sense of permanence and durability. This prepares organizations for the inevitable succession period when leaders move on.

Third, they build traditional balance sheets and stores of social capital that enhance credibility and flexibility in the marketplace and enable the taking on of new tasks and new approaches. The successful institutions in this book develop organizational cultures of informed risk taking, experimentation, and continuous learning and innovation. They deploy power rather than hoard it, make markets rather than follow them. They create mechanisms that aim to avoid the natural conservatism that builds in organizations as they grow, whether it's CICP's creation of new branded initiatives or CCD's taking on new responsibilities. Just as for startups and entrepreneurs, failure *is* an option as long as it is used to inform institutional evolution.

Fourth, they increasingly cross traditional public and private boundaries, reflecting the fundamental nature of cities as markets and networks. Some institutions, such as the Copenhagen City & Port Development, are purposefully hybrid organizations. Their public ownership enables the public sector to do what it does well—advance important objectives such as inclusion and sustainability and act on behalf of the entire citizenry rather than special interests. But private sector management also enables the maximization of value and public wealth and the smart leveraging of public, private, and civic capital.

Finally, they provide the catalyst for impact in both individual cities and cities collectively. As New Localism evolves, cities are no longer just looking to other cities for smart tactics and techniques. They are looking for institutional templates that can be adapted to places with different economic starting points and political and social cultures.

We are on the cusp of a new period of institutional evolution and creation. Public asset corporations. Public benefit banks. Scaled community development finance institutions. Regional venture funds. The common thread across all these institutions is that they are designed to use market power to raise capital, invest in the future, and bolster economic competitiveness and social inclusion.

TOWARD A NATION OF PROBLEM SOLVERS

We are left with some hard questions. How far can New Localism, in the absence of federal and state support, go in solving some of the hardest economic, social, and environmental challenges facing the United States and other nations? What is its potential to galvanize leadership and capital, what are its limitations? To what extent does it apply to places and communities that are economically struggling and increasingly socially isolated? How do we move New Localism from a loosely connected civic enterprise to a powerfully linked national and global movement?

Much is riding on the answers to these questions.

The promise of New Localism is to be a powerful vehicle for helping places and people adapt to the profound changes wrought by globalization, technological innovation, and demographic transformation, forces way beyond their control.

Cities and metropolitan communities are in many cases the right geographies to invent, apply, and test new methods and mechanisms for resolving the challenges of the modern era. They are also the right geographies for accessing large amounts of public, private, and philanthropic capital and putting it toward productive and visible use, for creating real wealth through economy shaping, placemaking, and talent preparing rather than the parasitic transfer of financial paper or manipulation of financial algorithms.

If solutions can be catalyzed and capitalized, New Localism can channel raging emotions on both the left and the right into productive activity.

The promise of New Localism, in essence, is not just to be an antidote to Angry Populism. It is to resolve many of the issues that stoked the fires of Angry Populism in the first place and, in so doing, repair the fraying fabric of society. It is also to heal the divisions that have emerged between the places where we live—urban, suburban, exurban, rural—even though these places are economically codependent and inextricably linked by common interest in metropolitan prosperity.

In the end, Angry Populism is a political movement subject to the ebbs and flows of electoral cycles. New Localism, by contrast, is a market and civic enterprise. That is its strength and potential.

How do we realize the full potential of this phenomenon?

First, cities need to be squarely and fully in the solution business. Problem solving, stripped to the basics, has two sides—the problem and the solution. Cities, the media, and many national and local constituencies spend a vast amount of time analyzing problems—examining, dissecting, assessing, quantifying, and ranking—through increasingly sophisticated means. But they spend less time designing, financing, delivering, and reporting on solutions.

We now need to shift to the other side of the equation. We need to apply as much time, talent, and energy to crafting solutions as we do to defining and analyzing problems. We need more methodological rigor in understanding how the features that enable solutions to work in one city can be adapted to places with different cultures, legal systems, and institutional structures. Problem *solving* must become a central part of our cultural and societal DNA.

Second, cities must recognize the assets they have and the hidden potential for productive, inclusive, and sustainable growth. In our view, they have been operating with only a portion of their potential, perhaps 50 to 60 percent of their inherent capacity. For those who protest, we recommend visiting those few places that have realized the full benefits of density and quality placemaking in their downtowns and along their waterfronts or have truly aligned academic centers of excellence and education and skills training with their special business competencies. The Pittsburgh, Indianapolis, and Copenhagen stories are successes precisely because these cities are maximizing their strengths and leveraging their assets in structured and organized ways.

But they are the exceptions. Most communities are leaving substantial capital and wealth on the table not because they lack the potential for growth but because they haven't organized themselves to grow.

Third, cities need to put all their talent to collective task. New Localism is a call for individuals who occupy traditional leadership positions to lead, with aspiration, confidence, and creativity. But it is also a call for a broader segment of urban citizens and constituencies to step up, take responsibility, and create their own solutions.

It is our observation that cities have more power than they think and more leaders than they think. Leaders are not unknown; in any given city they can be identified, enumerated, aggregated, and organized. In small cities they number in the hundreds. In medium-sized cities they number in the thousands. In large cities they number in the tens of thousands.

Our cities are rich in leadership and getting better at harnessing this human capital and wealth for collective impact. This is network intelligence at the city rather than corporate scale. As we have described, smart institutions play a substantial role. But technology could play a bigger role than it has to date. It is intriguing to imagine how the ability to link individuals through social networks could be expanded to connect leaders through problem-solving networks, within and across cities.

Fourth, cities need a frank institutional audit to assess whether the institutions that leaders inherit from prior generations are sharp enough, strong enough, and connected enough to get the job done in today's changing climate. Some cities will look at our stories and determine that existing institutions—public, private, philanthropic, or some combination— need to be repurposed. Others will decide to create new institutions that fit their economic moment and cultural realities. Cities, in short, are entering the twenty-first century equipped with twentieth-century institutions. A refresh is needed, city by city and metropolis by metropolis.

The result could be a burst of new institutional innovation that responds to the demand for systemic and continuous problem solving and engages the ample supply of talented individuals who want to put their expertise and experience to work. The challenge in most cities is one of organization as well as capacity.

We envision layers of new problem-solving institutions emerging. Some will, like the CICP, steward city and metro economies through reinvigorated leadership groups. Others will, like the Copenhagen City & Port Development, test new public-private models of urban regeneration and infrastructure finance. Still others will perfect and extend the new institutional models of entrepreneurial communities—1871 in Chicago, Innovation Depot Inc. in Birmingham, the Idea Factory in Santiago, Chile—that are proliferating throughout the world. These entities are already enabling solutions for the city that harness the affirmative energy and technical knowledge lying dormant and untapped in their communities. We imagine that future cities will host multiple innovation spaces—in city halls, universities, major corporations, business and social incubators, coworking spaces—to make problem solving routine and regular.

We need one other institutional advancement. Cities and suburban jurisdictions now share many common challenges—the growth of concentrated poverty, the misalignment of skills and new industries, a built environment that serves cars rather than people. Cracking these problems will require new mediating institutions that cross the artificial lines that divide city, suburb, and rural jurisdictions. Civil society must ultimately do what government cannot.

Fifth, cities—collectively, domestically, and globally—need a new set of intermediaries to help them realize the full potential of the New Localism. Some of these intermediaries must close the gap between new responsibilities and inadequate local capacity. Rockefeller's 100 Resilient Cities effort is a first mover in this space, enabling cities both to add new professional talent (chief resilience officers) for particular tasks and to engage the talent in a process of continual education that captures and codifies replicable solutions.

Some of these intermediaries must design a new metro finance system with cities and for cities. For the past decade, there has been endless talk about trillions of dollars sitting on the sidelines. There is not a lack of capital but rather a lack of connectivity and a lack of techniques to convert market power into tangible resources.

We predict that instruments, intermediaries, and institutions that connect cities and capital in productive and predictive ways will be a growth industry. Some vehicles will deliver competitive market returns by recognizing untapped sources (such as innovation districts); others will promise steady but less heady returns while meeting other investor interests (such as social enterprise). All will rely on sophisticated and seasoned analytics and trusted managers.

Sixth, the study of cities and city power must move beyond the straitjacket of government. In many respects, our diagnostics and prescriptions are limited by our antiquated perception of cities as governments rather than networks, as political wards of the state rather than centers of the economy and innovation. Urban researchers and observers are focusing too much on the governmental and political powers that cities don't have and too little on the market, fiscal, and financial powers they do have and how to leverage them. We need to view the urban world in its entirety.

Finally, all aspects of society need to celebrate and champion leadership as a high and honorable aspiration. Cities went through a period after urban renewal when the exercise of power was a dirty word. Cities put in place checks and balances and restrictions and prohibitions that have made the process of deploying power more like an Alice in Wonderland obstacle course than an inviting and reinforcing exercise. If cities are to survive and thrive in hostile times, city leaders must stop apologizing for leadership.

We are obviously not arguing for a return to the age of Robert Moses when autocratic rule, exercised by the few, was often rooted in racial prejudice and ethnic privilege. Rather, we are arguing for an activation of leadership across multiple dimensions and diverse constituencies that prioritize on tangible actions and concrete solutions.

Our efforts in this book to capture and define New Localism represent just an initial effort. If New Localism is to flourish, it demands intellectual and practical responses of equal ambition: new language to capture the disruptive dynamics under way, new metrics to measure urban prosperity across multiple dimensions, new solutions that are grounded and tested in practice, new kinds of public-private institutions and financial instruments to ensure that capital flows seamlessly to city needs, new forms of governance that both modernize local capacity and maximize the relationships between cities and higher levels of government, perhaps even new political institutions to hold federal and state representatives accountable to the needs of the communities that elected them rather than the rigid ideologies of parties and partisans that endorse them.

We need, in short, a theory and practice of New Localism that are as rich and as textured as cities themselves.

This is the way we reimagine power, redefine leadership, and create and repurpose effective institutions for this challenging age.

This is the way place trumps partisanship, community overcomes incivility, and cities thrive in the age of populism.

This is the way power will truly belong to the problem solvers.

Notes

Chapter 1

1. Philip Rucker and Robert Costa, "Bannon Vows a Daily Fight for Deconstruction of the Administrative State," *Washington Post*, February 23, 2017.

2. C. Eugene Steuerle, *Dead Men Ruling: How to Restore Fiscal Freedom and Rescue Our Future* (New York: Century Foundation Press, 2014).

3. U.S. Congressional Budget Office, "Updated Budget Projections: 2016 to 2026" (Congressional Budget Office, March 2016) (www.cbo.gov/sites/default/files/114th-congress-2015-2016/reports/51384-marchbaselineonecol.pdf).

4. Yuval Levin, *The Fractured Republic: Renewing America's Social Contract in the Age of Individualism* (New York: Basic Books, 2016), p. 5.

5. Daniel Patrick Moynihan, "President Reagan and Chairman Morrill: A Constitutional Reflection," address to the National League of Cities, March 24, 1985 (Daniel P. Moynihan Papers at the Library of Congress) (www.loc.gov/rr/mss/moynihan/moynihan-home.html).

6. Lizette Alvarez, "Mayors, Sidestepping Trump, Vow to Fill Void on Climate Change," *New York Times*, June 26, 2017.

7. "Blueprint for American Prosperity: Unleashing the Potential of a Metropolitan Area," Metropolitan Policy Program (Brookings, 2007), p. 7.

8. Rise of the Rest, "The Mission" (www.riseofrest.com/about/mission/).

Chapter 2

1. See, for example, Wendell Berry's essay collections, including *Another Turn of the Crank: Essays* (Berkeley, Calif.: Counterpoint Publishing, 2011); and, with Herman Daly, *What Matters? Economics for a Renewed Commonwealth* (Berkeley, Calif.: Counterpoint Publishing, 2010).

2. See the website of the Land Trust Alliance at www.landtrustalliance.org.

3. "About Us," Slow Food website (www.slowfood.com/about-us/). The global grassroots organization Slow Food was created to prevent the disappearance of local food cultures. The organization is among the forces inspiring consumers to seek out local ingredients, spurring interest in regional farmer's markets and community-supported agriculture (CSA) programs.

4. Beth Simon Noveck and Arnaud Sahuguet, "Participatory Democracy's Emerging Tools," *Governing*, March 11, 2015 (www.governing.com/columns/smart -mgmt/col-participatory-democracy-emerging-tools.html).

5. Edward Goetz and Susan Clarke, eds., *The New Localism: Comparative Urban Politics in a Global Era* (Thousand Oaks, Calif: Sage, 1993).

6. See, for example, Chris Tausanovitch and Christopher Warshaw, "Representation in Municipal Government," *American Political Science Review* 108, no. 3 (2014), pp. 605–41; Sapna Swaroop and Jeffrey D. Morenoff, "Building Community: The Neighborhood Context of Local Social Organization," PSC Research Report 04-549 (University of Michigan, Population Studies Center, Institute for Social Research, 2004); John Mollenkopf, *Contested City* (Princeton University Press, 1990); Bruce Katz and Scott Bernstein, "The New Metropolitan Agenda: Connecting Cities and Suburbs," *The Brookings Review* 16, no. 4 (1999), pp. 4–7; Bruce Katz, "Enough of the Small Stuff! Toward a New Urban Agenda," *The Brookings Review* 18, no. 3 (2000), pp. 6–11.

7. Juval Portugali, *Self-Organization and the City* (Berlin: Springer-Verlag, 2000).

8. See, for example, Bruce Katz and Jennifer Bradley, "Divided We Sprawl," *The Atlantic*, December 1999; Myron Orfield, *American Metropolitics* (Brookings Institution Press, 2002); and David Rusk, *Cities without Suburbs* (Washington: Woodrow Wilson Center Press, 1995).

9. Center on Budget and Policy Priorities, "Policy Basics: The Earned Income Tax Credit" (Washington: Center on Budget and Policy Priorities, October 21, 2016 [last update]) (www.cbpp.org/research/federal-tax/policy-basics-the-earned -income-tax-credit); Arloc Sherman, Danilo Trisi, and Sharon Parrott, "Various Supports for Low-Income Families Reduce Poverty and Have Long-term Positive Effects on Families and Children" (Washington: Center on Budget and Policy Priorities, July 30, 2013) (www.cbpp.org/research/various-supports-for -low-income-families-reduce-poverty-and-have-long-term-positive-effects); and Ingrid G. Ellen, Keren M. Horn, and Katherine M. O'Regan, "Poverty Concentration and the Low Income Housing Tax Credit: Effects of Siting and

Tenant Composition," *Journal of Housing Economics* 34 (December 2016), pp. 49–59.

10. Amy Liu and Alan Berube, "Matching Place-Based Strategies to the Scale of the Market" (Brookings, January 21, 2015) (www.brookings.edu/articles/matching -place-based-strategies-to-the-scale-of-the-market/).

11. William H. Frey, "A Big City Growth Revival?" (Brookings, May 28, 2013) (www.brookings.edu/opinions/a-big-city-growth-revival/).

12. Bruce Katz and Julie Wagner, "The Rise of Innovation Districts: A New Geography of Innovation in America" (Brookings, 2014); and Bruce Katz and Jennifer Bradley, *The Metropolitan Revolution* (Brookings Institution Press, 2013), pp. 113–43.

13. For an extensive analysis of urban decline, see Jennifer Vey, "Restoring Prosperity: The State Role in Revitalizing America's Older Industrial Cities" (Brookings, 2008) (www.brookings.edu/wp-content/uploads/2016/06/20070520 _oic.pdf).

14. *State of Metropolitan America: On the Front Lines of Demographic Transformation*, Metropolitan Policy Program (Brookings, 2010) (www.brookings.edu/wp -content/uploads/2016/07/metro_america_report1.pdf).

15. Audrey Singer, "Metropolitan Immigrant Gateways Revisited, 2014" (Brookings, December 2015) (www.brookings.edu/research/metropolitan-immigrant -gateways-revisited-2014/).

16. Richard Florida, *The Rise of the Creative Class: And How It's Transforming Work, Leisure, Community, and Everyday Life* (New York: Basic Books, 2014).

17. See, for example, Peter Calthorpe, *Urbanism in the Age of Climate Change* (Washington: Island Press, 2010).

18. NYPD CompStat Unit, "CompStat Report Covering the Week 5/1/2017 through 5/7/2017," *CompStat* 24, no. 18 (www.nyc.gov/html/nypd/downloads/pdf /crime_statistics/cs-en-us-city.pdf).

19. For more, see Hope Corman and Naci Mocan, "Carrots, Sticks and Broken Windows," NBER Working Paper 9061 (Cambridge, MA: National Bureau of Economic Research, July 2002) (www.nber.org/papers/w9061.pdf).

20. "Who We Are," National Network for Safe Communities website (nnscom munities.org/who-we-are/mission).

21. Lawrence Houstoun, "Business Improvement Districts: Partnering Local Governments and Business," *PM (Public Management) Magazine* 91, no. 7 (August 2009).

22. For a review of literature in favor of charter schools for their positive effects on student achievement, see Julian Betts and Y. Emily Tang, "The Effect of Charter Schools on Student Achievement: A Meta-analysis of the Literature" (University of Washington, National Charter School Research Project, October 2011); for the opposing view on charter schools, see Niraj Chokshi, "Charter Schools Are Hurting Urban Public Schools, Moody's Says," *Washington Post*, October 15, 2013 (www

.washingtonpost.com/blogs/govbeat/wp/2013/10/15/charter-schools-are-hurting
-urban-public-schools-moodys-says/?utm_term=.a65a474f3eef).

23. Henry G. Cisneros and Lora Engdahl, *From Despair to Hope: Hope VI and the New Promise of Public Housing in America's Cities* (Brookings Institution Press, 2009).

24. *State of Metropolitan America.*

25. James Manyika, Jaana Remes, Richard Dobbs, Javier Orellana, and Fabian Schaer, "Urban America: U.S. Cities in the Global Economy" (New York: McKinsey Global Institute, April 2012) (www.mckinsey.com/global-themes/urbanization/us
-cities-in-the-global-economy).

26. Angela Blanchard, "Refugees Don't Just Come to Nations; They Move to Cities" (Brookings, October 3, 2016) (www.brookings.edu/blog/metropolitan
-revolution/2016/10/03/refugees-dont-just-come-to-nations-they-move-to-cities/).

27. "The Delaware River Watershed," Coalition for the Delaware River Watershed, n.d. (www.delriverwatershed.org/the-watershed/).

28. Stephen Lee Davis, "Billions in Transit Measures Approved Tuesday: Unpacking the 2016 Election Results," *Transportation for America*, November 10, 2016 (t4america.org/2016/11/10/billions-in-transit-measures-approved-tuesday-unpacking
-the-2016-election-results/).

29. "Voluntary Pre-kindergarten (VPK)," Early Learning Coalition of Broward County, Inc., website (www.elcbroward.org/p/85/voluntary-pre-kindergarten
-vpk); Cornelius Frolik, "Dayton's Income Tax Hike Passes," *Dayton Daily News*, November 7, 2016; "2014 Election Results for Washington State," *Seattle Times*, November 21, 2014; and Josh Baugh and Maria Luisa Cesar, "Local Voters Decide to Put Their Money on Pre-K 4 SA," MySanAntonio.com, November 7, 2012 (www.mysanantonio.com/elections/article/Voters-approve-Castro-s-Pre-K-plan
-4014635.php).

30. "Maps 3," *News OK*, n.d. (newsok.com/maps3).

31. Bruce Katz, "Why Cities and Metros Must Lead in Trump's America," *Brookings*, November 21, 2016 (www.brookings.edu/research/why-cities-and
-metros-must-lead-in-trumps-america/#footnote-4). For K–12 education, see "School Funding," New America Foundation website (www.newamerica.org/education
-policy/policy-explainers/early-ed-prek-12/school-funding/); for transportation infrastructure, see "Funding Challenges in Highway and Transit: A Federal-State-Local Analysis" (Pew Charitable Trusts, February 24, 2015) (www.pewtrusts.org
/en/research-and-analysis/analysis/2015/02/24/funding-challenges-in-highway
-and-transit-a-federal-state-local-analysis).

32. Franklin D. Roosevelt, "Address at Oglethorpe University," speech delivered at Oglethorpe University, May 22, 1932.

33. Christian Paz, "Eric Cantor Rejects Short-Termism as Political Trend," *The Hoya*, March 18, 2016.

34. "About," C40 Cities Climate Leadership Group website (www.c40.org/about).

35. C40 Cities and ARUP, "Climate Action in Megacities 3.0: Networking Works, There Is No Global Solution without Local Action" (C40 and Arup, December 2015) (cam3.c40.org/images/C40ClimateActionInMegacities3.pdf).

Chapter 3

1. Robert E. Scott, "The Manufacturing Footprint and the Importance of U.S. Manufacturing Jobs," Economic Policy Institute Briefing Paper 388 (Washington: Economic Policy Institute, January 22, 2015) (www.epi.org/publication/the -manufacturing-footprint-and-the-importance-of-u-s-manufacturing-jobs/#epi -toc-8).

2. Branko Milanovic, *Global Inequality: A New Approach for the Age of Globalization* (Cambridge, MA: Harvard University Press, 2016).

3. Pedro Nicolaci da Costa, "The Richest U.S. Families Own a Startling Proportion of America's Wealth," *Business Insider,* June 28, 2017 (www.businessinsider .com/richest-us-families-own-a-startling-proportion-of-americas-wealth-2017-6).

4. "The American Middle Class Is Losing Ground" (Pew Research Center, December 9, 2015) (www.pewsocialtrends.org/2015/12/09/the-american-middle-class -is-losing-ground/).

5. Federica Cocco, "Most US Manufacturing Jobs Lost to Technology, Not Trade," *Financial Times,* December 2, 2016; Scott Andes and Mark Muro, "Don't Blame the Robots for Lost Manufacturing Jobs" (Brookings, April 29, 2015) (www.brookings.edu/blog/the-avenue/2015/04/29/dont-blame-the-robots-for -lost-manufacturing-jobs/); and Georg Graetz and Guy Michaels, "Robots at Work," CEP Discussion Paper 1335 (London School of Economics, Centre for Economic Performance, June 22, 2017) (http://cep.lse.ac.uk/pubs/download/dp 1335.pdf).

6. Department of Homeland Security, "Persons Obtaining Lawful Permanent Resident Status by Type of Admission and Region and Country of Nationality: Fiscal Year 2017" (Department of Homeland Security, June 27, 2017) (www.dhs.gov /immigration-statistics/special-reports/legal-immigration#File_end); and Office of Immigration Statistics, "2012 Yearbook of Immigration Statistics" (Department of Homeland Security, July 2013) (www.dhs.gov/sites/default/files/publications /Yearbook_Immigration_Statistics_2012.pdf).

7. Jens Manuel Krogstad and Richard Fry, "Dept. of Ed. Projects Public Schools Will Be 'Majority-Minority' This Fall" (Pew Research Center, August 18, 2014) (www.pewresearch.org/fact-tank/2014/08/18/u-s-public-schools-expected-to -be-majority-minority-starting-this-fall/).

8. "Languages Spoken at ASD," Anchorage School District website (www .asdk12.org/aboutasd/languages/).

9. See, for example, Seth J. Schwartz, J. B. Unger, B. L. Zamboanga, and J. Szapocznik, "Rethinking the Concept of Acculturation: Implications for Theory and Research," *American Psychologist* 65, no. 4 (2010).

10. William H. Frey, *Diversity Explosion* (Brookings Institution Press, 2017), pp. 191–95.

11. Gretchen Livingston and Anna Brown, "Intermarriage in the U.S. 50 Years After Loving v. Virginia" (Pew Research Center, May 2017) (file:///C:/Users/BEby/Downloads/Intermarriage-May-2017-Full-Report.pdf).

12. Tom Clark, "EU Voting Map Lays Bare Depth of Division across Britain," *The Guardian*, June 24, 2016.

13. Saskia Sassen, *The Global City: New York, London, and Tokyo* (Princeton University Press, 2001).

14. United Nations, "Urban and Rural Areas 2009" (United Nations, 2009) (www.un.org/en/development/desa/population/publications/urbanization/urban-rural.shtml). In 2009, the UN Department of Economic and Social Affairs reported that the number of people living in urban areas (3.42 billion) had surpassed the number living in rural areas (3.41 billion). The report noted that disparities existed with regard to urbanization of the less developed world, anticipating that it would take another decade (to 2020) for half the population of underdeveloped regions to live in urban areas. The department expects the world's urban population to continue its growth, reaching approximately 84 percent by the year 2050.

15. United Nations, "World's Population Increasingly Urban with More Than Half Living in Urban Areas" (United Nations, July 14, 2014) (www.un.org/en/development/desa/news/population/world-urbanization-prospects-2014.html).

16. Population Reference Bureau, "Human Population: Urbanization" (Washington: Population Reference Bureau, n.d.) (www.prb.org/Publications/Lesson-Plans/humanpopulation/Urbanization.aspx). The Population Reference Bureau used megacities, densely inhabited urban areas with populations of over 10 million people, as a measure of current and projected urbanization. It is anticipated that twenty-seven megacities will exist by 2025, with twenty-one in less developed countries. Additionally, the growth of urban agglomerations by the year 2025 is projected to be most rapid in less developed countries. With the exception of Japan, the six countries with the highest projected population growth in urban areas are considered underdeveloped in the Population Reference Bureau's study.

17. Johan Nylander, "China's Investment in Elite Universities Pays Off: New Ranking," *Forbes*, September 14, 2015.

18. Ruth Schuster, "The Secret of Israel's Water Miracle and How It Can Help a Thirsty World," *Haaretz*, July 4, 2017.

19. Thomas L. Friedman, *The World Is Flat: A Brief History of the Twenty-first Century* (New York: Farrar, Straus, and Giroux, 2005).

20. Vivienne Walt and Naina Bajekal, "Muslims in Neglected Paris Suburbs Worry Conditions Could Produce More Terrorists," *Time*, January 10, 2015.

21. See, for example, Charles Postel, *The Populist Vision* (Oxford University Press, 2009); Robert C. McMath Jr., *American Populism: A Social History 1877–1898* (New York: Hill and Wang, 1993); Lawrence Goodwyn, *The Populist*

Moment: A Short History of the Agrarian Revolt in America (Oxford University Press, 1978); Lawrence Goodwyn, *The Democratic Promise: The Populist Movement in America* (Oxford University Press, 1976), and Daniele Albertazzi and Duncan McDonnell, eds., *Twenty-First Century Populism: The Spectre of Western European Democracy* (Basingstoke: Palgrave Macmillan, 2008).

22. Pierre Manent, "Populist Demagogy and the Fanaticism of the Center," *American Affairs Journal* 1, no. 2 (Summer 2017).

23. William Greider, *Secrets of the Temple: How the Federal Reserve Runs the Country* (New York: Simon and Schuster, 1989); Postel, *The Populist Vision*; and Goodwyn, *The Populist Moment.*

24. Christopher Lasch, *The Revolt of the Elites and the Betrayal of Democracy* (New York: W. W. Norton, 1996). Lasch provides an "expansive definition" of the privileged class, including nearly one-fifth of the U.S. population in his analysis of "the new meritocracy." Characterizing the efforts of the new elites as a "betrayal of the American dream," Lasch attributes shifts in the "overriding goals of public policy" to the political advocacy of wealthy professionals. Lasch later argues that heightened partisanship is the product of new elites' appropriation of American political discourse, establishing an unprecedented culture of disdain and ideological dogmatism in modern public debate. José Ortega y Gasset in *The Revolt of the Masses* (Barcelona: El Sol, 1929), while similarly critical of mass portions of the population, avoids referring to specific social classes in his work. His primary focus is the "bourgeois educated man," or those who irresponsibly attempt to extend their worldly knowledge to their largely ignorant peers. Ortega identifies the recklessly educated as the root of society's struggles in social and professional development.

25. Ryan Teague Beckwith, "Read Donald Trump's Speech on the Orlando Shooting," *Time*, June 13, 2016 (last update) (time.com/4367120/orlando-shooting-donald-trump-transcript/).

26. Goodwyn, *The Populist Moment.*

Chapter 4

1. U.S. Nuclear Regulatory Commission, "Backgrounder on the Three Mile Island Accident" (U.S. Nuclear Regulatory Commission, February 2013) (www.nrc.gov/reading-rm/doc-collections/fact-sheets/3mile-isle.html#animated).

2. "Oral-History: Red Whittaker," interview by Peter Asaro with Selma Šabanovic (IEEE History Center, November 23, 2010).

3. John Markoff, "The Creature That Lives in Pittsburgh," *New York Times*, April 21, 1991.

4. Rick Michal, "Red Whittaker and the Robots That Helped Clean Up TMI-2," *Nuclear News* 52, no. 13 (2009), pp. 37–40.

5. John Edwards, "Carnegie Mellon: The World's Premier Robotics Institute?," *Robotics Business Review*, June 6, 2014. In 1994, Reddy received the Turing Award, the computer science equivalent to the Nobel Prize.

6. Joanne Pransky, "The Pransky interview: Dr William 'Red' Whittaker, Robotics Pioneer, Professor, Entrepreneur," *Industrial Robot: An International Journal* 43 no. 4 (2016), pp. 349–53.

7. Clive Thompson, "Uber Would Like to Buy Your Robotics Department," *New York Times*, September 11, 2015. Personal communication with Tim McNulty indicates that the Robotics Institute actually works more on projects at Levels 1 and 2, while the National Robotics Engineering Center's work spans Levels 1 to 4. Research partners extend the collaboration to Level 9, and the buildings around NREC currently house Level 9 work.

8. Rebecca Nuttall, "Roboburgh: Pittsburgh Has Always Been a Leader in the Robotics Revolution," *Pittsburgh City Paper*, April 27, 2016.

9. "Innovation Works" (www.innovationworks.org/). AlphaLab, which started in 2008, helps technology companies maximize their early progress through customer discovery and product development in a rapid, iterative approach. AlphaLab Gear, which launched in 2013, is a hardware accelerator program that provides resources and expertise in areas specific to physical product companies, including product design, manufacturing, supply chain, and retail distribution.

10. Kate Rogers, "A 'Silicon Strip' That's Rising in America's Rust Belt," CNBC, June 17, 2016.

11. Steve Twedt, "Lawrenceville-Based Robotics Engineers Target Disabilities, Dynamite," *Pittsburgh Post-Gazette*, January 2, 2015. For example, the Patient Assist Robotic Arm can attach to a power wheelchair and, with the aid of a sling, help people transfer from a wheelchair to a car, toilet, or couch.

12. Vaish Krishnamurthy, "Could my dream of starting a robotics company have come true had it not been for Pittsburgh?" (blog entry), *Clean Robotics*, April 4, 2016 (www.cleanrobotics.com/2016/04/04/Ode-to-Pittsburgh/).

13. Byron Spice, "Pittsburgh Colleges and Industry Create Associate Degree Program to Teach Skills for Building, Servicing Robots and Embedded Systems," *Carnegie Mellon University News*, February 23, 2009 (www.cs.cmu.edu/news /pittsburgh-colleges-and-industry-create-associate-degree-program-teach-skills -building).

14. Tim Henderson, "Millennials Bring New Life to Some Rust Belt Cities" (Pew Charitable Trusts, July 25, 2016) (www.pewtrusts.org/en/research-and-analysis /blogs/stateline/2016/07/25/millennials-bring-new-life-to-some-rust-belt-cities).

15. Dan Majors, "Pittsburgh's Youth Exodus Reverses: Millennials Are Being Drawn to the City," *Pittsburgh Post-Gazette*, August 8, 2016.

16. "The Pittsburgh-India Connection Has Paid Off for Pittsburgh," *Pittsburgh Post-Gazette*, May 1, 2011.

17. Patty Tascarella, "iGate Founders Plan to Invest $40M in Tech Startups," *Pittsburgh Business Times*, April 8, 2016.

18. Byron Spice, Ken Walters, and Kristin Carvell, "Uber, Carnegie Mellon Announce Strategic Partnership and Creation of Advanced Technologies Center in Pittsburgh," *Carnegie Mellon University News*, February 2, 2015.

19. Mike Ramsey and Douglas MacMillan, "Carnegie Mellon Reels after Uber Lures Away Researchers," *Wall Street Journal*, May 31, 2015.

20. Richard Florida, "How Uber's Driverless Cars Could Make Pittsburgh America's Next Great Tech Hub," *CityLab*, June 3, 2015 (www.citylab.com/life /2015/06/how-ubers-driverless-cars-could-make-pittsburgh-americas-next-great -tech-hub/394691/).

21. Sherry Stokes and Ken Walters, "Carnegie Mellon Spinoff Ottomatika Acquired by Delphi," *Carnegie Mellon University News*, August 4, 2015.

22. "Ford Invests in Argo AI, A New Artificial Intelligence Company, In Drive for Autonomous Vehicle Leadership" (Ford Motor Company Media Center, February 10, 2017) (media.ford.com/content/fordmedia/fna/us/en/news/2017/02 /10/ford-invests-in-argo-ai-new-artificial-intelligence-company.html).

23. Aaron Aupperlee, "Aurora Innovation Joins Pittsburgh's Self-driving Car Ecosystem," *TribLive*, May 3, 2017 (triblive.com/local/allegheny/12256468-74 /aurora-innovation-joins-pittsburghs-self-driving-car-ecosystem).

24. Aarian Marshall and Alex Davies, "How Pittsburgh Birthed the Age of the Self-driving Car," *Wired*, August 19, 2016.

25. "Andrew W. Moore Biography," School of Computer Science at Carnegie Mellon University web page (www.cs.cmu.edu/~awm/biography.html).

26. Vaish Krishnamurthy, "Could My Dream of Starting a Robotics Company Have Come True Had It Not Been for Pittsburgh?," *Clean Robotics*, April 4, 2016 (www.cleanrobotics.com/2016/04/04/Ode-to-Pittsburgh/).

27. Kris B. Mamula, "Pitt Ranked Fifth Nationally in Federal Health Research Funding," *Pittsburgh Post-Gazette*, June 13, 2016.

28. Adam Reinherz, "World-Renowned Opthalmologist Foresees Future in Pittsburgh," *Jewish Chronicle*, n.d. (thejewishchronicle.net/view/full_story/27238571 /article-world-renowned-ophthalmologist-foresees-future-in-pittsburgh).

29. Scott Andes, John Ng, Carolyn Gatz, and Mark Muro, "From Health Care Capital to Innovation Hub: Positioning Nashville as a Leader in Health IT" (Brookings, August 2016) (www.brookings.edu/wp-content/uploads/2016/08/metro _20160824_nashvillehealthit.pdf).

30. Scott Andes, Mitch Horowitz, Ryan Helwig, and Bruce Katz, "Capturing the Next Economy: Pittsburgh's Rise to a Global Innovation City" (Brookings, 2017).

31. Chris Potter, "Pittsburgh Mayor Peduto Says Uber Must 'Fight for More Than Profit,'" *Pittsburgh Post-Gazette*, April 3, 2017.

32. Matthew Taylor, "21st Century Enlightenment Revisited" (London: Royal Society for the Encouragement of Arts, Manufactures and Commerce, December

13, 2016) (www.thersa.org/discover/publications-and-articles/matthew-taylor-blog/2016/12/21st-century-enlightenment-revisited).

33. Edward Glaeser and William Kerr, "What Makes a City Entrepreneurial?" (Harvard Kennedy School, February 2010) (www.hks.harvard.edu/index.php/content/download/68625/1247310/version/1/file/entrepreneurs.pdf); and Vivek Wadhwa, AnnaLee Saxenian, Ben Rissing, and Gary Gereffi, "America's New Immigrant Entrepreneurs" (faculty paper, University of California, Berkeley, January 4, 2007) (people.ischool.berkeley.edu/~anno/Papers/Americas_new_immigrant_entrepreneurs_I.pdf).

34. Hao Zhao and Scott E. Seibert, "The Big Five Personality Dimensions and Entrepreneurial Status: A Meta-Analytical Review," *Journal of Applied Psychology* 91, no. 2 (2006), pp. 259–71.

35. Antoine van Agtmael and Fred Bakker, *The Smartest Places on Earth: Why Rustbelts Are the Emerging Hotspots of Global Innovation* (New York: Public Affairs, 2016), pp. 27–28.

36. Ibid, pp. 8–16.

37. Ibid, p. 17.

38. Bruce Katz, "Closing Remarks," presentation at a conference, "The Smartest Places on Earth: Why Rustbelts Are the Emerging Hotspots of Global Innovation, with Authors Antoine Van Agtmael and Fred Bakker," Brookings Institution, April 6, 2016 (www.brookings.edu/wp-content/uploads/2016/03/20160406_rustbelt_innovation_transcript.pdf).

39. Mark Muro, Jonathan Rothwell, Scott Andes, Kenan Fikri, and Siddharth Kulkarni, "America's Advanced Industries: What They Are, Where They Are, and Why They Matter" (Brookings, February 2015) (www.brookings.edu/wp-content/uploads/2015/02/advancedindustry_finalfeb2lores-1.pdf).

40. Jonathan Rothwell, "The Hidden STEM Economy" (Brookings, June 2013) (www.brookings.edu/wp-content/uploads/2016/06/TheHiddenSTEMEconomy610.pdf).

41. James Manyika, Michael Chui, Jacques Bughin, Richard Dobbs, Peter Bisson, and Alex Marrs, "Disruptive Technologies: Advances That Will Transform Life, Business, and the Global Economy" (New York: McKinsey Global Institute, May 2013).

42. See, for example, Joseph A. Schumpeter, *Capitalism, Socialism, and Democracy* (New York: Harper and Brothers, 1942).

43. Andes and others, "Capturing the Next Economy."

44. Mariana Mazzucato, *The Entrepreneurial State: Debunking Public vs. Private Sector Myths* (London: Anthem Press, 2013).

45. Foundation Center, "Fiscal Totals of the 50 Largest Foundations in the U.S. by Total Assets, 2014" (data.foundationcenter.org/#/foundations/all/nationwide/top:assets/list/2014).

46. Heinz Endowments, *2014 Annual Report*, (www.heinz.org/UserFiles/Library /2014_Annual_Report.pdf).

47. National Center for Charitable Statistics, analysis of 2005–2009 American Community Survey 5-Year Estimates (accsweb.urban.org/pubapps/geoshowvals .php?Id=306453&code=6280&v=pf&lev=#selectedcontent).

48. Jeffery Fraser, "Ground Work," *H Magazine*, no. 1, 2017 (www.heinz.org /userfiles/library/2017_issue_1-ground_work.pdf).

49. City of Pittsburgh, County of Allegheny Board of County Commissioners, University of Pittsburgh, and Carnegie-Mellon University, "Strategy 21: Pittsburgh/Allegheny Economic Development Strategy to Begin the 21st Century: A Proposal to the Commonwealth of Pennsylvania," June 1985 (www.briem.com/files /strategy21.pdf).

50. Robert Mehrabian and Thomas H. O'Brien, "The Greater Pittsburgh Region: Working Together to Compete Globally," November 1994 (di26aiwl9i0hv .cloudfront.net/wp-content/uploads/2013/10/pittsburgh.pdf).

51. Donald K. Carter, *Remaking Post-Industrial Cities: Lessons from North America and Europe* (Abingdon: Routledge, 2016), 113.

52. Donald K. Carter, phone interview by the authors, April 18, 2017.

53. Andrew Carnegie, "The Road to Business Success: A Talk to Young Men," address to the students of Curry Commercial College, Pittsburgh, June 23, 1885.

54. Cited in Rebecca Nuttall, "Roboburgh: Pittsburgh Has Always Been a Leader in the Robotics Revolution," *Pittsburgh City Paper*, April 27, 2016.

55. Cited in Glenn Thrush, "The Robots That Saved Pittsburgh," *Politico Magazine*, February 4, 2014.

56. Pascal-Emmanuel Gobry, "Facebook Investor Wants Flying Cars, Not 140 Characters," *Business Insider*, July 30, 2011 (www.businessinsider.com/founders-fund-the-future-2011-7).

57. "Pittsburgh Engineering: Robotics at Carnegie Mellon University," video, WQED Pittsburgh, filmed [July 2010], YouTube video, 6:04 (www.youtube.com /watch?v=wBWM0P-HiwM).

58. Bruce Katz and Jennifer Bradley, "The Rise of Innovation Districts," in *The Metropolitan Revolution: How Cities and Metros Are Fixing Our Broken Politics and Fragile Economy* (Brookings Institution Press, 2014); and Bruce Katz and Julie Wagner, "The Rise of Innovation Districts: A New Geography of Innovation in America" (Brookings, May 2014) (c24215cec6c97b637db6-9c0895f07c3474f66 36f95b6bf3db172.ssl.cf1.rackcdn.com/content/metro-innovation-districts/~ /media/programs/metro/images/innovation/innovationdistricts1.pdf).

59. National Science Foundation, "Higher Education and Research and Development Survey, Fiscal Year 2015," November 2016.

60. "Carnegie Mellon and Tata Consultancy Services Break Ground on Global Research Facility in the U.S.," *CMU News*, April 13, 2017.

61. Joe Cortright, "Young and Restless," *City Observatory*, October 19, 2014.

62. Quoted in Justine Coyne, "CMU's Building Boom," *Pittsburgh Business Times*, October 30, 2015.

63. Robin Micheli, "Rebooting Chattanooga's Fortunes," CNBC, November 18, 2013.

64. Tennessee Aquarium, "Tennessee Aquarium History" (www.tnaqua.org/about -us/tennessee-aquarium-history).

65. David Talbot and Maria Paz-Canales, "Smart Grid Paybacks: The Chattanooga Example," Municipal Fiber Project, Berkman Klein Center for Internet and Society Research, Harvard University, February 2017 (dash.harvard.edu/bitstream /handle/1/30201056/2017-02-06_chatanooga.pdf?Sequence=1).

66. Andy Berke, interview by Bruce Katz, "The Rise of Innovation Districts: A New Geography of Innovation in America," The Brookings Institution, Washington, D.C., June 9, 2014.

67. Dominic Rushe, "Chattanooga's Gig: How One City's Super-Fast Internet Is Driving a Tech Boom," *The Guardian*, August 30, 2014.

68. Bruce Katz, "An Innovation District Grows in Chattanooga" (Brookings, September 29, 2015) (www.brookings.edu/blog/the-avenue/2015/09/29/an-innovation -district-grows-in-chattanooga/).

69. Mike Pare, "Oak Ridge National Laboratory's New Chattanooga Office to Link Lab to Companies," *Times Free Press*, October 21, 2016.

70. Steven Johnson, *Where Good Ideas Come From* (New York: Riverhead Books, 2011).

Chapter 5

1. "William Hudnut III, Mayor Who Revitalized Downtown Indianapolis, Dies at 84," *Washington Post*, December 20, 2016. Mayor Hudnut was elected in 1975, when Indianapolis was a hollowed-out rust belt city struggling to revitalize its postmanufacturing economy. White flight drove out local businesses and the city's population reached historically low numbers.

2. "Star of the Snow Belt: Indianapolis Thrives on Partnership of City, Business, Philanthropy," *Wall Street Journal*, July 14, 1982. Population figures are from U.S. Census, "Annual Estimates of the Resident Population for Incorporated Places of 50,000 or More, Ranked by July 1, 2016 Population: April 1, 2010 to July 1, 2016," *U.S. Census American FactFinder*, May 2017.

3. "Q&A: Indianapolis Sports Strategy," *American Outlook* (Winter 2011) (www.americanoutlook.org/uploads/1/3/3/1/13311122/final_winter2011_web.pdf).

4. Dawn Mitchell, "National Sports Festival Sparked City's Sports Prominence," *Indy Star*, August 21, 2016.

5. David Bodenhamer and Robert Graham, *The Encyclopedia of Indianapolis* (Indiana University Press, 1994).

6. Phillip B. Wilson, "Thirty Years Later, Remembering How Colts' Move Went Down," *USA Today*, March 29, 2014.

7. Mark Alesia, "NCAA Approaching $1 Billion Per Year amid Challenges by Players," *Indy Star*, March 27, 2014.

8. David Johnson, email exchange with Bruce Katz, April 28, 2017.

9. Ted Gayer, Austin J. Drukker, and Alexander K. Gold, "Tax-Exempt Municipal Bonds and the Financing of Professional Sports Stadiums" (Brookings, 2016); and Roger G. Noll and Andrew Zimbalist, *Sports, Jobs, and Taxes: The Economic Impact of Sports Teams and Stadiums* (Brookings Institution Press, 1997). In their report, Gayer, Drukker, and Gold found weak evidence for spillover gains to the local economy, which are often used as the justification for government subsidies of sports stadiums. Additionally, the tax-exempt status of stadium financing results in considerably large and inefficient federal subsidies. These findings were preceded by Noll and Zimbalist's 1997 book, which similarly concludes that sports facilities do not significantly contribute to local economic growth and employment, and further, that the magnitude of net subsidies for stadiums exceeds the financial benefits.

10. David Johnson, email exchange with Bruce Katz, April 28, 2017.

11. Corporate Community Council, internal document, "Corporate Community Council Task Force Report: A New Approach to Central Indiana Growth and Opportunity," July 21, 1998.

12. Ibid.

13. David Johnson, email exchange with Bruce Katz, April 28, 2017.

14. Central Indiana Corporate Partnership (CICP), internal document, "Central Indiana Corporate Partnership Mission Overview and Evolution, 1999–2017."

15. Ibid., emphasis added.

16. "About the Indy Chamber," Indy Chamber website (www.indychamber .com/belong/about/).

17. CICP, 2016 *Central Indiana Corporate Partnership Annual Report* (www .cicpindiana.com/wp-content/uploads/2017/03/CICP_2016-Annual-Report _WEB.pdf).

18. CICP, "About Us" (www.cicpindiana.com/about-cicp/).

19. CICP, internal document, "Central Indiana Corporate Partnership Mission Overview and Evolution, 1999–2017."

20. "Four-Year Doctor of Medicine (MD) Degree Program," Indiana University School of Medicine website (medicine.iu.edu/education/md/).

21. Northeast Indiana Regional Partnership, "Medical Devices" (neindiana .com/doing-business-here/target-industries/medical-devices/?contrast=off).

22. Battelle Memorial Institute, *Nurturing Central Indiana's Pillar Industries for 21st Century Midwestern Pre-eminence*, report prepared for the CICP, executive

summary, December 2000 (www.cicpindiana.com/wp-content/uploads/2015/01/battelle-cluster-executive-summary.pdf).

23. BioCrossroads, "Where Ideas Find Life: The Evolution of BioCrossroads 2002–2012," 2012, p. 3 (www.biointellex.com/wp-content/uploads/2014/08/BIOX _evolution-brochure_final.pdf).

24. Ibid., pp. 4 and 5.

25. Ibid., p. 14.

26. BioCrossroads, internal document, "BioCrossroads History to 2017," pp. 8–9.

27. BioCrossroads, "Where Ideas Find Life," p. 17.

28. Ibid., p. 8.

29. Ibid., p. 4.

30. Ibid., p. 11.

31. Ibid.

32. Brian Eason, "City-County Council OKs $75M for Indianapolis Tech Park," *Indianapolis Star*, November 10, 2015.

33. BioCrossroads, "Indiana's Life Sciences Industry Economic Impact Climbs to $63 Billion," *BioSpeak Indiana*, February 21, 2017 (www.biocrossroads.com/1701-2/).

34. Internal documents from Brian Stemme, "2016 Metrics, Indiana Life Sciences Sector"; and BioCrossroads, *2016 Annual Report* (www.biointellex.com/wp-content/uploads/2017/04/2016-Annual-report.pdf).

35. Quoted in Charlotte-Mecklenburg Opportunity Task Force, "Context," in *Leading on Opportunity* (leadingonopportunity.org/introduction/executive-summary/). The task force responded to Reeves as follows: "We recognize that creating a task force when a sticky issue arises is the 'Charlotte way.' We wanted to do things differently. Our Task Force was not a group of 'the usual suspects,' the people who are always asked to sit at the table. Many of us had never been involved in community change work. Some of us came to the issue of economic mobility and opportunity somewhat uninformed. For others, our first-hand knowledge of inequality and lack of opportunity is deeply personal. We represent a wide range of backgrounds and perspectives."

36. Battelle Memorial Institute, *Nurturing Central Indiana's Pillar Industries for 21st Century Midwestern Pre-eminence*, executive summary, p. 6.

37. BioCrossroads, "Where Ideas Find Life," p. 21, emphasis added.

38. Ibid., p. 22.

39. Internal document, "Conexus Indiana Timeline"; internal document, "Agrinovus Indiana Historical Profile."

40. Internal document, "Ascend Indiana Overview."

41. Craig Fehrman, "Bill Hudnut: A Man of His Word," *Indianapolis Monthly*, June 20, 2016.

42. See, for example, Richard Feiock and Jered Carr, "A Reassessment of City/County Consolidation: Economic Development Impacts," *State and Local Government Review* 29, no. 3 (1997), pp. 166–71.

43. David Lawther Johnson, "Clusters, Communities, and Competitiveness: An Emerging Model from America's Midwest," in *The Oxford Handbook of Local Competitiveness*, ed. David B. Audretsch, Albert N. Link, and Mary Walshok (Oxford University Press, 2015), p. 407.

44. Sean Safford, *Why the Garden Club Couldn't Save Youngstown: The Transformation of the Rust Belt* (Harvard University Press, 2009).

45. CICP, "Central Indiana Corporate Partnership Mission Overview and Evolution, 1999–2017."

46. Indy Johar, "We Don't Face a Crisis of Government but a Crisis of Governance . . ." (blog entry), *Dark Matter Laboratories*, June 11, 2015 (provocations.darkmatterlabs.org/future-of-goverance-draft-284790e4f087).

47. Lilly Endowment, *2015 Lilly Endowment Annual Report* (Indianapolis, 2015) (www.lillyendowment.org/annualreports/2015/LE15_annual-report.pdf).

48. Lester M. Salamon, "The New Governance and the Tools of Public Action: An Introduction," in Lester M. Salamon and Odus V. Elliott, *The Tools of Government: A Guide to the New Governance* (Oxford University Press, 2002), p. 2.

49. Leslie Brokaw, "Six Lessons from Amsterdam's Smart City Initiative" (blog entry), *MIT Sloan Management Review*, May 25, 2016 (sloanreview.mit.edu/article/six-lessons-from-amsterdams-smart-city-initiative/).

50. Royce Hanson and Donald F. Norris, "Corporate Citizenship and Urban Governance in Baltimore: Implications of Restructuring and Globalization of the Economy" (Brookings, September 2006) (www.brookings.edu/wp-content/uploads/2016/07/20060901_baltimore.pdf).

51. Sam A. Williams, *The CEO as Urban Statesman* (Mercer University Press, 2014).

52. Royce Hanson, Hal Wolman, and David Connolly, "Finding a New Voice for Corporate Leaders in a Changed Urban World: The Greater Cleveland Partnership," case study prepared for the Brookings Institution Metropolitan Policy Program (Brookings, September 2006) (www.brookings.edu/wp-content/uploads/2016/07/20060901_cleveland.pdf).

53. Ibid., pp. 7–8.

54. Ibid., p. 6.

55. Brent Larkin, "Richard Shatten: A Genius, and Much More" (Cleveland City Planning Commission, February 14, 2002) (planning.city.cleveland.oh.us/CWP/DEDICATION.HTM).

56. Bruce Katz and Jeanne Shatten, "Prize Inspires Students to Continue Shatten's Work" (Brookings, 2005).

57. Hanson, Wolman, and Connolly, "Finding a New Voice for Corporate Leaders in a Changed Urban World."

58. Cincinnati Center City Development Corporation (3CDC), "About 3CDC" (www.3cdc.org/about-3cdc/).

59. 3CDC, "3CDC Real Estate Projects" (www.3cdc.org/projects/).

60. Cortex Innovation Community, "Who We Are" (cortexstl.com/who-we-are/); and Julie Wagner, "In St. Louis, a Gateway to Innovation and Inclusion," *Metropolitan Revolution* (blog), (Brookings, May 2016) (www.brookings.edu/blog/metropolitan -revolution/2016/05/05/in-st-louis-a-gateway-to-innovation-and-inclusion/).

61. Ibid.

62. Janelle Gelfand and Bowdeya Tweh, "How 3CDC Built a Local Events Empire," Cincinnati.com, February 9, 2017 (www.cincinnati.com/story/news/2017 /02/09/3cdc-really-wants-you-have-fun-downtown/97280348/).

63. Goktug Morcol, "Center City District: A Case of Comprehensive Downtown BIDs," *Drexel Law Review* 3, no. 271 (2010).

64. Patrick Kerkstra, "How Paul Levy Created Center City," *Philadelphia*, November 22, 2013.

65. Lawrence Houstoun, "Business Improvement Districts: Self-Help Downtown," International Economic Development Council: A Compilation of Articles 1988–2011 (2011).

66. Paul Levy, "Diversifying Downtown from the Ground Up," *Economic Development Journal* 12, no. 2 (2013), p. 9.

67. Kerkstra, "How Paul Levy Created Center City."

68. Central Philadelphia Development Corporation, *2017 State of Center City, Philadelphia* (www.centercityphila.org/uploads/attachments/cj1i05wbm09 bz0oqdba7q23g5-17-socc-full.pdf).

69. Peter Bogason and Juliet Musso, "The Democratic Prospects of Network Governance," *American Review of Public Administration* 36, no. 1 (March 2006), p. 318.

70. Michael Powell, "Parks Department Takes a Seat behind Nonprofit Conservancies," *New York Times*, February 3, 2014.

71. Kerkstra, "How Paul Levy Created Center City."

72. Max Rivlin-Naylor, "Business Improvement Districts Ruin Neighborhoods," *New Republic*, February 19, 2016.

73. Gerry Stoker, "Public Value Management: A New Narrative for Networked Governance?," *American Review of Public Administration* 36, no. 1 (March 2006), p. 53.

Chapter 6

1. This section draws from Bruce Katz and Luise Noring, "The Copenhagen City and Port Development Corporation: A Model for Regenerating Cities" (Brookings, 2017) (www.brookings.edu/research/copenhagen-port-development/).

2. Holger Bisgaard, "Kobenhavn er genrejst: Men hvad nu?," *Politiken*, April 25, 2010.

3. CPH City & Port Development, "From Idea to Project" (CPH City & Port Development in collaboration with Cobe, Sleth, Polyform, and Rambøll, August 2012).

4. Stefan Fölster and Dag Detter, *The Public Wealth of Nations* (New York: Palgrave Macmillan, 2015); and Dag Detter and Stefan Fölster, *The Public Wealth of Cities* (Brookings Institution Press, 2017).

5. OECD, "Territorial Reviews: Copenhagen, Denmark" (Paris: OECD, 2009).

6. Bruce Katz and Luise Noring, "Why Copenhagen Works" (Brookings, February 17, 2016) (www.brookings.edu/research/why-copenhagen-works/).

7. Mads Lebech, interview by Luise Noring, Danish Industry Foundation, Copenhagen, October 6, 2016.

8. *City of Cleveland, Ohio: Comprehensive Annual Financial Report for the Year Ended December 31, 2014* (City of Cleveland, Department of Finance, 2015) (www.city.cleveland.oh.us/sites/default/files/forms_publications /2014CAFR.pdf).

9. IFRS requires market value for financial instruments and realizable non-current assets, but not for plant, machinery, and equipment.

10. Fölster and Detter, *The Public Wealth of Nations*; and Detter and Fölster, *The Public Wealth of Cities*, p. 92.

11. Lars Rohde, interview by the authors, National Bank of Denmark, Copenhagen, September 26, 2016.

12. Carsten Koch, interview by Luise Noring, CPH City & Port Development, September 16, 2016.

13. Peter Damgaard Jensen, interview by Luise Noring, PKA Real Estate, Hellerup, Denmark, November 10, 2016.

14. Carsten Koch, interview by Luise Noring, CPH City & Port Development, September 16, 2016.

15. Michael Nielsen, interview by Luise Noring, ATP Real Estate, Copenhagen, Denmark, November 7, 2016.

16. The Pittsburgh and Indianapolis case studies examined in chapters 4 and 5 have similar effects. The Robotics Institute in Pittsburgh was founded in 1979. The Central Indiana Corporate Partnership was launched in 1999.

17. Airports Council International, "The Ownership of Europe's Airports: 2016" (ACI Europe, 2016) (newairportinsider.com/wp-content/uploads/2016/04/ ACIEUROPEReportTheOwnershipofEuropesAirports2016.pdf).

18. Buzz Bissinger, *A Prayer for the City* (New York: Vintage Publishing, 1998); and *House of Cards*, "Chapter 4," directed by James Foley, written by Rick Cleveland and Beau Willimon, Netflix, February 1, 2013.

Chapter 7

1. See Arindrajit Dube, "Minimum Wage and Job Loss: One Alarming Seattle Study is Not the Last Word," *New York Times*, July 20, 2017. Dube summarizes the results of several recent minimum wage studies: Ekaterina Jardim, Mark C. Long, Robert Plotnick, Emma van Inwegen, Jacob Vigdor, and Hilary Wething, "Minimum Wage Increases, Wages, and Low-Wage Employment: Evidence from Seattle," NBER Working Paper 23532 (Cambridge, MA: National Bureau of Economic Research, June 2017); Michael Reich, Sylvia Allegretto, and Anna Godoey, "Seattle's Minimum Wage Experience 2015–2016," Center on Wage and Employment Dynamics Policy Brief (Berkeley: University of California, Institute for Research on Labor and Employment, June 2017) (irle.berkeley.edu/files/2017 /Seattles-Minimum-Wage-Experiences-2015-16.pdf); and Doruk Cengiz and others, "The Effect of Minimum Wages on the Total Number of Jobs: Evidence from the United States Using a Bunching Estimator," Sole-Jole.org, April 30, 2017 (www.sole-jole.org/17722.pdf).

2. Center City District and Central Philadelphia Development Corporation, "2017 State of Center City: Philadelphia," 2017 (centercityphila.org/uploads /attachments/cj1i05wbm09bz0oqdba7q23g5-17-socc-full.pdf).

3. University City District, "The State of University City: 2017," University City District Report, 2017 (www.universitycity.org/sites/default/files/documents /The%20State%20of%20University%20City%202017_0.pdf).

4. "Philadelphia: The State of the City" (Pew Charitable Trusts, March 2016) (www.pewtrusts.org/~/media/assets/2016/03/philadelphia_the_state_of_the_city _2016.pdf).

5. Molly Webb, "The Long and Troubling History of Penntrification in West Philly," *Curbed Philadelphia*, July 11, 2013.

6. Judith Rodin, *The University and Urban Revival: Out of the Ivory Tower and Into the Streets: The City in the Twenty-First Century* (University of Pennsylvania Press, 2007).

7. Penn Alexander School, "About Penn Alexander School" (www.pennalex school.org/about-us).

8. "New Public School to Open in West Philadelphia with Support of $1.8 Million Philadelphia School Partnership Grant," *Drexel Now*, February 10, 2016 (drexel.edu/now/archive/2016/February/SLA-MS-to-Open-at-Dornsife -Center/).

9. Susan Snyder, "College President as Urban Planner," *Philadelphia*, May 15, 2016.

10. "West Philly Neighborhood in Philadelphia, Pennsylvania," City-data.com (www.city-data.com/neighborhood/West-Philly-Philadelphia-PA.html).

11. Melissa Romero, "New Schuylkill Yards Renderings Revealed," *Curbed Philadelphia*, March 27, 2017 (philly.curbed.com/2017/3/27/15071252/new-schuylkill -yards-renderings-drexel).

12. Scott Andes and others, "Connect to Compete: How the University City–Center City Innovation District Can Help Philadelphia Excel Globally and Serve Locally" (Brookings, May 2017) (www.brookings.edu/wp-content/uploads/2017/05/csi_20170511_philadelphia_innovationdistrict_report1.pdf).

13. See, for example, M. Night Shyamalan, *I Got Schooled* (New York: Simon and Schuster, 2013); and Ira Katznelson and Margaret Weir, *Schooling for All: Class, Race, and the Decline of the Democratic Ideal* (University of California Press, 1988).

14. See, for example, Drew Desilver, "U.S. Students' Academic Achievement Still Lags That of Their Peers in Many Other Countries" (Pew Research Center, February 15, 2017) (www.pewresearch.org/fact-tank/2017/02/15/u-s-students-internationally-math-science/).

15. Jonathan Rothwell, "The Declining Productivity of Education" (Brookings, December 23, 2016) (www.brookings.edu/blog/social-mobility-memos/2016/12/23/the-declining-productivity-of-education/).

16. Shyamalan, *I Got Schooled.*

17. See, for example, the work of the Springboard Collaborative: "The Problem" (Philadelphia: Springboard Collaborative, n.d.) (springboardcollaborative.org/the-problem-2/).

18. K. J. Dell'Antonia, "The Families That Can't Afford Summer," *New York Times,* June 4, 2016.

19. Arne Duncan, "Escaping the Constraints of 'No Child Left Behind,'" *Washington Post,* January 6, 2012.

20. See, for example, Grace Chen, "At the 20-Year Mark, Are Charter Schools Making the Grade?," *Public School Review,* September 21, 2016.

21. National Alliance for Public Charter Schools, "A Closer Look at the Charter School Movement," PublicCharters.org, n.d. (www.publiccharters.org/wp-content/uploads/2016/02/New-Closed-2016.pdf).

22. Diana Rocco, "Mast Charter School Holds Competitive Lottery to Determine Admission," CBS Philly, February 16, 2016 (philadelphia.cbslocal.com/2016/02/16/mast-charter-school-holds-competitive-lottery-to-determine-admission/).

23. National Alliance for Public Charter Schools, "A Growing Movement: America's Largest Charter School Communities," PublicCharters.org, November 2015 (www.publiccharters.org/wp-content/uploads/2015/11/enrollmentshare_web.pdf).

24. CREDO (Center for Research on Education Outcomes), *National Charter School Study 2013* (Stanford University, 2013) (credo.stanford.edu/documents/NCSS%202013%20Final%20Draft.pdf).

25. Mathematica Policy Research, *Understanding the Effect of KIPP As It Scales: Vol. 1. Impacts on Achievement and Other Outcomes* (Washington: Mathematica Policy Research, on behalf of the KIPP Foundation, San Francisco,

September 17, 2015) (www.kipp.org/wp-content/uploads/2016/09/kipp_scale-up _vol1-1.pdf).

26. Niraj Chokshi, "Charter Schools Are Hurting Urban Public Schools, Moody's Says," *Washington Post*, October 15, 2013.

27. Dian Schaffhauser, "Report: Education Tech Spending on the Rise," *The Journal*, January 19, 2016.

28. See, for example, the Springboard Collaborative's "What We Do" (Philadelphia: Springboard Collaborative, n.d.) (springboardcollaborative.org/the-problem -2/), and "About Us" on the Relay Graduate School of Education's website (www .relay.edu/about-us).

29. National Catholic Education Association, "United States Catholic Elementary and Secondary Schools 2016-2017: The Annual Statistical Report on Schools, Enrollment, and Staffing," NCEA.org, March 2017 (www.ncea.org/NCEA /Proclaim/Catholic_School_Data/Catholic_School_Data.aspx).

30. Mark E. Courtney, Amy Dworsky, Adam Brown, Colleen Cary, Kara Love, and Vanessa Vorhies, "Midwest Evaluation of the Adult Functioning of Former Foster Youth: Outcomes at Age 26" (Chicago: Chapin Hall at the University of Chicago, 2011) (www.chapinhall.org/sites/default/files/Midwest%20Evaluation _Report_4_10_12.pdf).

31. "The Social Genome Project" (Center on Children and Families at Brookings, n.d.) (www.brookings.edu/the-social-genome-project/).

32. Isabel V. Sawhill and Quentin Karpilow, "How Much Could We Improve Children's Life Chances by Intervening Early and Often?," CCF Brief 54 (Center on Children and Families at Brookings, July 2014) (www.brookings.edu/wp -content/uploads/2016/06/improve_child_life_chances_interventions_sawhill .pdf).

33. James J. Heckman, "Skill Formation and the Economics of Investing in Disadvantaged Children," *Science* 312 (June 30, 2006); Sneha Elango, Jorge Luis Garcia, James J. Heckman, and Andres Hojman, "Early Childhood Education," NBER Working Paper WP 21766 (Cambridge, MA: National Bureau of Economic Research, November 2015) (www.nber.org/papers/w21766.pdf).

34. Jack P. Shonkoff and Deborah A. Phillips, *From Neurons to Neighborhoods: The Science of Early Childhood Development*, (Washington: National Academy Press, 2000).

35. Errin Haines Whack, "Philadelphia Launches Pre-K Program Funded by Soda Tax," Associated Press, January 6, 2017; and City of Seattle, "The Seattle Preschool Program Implementation Plan" (www.seattle.gov/Documents /Departments/OFE/AboutTheLevy/EarlyLearning/SPP%20Implementation%20 Plan.April%201.PostCommittee.pdf).

36. See, for example, the Philadelphia Youth Build program's "About Us" on the Youth Build Philly website (youthbuildphilly.org/about/).

37. Chicago Public Schools, "Cohort Dropout and Graduation Rates, Prior Method (1999–2014)," CPS School Data (cps.edu/SchoolData/Pages/SchoolData .aspx).

38. City Colleges of Chicago, "Chicago Star Scholarship" (www.ccc.edu /departments/Pages/chicago-star-scholarship.aspx).

39. Greg Fischer, "Cradle to Career Initiative" (U.S. Department of Education, Center for Faith-Based and Neighborhood Partnerships, May 12, 2015) (sites.ed.gov /fbnp/cradle-to-career-initiative/); and Bruce Katz and Greg Fischer, "US Lessons for UK Metro Mayors: The Hard Impact of Soft Power," *Metropolitan Revolution* (blog) (Brookings, February 9, 2017) (www.brookings.edu/blog/metropolitan-revolution /2017/02/09/us-lessons-for-uk-metro-mayors-the-hard-impact-of-soft-power/).

40. "Cradle to Career: Louisville" (Louisville, KY: Mayor's Office, December 2014) (louisvilleky.gov/sites/default/files/safe_neighborhoods/vii_b_cradleto careerlouisville_0_5.pdf).

41. Bluegrass Economic Advancement Movement and the Brookings Institution Metropolitan Policy Program, "Seizing the Manufacturing Moment: An Economic Growth Plan for the Bluegrass Region of Kentucky" (Brookings, November 2013) (www.brookings.edu/wp-content/uploads/2016/07/BMPP_BluegrassNov18Lores .pdf); and Katz and Fischer, "US Lessons for UK Metro Mayors."

42. Robert Putnam, *Bowling Alone: The Collapse and Revival of American Community* (New York: Simon and Schuster: 2000).

43. Jeffrey Gettleman, "Fire Kills Mother and Children at Home," *New York Times*, October 17, 2002.

44. Michael Gecan, *Going Public: An Organizer's Guide to Citizen Action* (New York: Anchor, 2004); and William Greider, *Who Will Tell the People* (New York: Simon and Schuster, 1993).

45. Robert Linthicum, "What Is Power, and How Can It Be Used for the Common Good?," Inland Communities Organizing Network website (www.icon -iaf.org/resources/what-is-power/).

46. Lincoln Institute of Land Policy and Minnesota Center for Fiscal Excellence, "50-State Property Tax Comparison Study," June 2016 (www.lincolninst .edu/sites/default/files/pubfiles/50-state-property-tax-study-2016-full.pdf).

47. Merrit Kennedy, "Lead-Laced Water in Flint: A Step-by-Step Look at the Makings of a Crisis," NPR, April 20, 2016.

48. Nick Paumgarten, "The Death and Life of Atlantic City," *New Yorker*, September 7, 2015.

Chapter 8

1. "A Widening Gap in Cities: Shortfalls in Funding for Pensions and Retiree Health Care" (Pew Charitable Trusts, January 2013) (www.pewtrusts.org/~ /media/legacy/uploadedfiles/pcs_assets/2013/pewcitypensionsreportpdf.pdf);

Terry Savage, "Don't Count on That Government Pension," *Chicago Tribune*, April 17, 2017; "The Houston Pension Question: How the City's Liability Grew and the Options for Reform" (Houston: Rice Kinder Institute for Urban Research, n.d.) (kinder.rice.edu/uploadedFiles/Kinder_Institute_for_Urban_Research/Programs /Urban_Governance/PENSION_REPORT_FINAL_SINGLEPAGE.pdf); Claudia Vargas, "Big Pensions Add to City's Retirement Fund Woes," Philly.com, May 23, 2016; and Peter Jamison, "Paying for Public Retirees Has Never Cost L.A. Taxpayers More: And That's after Pension Reform," *Los Angeles Times*, November 18, 2016.

2. Matthew Dolan, Susan Tompor, and John Gallagher, "Detroit Rising: Life after Bankruptcy," *Detroit Free Press*, November 8, 2015; and Travis H. Brown, "Hartford, Hit with Brunt of Connecticut Tax Hike, Hires Bankruptcy Attorney," *Forbes*, July 10, 2017.

3. Laurence J. Kotlikoff and Scott Burns, *The Coming Generational Storm: What You Need to Know about America's Economic Future* (MIT Press, 2004); and Susan M. Wachter, ed., *Public Pensions and City Solvency* (University of Pennsylvania Press, 2015).

4. Amy B. Monahan, "The Law and Politics of Municipal Pensions," in Wachter, ed., *Public Pensions and City Solvency.*

5. "The Houston Pension Question."

6. Pennsylvania Independent Fiscal Office, "Amendments 01354 and 01558 to Senate Bill 1, Printer's Number 853," June 3, 2017.

7. Julie Bosman and Monica Davey, "'Everything's in Danger': Illinois Approaches 3rd Year without Budget," *New York Times*, June 29, 2017; and Rick Pearson and Kim Geiger, "Illinois Supreme Court Rules Landmark Pension Law Unconstitutional," *Chicago Tribune*, May 8, 2015.

8. Rana Foroohar, *Makers and Takers: The Rise of Finance and the Fall of American Business* (New York: Crown, 2016); Simon Johnson and James Kwak, *13 Bankers: The Wall Street Takeover and the Next Financial Meltdown* (New York: Vintage Books, 2011); Michael Lewis, *The Big Short: Inside the Doomsday Machine* (New York: W. W. Norton, 2011); Lawrence E. Mitchell, *The Speculation Economy: How Finance Triumphed over Industry* (Oakland, Calif.: Berrett Koehler Publishers, 2008); and Jeff Madrick, *Age of Greed: The Triumph of Finance and the Decline of America, 1970 to the Present* (New York: Vintage Books, 2012).

9. Lendol Calder, *Financing the American Dream: A Cultural History of Consumer Credit* (Princeton University Press, 2001).

10. Raghuram G. Rajan, *Fault Lines: How Hidden Fractures Still Threaten the World Economy* (Princeton University Press, 2011).

11. Federal Reserve Bank of New York, "Quarterly Report on Household Debt and Credit," February 2017 (www.newyorkfed.org/medialibrary/interactives/house holdcredit/data/pdf/HHDC_2016Q4.pdf).

12. Federal Reserve, "Insured U.S.-Chartered Commercial Banks That Have Consolidated Assets of $300 Million or More, Ranked by Consolidated Assets," *Federal Reserve Statistical Release*, December 31, 2016 (www.federalreserve.gov /releases/lbr/current/).

13. Federal Deposit Insurance Corporation, "FDIC Community Banking Study," FDIC.gov, December 2012 (www.fdic.gov/regulations/resources/cbi/report /cbi-full.pdf).

14. Preqin, *2017 Preqin Global Private Equity & Venture Capital Report* (New York: Prequin, 2017) (www.preqin.com/item/2017-Preqin-Global-Private-Equity -and-Venture-Capital-Report/1/16504).

15. Muhammad Yunus, *Banker to the Poor: Micro-lending and the Battle Against World Poverty* (New York: Public Affairs, 2008).

16. "About Us," U.S. Department of the Treasury Community Development Financial Institutions Fund website (www.cdfifund.gov/about/Pages/default .aspx).

17. Jeremy Nowak, "CDFI Futures: An Industry at a Crossroads," Opportunity Finance Network website, March 2016 (ofn.org/sites/default/files/resources/PDFs /Publications/NowakPaper_FINAL.pdf).

18. Global Impact Investing Network, "Impact Investing" (thegiin.org/impact -investing/).

19. James M. Willcox, *A History of the Philadelphia Savings Fund Society, 1816–1916* (London: Forgotten Books, 2016).

20. David Mason, *From Buildings and Loans to Bail-Outs: A History of the American Savings and Loan Industry, 1831–1995* (Cambridge University Press, 2004); and J. Carroll Moody and Gilbert C. Fite, *The Credit Union Movement* (University of Nebraska Press, 1971).

21. John J. Havens and Paul G. Schervish, "Why the $41 Trillion Wealth Transfer Estimate Is Still Valid: A Review of the Challenges and Questions" (Boston College Social Welfare Research Institute, January 6, 2003) (www.bc.edu/content /dam/files/research_sites/cwp/pdf/41trillionreview.pdf).

22. Steven Overly, "Universities Are Venturing into New Territory: Funding Start-Up Businesses," *Washington Post*, February 14, 2015.

23. University of Missouri-Kansas City Innovation Center, *We Create Capital* (June 2015) (www.kcchamber.com/KCChamber/media/Big5Media/Entrepre neurship/We-Create-Capital_2015.pdf); "Scaling up Business in Kansas City," University of Missouri-Kansas City website (info.umkc.edu/research/scaling-up -business-in-kansas-city/).

24. Alaina J. Harkness and Emily Gustafsson-Wright, "The Market Makers: Local Innovation and Federal Evolution for Impact Investing," *Metropolitan Revolution* (blog) (Brookings, April 28, 2016) (www.brookings.edu/blog/metropolitan -revolution/2016/04/28/the-market-makers-local-innovation-and-federal-evolution -for-impact-investing/).

25. Social Finance Ltd., "Social Impact Bonds" (www.socialfinance.org.uk /services/social-impact-bonds/).

26. Jeff Edmonson, Bill Crim, and Allen Grossman, "Pay-for-Success Is Working in Utah," *Stanford Social Innovation Review*, October 27, 2015 (ssir.org/articles /entry/pay_for_success_is_working_in_utah).

27. Abby Martin, "A Pioneering Environmental Impact Bond for DC Water" (Conservation Finance Network, Yale Center for Business and the Environment, January 2, 2017), (www.conservationfinancenetwork.org/2017/01/02/pioneering -environmental-impact-bond-for-dc-water).

28. Ira Goldstein, Lance Loethen, Edward Kako, and Cathy Califano, "CDFI Financing of Supermarkets in Underserved Communities: A Case Study" (Philadelphia: Reinvestment Fund, August 1, 2008) (www.reinvestment.com/wp-content /uploads/2015/12/CDFI_Financing_of_Supermarkets_in_Underserved _Communities_A_Case_Study-Report_2008.pdf).

29. Pennsylvania Fresh Food Financing Initiative website (www.reinvestment .com/success-story/pennsylvania-fresh-food-financing-initiative/).

30. "Who We Are," Uplift Solutions website (upliftsolutions.org/).

Chapter 9

1. For more on Philadelphia's innovation district, see Jennifer S. Vey, Scott Andes, Jason Hachadorian, and Bruce Katz, "Connect to Compete: How the University City-Center City Innovation District Can Help Philadelphia Excel Globally and Serve Locally" (Brookings, 2017) (https://www.brookings.edu/research /connect-to-compete-philadelphia/); Scott Andes, Mitch Horowitz, Ryan Helwig, and Bruce Katz, "Capturing the Next Economy: Pittsburgh's Rise to a Global Innovation City" (Brookings, 2017).

2. "The Story So Far," King's Cross website (www.kingscross.co.uk/the-story -so-far).

3. Alex Hern and Rob Davies, "Google Commits to Massive New London Headquarters," *The Guardian*, November 16, 2016.

4. Judith Evans, "UK Sells Stake in King's Cross Redevelopment," *Financial Times*, January 22, 2016.

5. Erika Becker-Medina, "Public-Employee Retirement Systems State- and Locally-Administered Pensions Summary Report: 2010" (U.S. Census, Governments Division, April 20, 2012) (www.census.gov/prod/2012pubs/g10-aret-sl.pdf): "As of 2010, there were in total 3,418 state- and locally administered pension systems in the United States. The vast majority of these systems were at the local level, with only 222 state-administered pension systems in the country. The states with the most pension systems were Pennsylvania (1,425 systems), Illinois (457 systems), and Florida (303 systems)."

6. David Oakley, "Sweden Transforms Public Finance," *Financial Times*, October 16, 2016.

7. Nick Malawskey, "Pa County to Fix 33 Bridges in First-of-Its-Kind Project," *PennLive*, February 15, 2017.

8. "Overview," Florida's Children's Council website (www.flchildrenscouncil .org/about-cscs/overview/).

9. Margaret Brodkin, "Creating Local Dedicated Funding Streams for Kids" (Funding the Next Generation, November 2015) (www.fundingthenextgeneration .org/nextgenwp/wp-content/uploads/2016/03/FTNG-Toolkit-Edition1a-Nov2015 .pdf).

10. Ibid.

11. Boone County Community Services Department, *2015 Annual Report and Program Directory* (www.showmeboone.com/communityservices/common /pdf/2015%20Annual%20Report.pdf).

Chapter 10

1. Alex Friedhoff, Howard Wial, and Harold Wolman, "The Consequences of Metropolitan Manufacturing Decline: Testing Conventional Wisdom" (Brookings, 2010).

2. Jim Martin, "Erie Insurance Plans $135 Million Expansion, 600 New Jobs," *Go Erie*, November 11, 2016.

3. "ECF Awards Mercyhurst $4 Million for Innovation District" (Mercyhurst University, October 12, 2016) (www.mercyhurst.edu/news/ecf-awards-mercyhurst -4-million-innovation-district).

4. Gerry Weiss, "Mercyhurst University, Erie Insurance to Collaborate on Risk Management Program," *Go Erie*, February 3, 2017.

5. Peter Hirshberg and Marcia Kadanoff, "Maker Cities: If You Can Imagine It, You Can Build It," *U.S. News & World Report*, May 23, 2017.

6. Davie Bruce, "Saint Vincent Unveils Plan for $115 Million Investment," *Go Erie*, February 10, 2017.

7. James Fallows, "Erie's Unlikely Benefactor: Its Casino," *The Atlantic*, September 11, 2016.

8. Reid Hoffman, "Network Intelligence: Your Company Can't Thrive without It," slide deck, February 23, 2015 (www.slideshare.net/reidhoffman/network -intelligence-your-company-cant-thrive-without-it/22-There_are_moresmart _people_inthe).

9. Gary McCaleb, personal communication with the authors, May 5, 2017.

10. Alaina Harkness and others, "Leading beyond Limits: Mayoral Powers in the Age of New Localism" (Brookings, 2017).

11. Lawrence Houstoun, *Business Improvement Districts* (Washington: Urban Land Institute, 2003).

12. Bruce Katz and Jennifer Bradley, *The Metropolitan Revolution* (Brookings Institution Press, 2013), p. 197.

13. See, for example, the efforts under way in Chicago as highlighted in Sean Thornton, "Open Data in Chicago: A Comprehensive History," Data Smart City Solutions (Ash Center for Democratic Governance and Innovation, Harvard Kennedy School of Government, 2013) (datasmart.ash.harvard.edu/news/article /open-data-in-chicago-a-comprehensive-history-311).

14. James Fallows, "Erie and America," *The Atlantic*, August 25, 2016.

15. Bruce Katz, "Converging Possibilities; Oklahoma City's Innovation District" (Brookings, April 25, 2017) (www.brookings.edu/blog/metropolitan-revolution /2017/04/25/converging-possibilities/).

16. Steven Johnson, *Where Good Ideas Come From* (New York: Riverhead Books, 2011), p. 245.

17. Erin Carson, "Fighting Fire in Louisville, the Hackathon Way," CNET, October 26, 2016 (www.cnet.com/news/fighting-fire-in-louisville-the-hackathon -way/).

18. Hirshberg and Kadanoff, "Maker Cities."

Index

Reader's Guide

1. In the first chapter we show how the exercise of power is changing from top-down, command-and-control political systems to more horizontal relationships that involve multiple sectors—civic, public, and private—within local communities. Does this resonate with your experience?

2. In the same chapter we note that in the future, power will belong to problem solvers. This is a very different notion of conventional ideas of power based on the ability to effect (even coerce) behavior and decisions. Can you give examples where power accrues to problem solvers? How is this reshaping our world?

3. Many forces have contributed to the renewal of many American cities over the past few decades: the knowledge economy, demography, culture, and governance innovations. What other issues have affected urban change since the 1980s? Do you think the present urban renaissance is sustainable? What will sustain or destabilize urban growth?

4. *The New Localism* is a book about the collaborative efforts of public, private, and civic engagement. We think those interactions form the DNA of social change today. Do you have experiences with cross-sector efforts? How have they worked out? What issues emerge in working across domains? Do you see possibilities for this kind of collaboration in your community that is not being actualized today? Who can lead its formation?

5. The globalization of economic relations has led to political reactions around increased levels of income inequality, a perceived loss of national sovereignty, the loss of manufacturing, and discontent with trade deals. How have those reactions affected American politics? What are the differences between populism on the right and populism on the left in this new context? How do you think American politics will manage these issues over time? What will the role be of local development versus national policy?

6. Technology and global trade create a globally connected society hard to imagine even a few decades ago. We think globalization has also imbued locality with new significance. How do you think the local and global converge in the new economy? Will the nation-state become less relevant? Why or why not?

7. The core of this book consists of three case studies in two American cities and in one European city: Pittsburgh, Indianapolis, and Copenhagen. We offer these case studies to illustrate new models of growth, governance, and finance, respectively. In the 1970s as Pittsburgh was losing its steel plants, it would have been very difficult to predict that it would become a technological powerhouse in a post-manufacturing economy. Is the Pittsburgh growth example replicable? Why or why not?

8. The Indianapolis case study illustrates what we call networked governance. We think this emerging model is not well understood and certainly understudied. What do we need to understand about networked governance to enable its growth? Are the public officials in your community cognizant of the limits of the public sector and their need to collaborate across sectors? Can this kind of governance lead to increased levels of democratic participation or does the shifting role of the public sphere lead to less democracy?

9. Copenhagen illustrates a different model of public asset management from ones with which most of us are familiar. We think this example holds significant opportunities for adoption in the United States and elsewhere. Do you agree? Why or why not? What are examples of public assets in your community that could yield greater returns to be plowed back into the public sector?

10. Economic inclusion is vital to the growth and development of American cities and other communities. New norms of growth, governance, and finance have to take that into account. In our chapter on inclusion we focus a great deal on work force, schools, and human capital. What other issues are critical to look at and explore? How is your community addressing these issues? What more should they do? What are the constraints to action or change?

11. The chapter on finance, chapter 8, presents the elements of what we term "metro finance": new instruments and intermediaries that stretch the canvas from market viability to public purpose. We note the importance of these elements in the context of tight public budgets and private capital that is plentiful but less connected to place than in the past. What do you think of the way we framed these issues? Have you worked with sources of finance that take a dual perspective on financial and social returns?

12. Our way of talking about investing in the future comes down to three Is: *innovation, infrastructure, and inclusion.* We offer some ideas that could be useful for communities nationally and globally. Which of these ideas or issues are most critical to your community's future? What are other ways that you would define making investments in the future?

13. We conclude the book with a call to action. Can we become a nation of problem solvers? What will it take in terms of a shift in our culture and politics to accelerate pragmatic models of social change? What are the consequences of retreating from a solutions orientation?

14. *The New Localism* was written at a time when political dysfunction and stalemate grab all the headlines, and national political discourse obscures the progress we see happening on the ground. Does the book make the case that there is a new local practice emerging in American communities that may end up being more important over the long haul than the grievances of the moment? What other issues should we have covered to make the argument more effectively?